IN AMMA'S HEALING ROOM

IN AMMA'S
HEALING
ROOM

INDIANA UNIVERSITY PRESS
BLOOMINGTON AND INDIANAPOLIS

GENDER AND VERNACULAR ISLAM IN SOUTH INDIA

Joyce Burkhalter Flueckiger

This book is a publication of

Indiana University Press
601 North Morton Street
Bloomington, IN 47404-3797 USA

http://iupress.indiana.edu

Telephone orders 800-842-6796
Fax orders 812-855-7931
Orders by e-mail iuporder@indiana.edu

© 2006 by Joyce Burkhalter Flueckiger

The paper used in this publication meets the
minimum requirements of American National
Standard for Information Sciences—Permanence
of Paper for Printed Library Materials, ANSI
Z39.48-1984.

Manufactured in the United States of America

**Library of Congress Cataloging-in-
Publication Data**
Flueckiger, Joyce Burkhalter.
  In Amma's healing room : gender and
vernacular Islam in South India / Joyce
Burkhalter Flueckiger.
    p. cm.
  Includes bibliographical references and index.
  ISBN 0–253-34721–1 (cloth : alk. paper)—
ISBN 0–253-21837–3 (pbk. : alk. paper)
  1. Muslim women—India—Hyderabad
(District) 2. Healers—India—Hyderabad
(District)—Biography.   3. Hyderabad (India :
District)—Social life and customs.   I. Title.
  HQ1744.M93F58 2006
  305.48'69739—dc22
2005019837
      1 2 3 4 5   11 10 09 08 07 06

Dedicated to Amma and Abba
Who opened their home, healing room, and hearts, and
Who continue to influence many lives on both sides of the seven seas

Amma and Abba, 1996

No matter how many books you write, Jo-ice, that knowledge will be incomplete. No matter how much you write, it won't be enough. Even if you used all the trees in the universe as pens, even then.

Allah has decreed that even if you use up all the ink of the water of the oceans and all the pens from the trees of the world, even then, you won't have finished the history of the *kalmā*.

—Amma, March 2, 1995

CONTENTS

Preface

This book is an ethnographic study of Islamic practices centered around a Muslim female spiritual healer, Amma, who lives and practices in the South Indian city of Hyderabad. Her healing practice represents a form of vernacular Islam as it has taken root in and grown out of a particular locality. Two features are particularly noticeable at this site of vernacular practice in Amma's healing room: gender roles and negotiations and the ways in which Islam has taken shape in its Indian context. Because of Amma's unusual ritual role as a female Muslim healer practicing in the public realm, many of the actors in the healing room articulate issues of gender roles and possibilities. As a woman, Amma has to continually recreate and maintain her authority as a healer to meet the 'public', which includes Hindus and Muslims, men and women. At the same time, many of her patients come to her *because* she is a woman who is thought to be more patient and loving than male healers.

A second characteristic of the healing room is that patients come to Amma for spiritual healing from several different Indian religious traditions: Islam, Hinduism, and Christianity. For scholars and students of religion, this raises the question What makes religious healing possible across religious boundaries? One indigenous answer, as Amma gives it, is that in the healing room, these boundaries of difference collapse. Patients share a cosmology that articulates healing as a spiritual idiom in which spiritual beings or forces intervene in the physical and social world to cause illness. A ritual grammar is shared, and many narrative repertoires and motifs are shared across religious boundaries. At this level of spiritual practice, seemingly rigid boundaries between Indian religious traditions are porous and unsettled. *In Amma's Healing Room* is a study of particular expressions of vernacular Islam that reveal to us the potential flexibility and creativity of Islam, a tradition that is often viewed by both Muslims and non-Muslims alike to be universal, singular, and monolithic.

Religious healing practices are more often written about by medical anthropologists than religious studies scholars. But since practitioners of the kinds of healing Amma engages in think of themselves primarily as religious practitioners, it is important for scholars of religion to expand the boundaries of "what counts" to include these expressions of vernacular religious traditions. Even as I have made clear that my primary interest in my work with Amma is to understand how her healing practice works internally as a religious system and, more particularly, how gendered and religious identities are performed and/or negotiated at this level of practice, audience members who have heard me speak about this healing practice (at numerous conferences, in classes, etc.) frequently push me to answer whether or not I think it "works." When they ask "How does it work?" they are really interested in knowing Does it work according to the terms in which "we" who live outside this social/religious system would identify as successful? So here in the preface, I will attempt to address this question.

Let me begin with a story. When I first met Amma in January 1989, I was not employed as a university professor but was working part-time as an editor and was between two postdoctoral research grants. Amma and her patients were slightly aghast that I did not have a permanent academic position when I had had a Ph.D. for five years. And so, at the end of that first extended three-week visit to Amma's healing room, she gave me an amulet so I would get a permanent position. I accepted the amulet as a gift of love and carried it with me in my handbag, as Amma had instructed, but did not really think about its potential effects. However, a series of events followed (and had preceded) that, in retrospect, seem serendipitous: due to an unexpected tangle of bureaucratic decisions by the government of India, I was unable to return to the site where I had done my Ph.D. fieldwork in Chhattisgarh. Because of this I was free to return to work with Amma the following year instead of going back to Chhattisgarh. Before I returned to do this work, I had mentally taken myself off the market for jobs in the field of Hindi language and literature, for which there had only been four openings in the previous eight years.

My Ph.D. fieldwork had been ethnographic but in the field of folklore; my resulting book, *Gender and Genre in the Folklore of Middle India* (1996), concerns indigenous conceptions of genre—something I had thought could be stretched as relevant to teaching South Asian languages and literatures. By taking myself off this job market, I was free to conduct ethnographic fieldwork that could not in any way be construed as contributing to the field of literature.

When I returned from my first fieldwork stint (of two months) with Amma, a tenure-track position was advertised at Emory University in the Department of Religion for someone who did "performance studies"; preference would be given to someone who worked with nonwestern traditions and gender, and, if all other things were equal, preference would be given to someone who worked with Islamic traditions. My work with Amma fulfilled these requirements in a way that my earlier fieldwork in Chhattisgarh did not. My job talk for this position was based on those first two months of fieldwork with Amma, and I was offered the position. Amma would say that it was her amulet that led to this successful conclusion, and indirectly, I would have to concur: meeting Amma changed the direction of my research interests and introduced me to Islam on a personal and intellectual level that I had not been exposed to earlier, and my work with Amma gave me courage to apply to a position that was "outside" my interdisciplinary field of South Asian Languages and Literatures.

But this story rarely satisfies the questioner; s/he is not satisfied with the ambiguities and multiple interpretations of a story. S/he usually persists: "But does it *work* for the women who come to Amma for abusive husbands, runaway children, and trouble in the house?" And here I would have to answer, if forced by such a direct question, that yes, I think healing at Amma's table often works on a psychological level, empowering women to go home to their families with a different sense of self-esteem and possibility than they came with. They find that they are not alone in whatever manifestation "trouble"/*pareśānī* has taken in their own lives. They sit with other patients while waiting their turn at Amma's table and share their stories with each other. They tell their stories to Amma, who declares with confidence that they will find a satisfactory ending if they follow her prescriptions; she gives coherence to narratives that patients experience to be without reason. Amma provides comfort, creates mean-ingful relationships, and sends patients home with a sense of confidence that their situations can and will change.

But these are not Amma's explanations. She diagnoses and prescribes according to the spiritual forces that have intruded into the social/physical world. She does not live and prescribe in an explicitly psychological or psychoanalytic world—and thus, in this book, I do not analyze her ex-periences and practices in these terms. Nor am I trained to do so. Readers who are interested in this kind of analysis might fruitfully consult Sudhir Kakar's *Shamans, Mystics, and Doctors: A Psychological Inquiry into India and Its Healing Traditions* (1982). Kakar, who is trained as an analyst, looks for correspondences between what he calls "demonological [spiri-tual] and psychological idioms" of illness and healing, even as he acknowl-edges that "if your worldview is demonological . . . then any task of buried feelings toward fathers is irrelevant and certainly very irreverent" and "if one's framework is psychological . . . then talk of. . . . demons is patently absurd" (1982, 23). He asserts that both systems, however, are "languages of psychic disturbance and healing which can be [imperfectly] translated into each other" (29).

I have written this book with an audience in mind modeled on one with which I have interacted regularly over the years I have worked with Amma—the undergraduate students who have enrolled in my class "Women, Religion and Ethnography." I have tried to write so that these traditions will be accessible to the nonspecialist in a narrative style similar to the one Amma and Abba often use to teach, attempting not to over-whelm their story with academic jargon or apparatus. It is my hope that this book will also be accessible and understandable to Amma's English-reading grandsons and disciples if one day they read the book I will send them. I have, however, included the key Dakini Urdu terms for many of my translations, so that scholars of South Asia and Islam will be able to make their own comparisons to traditions that may or may not share concepts and vocabulary.

Acknowledgments

For a book whose research and writing has spanned over a decade, the network of family, friends, colleagues, and supporting institutions to which thanks are given extends far beyond what can be contained by the written page. I first offer my deepest gratitude and honor to Amma and Abba and their family, thanks for who they are and for opening their lives and home to me. From the beginning of our relationship, both Amma and Abba saw themselves as my teachers; they cannot have imagined the many levels at which I learned from them. I treasure Amma's blessings of my children and her intuitions about their personalities and potential.

Over many returns to Hyderabad between 1989 and the present, Revati and Thanganne Thangavelu and their extended families have graciously offered me an open home and table, wisdom when I needed to make difficult decisions about research strategies, and daily encouragement. In 1990, they gave over their living room to my fieldwork associate Lakshmi and me for seven weeks when they barely knew us. In those initial days of fieldwork in the healing room, Revati understood the conflicting demands of research and families and friends; she often kept us on task to "do our work." Thanganne's special gift was morning cups of tea. Both Revati and Thanganne have been wonderful conversation partners, friends, and family.

Diane and Andreas D'Souzas of the Henry Martyn Institute in Hyderabad similarly offered an open home, rich cups of South Indian coffee, and lively conversation. Their experiences of and insights into vernacular Islam in Hyderabad were invaluable, against which I could check my own experiences and interpretations. They understand well the dominant textual orientations of the study of Islam in the western academy; thus, their encouragement was particularly important. I also want to thank their children, Tara, Noel, and Mira, for the reminders they gave me of the joy, spontaneity, and balance that children can give, when my own children were far away.

For much of 1994–1995 and for shorter visits to Hyderabad thereafter, I stayed in the hostel of the American Studies Research Center (ASRC) on Osmania University campus (a half-hour walk from Amma's healing room). The hostel manager, Srinivas, found room for me when I was not quite the "standard" guest, and the entire staff of the hostel and library welcomed me and accommodated my sometimes erratic schedule. I am particularly grateful for the e-mail access that was given to me at the library. At the hostel I met young scholars from all over India who had come to the library to conduct research on American Studies topics. We exchanged American and Indian experiences and our knowledge of histories, politics, and literature; these lively conversations provided much-needed breaks from transcribing tapes and writing up fieldnotes.

A. R. Khaleel is one of the friends I met at the ASRC in 1994. Khaleel is a Hyderabadi in all the best senses of the word, steeped in Hyderabadi culture, language, and history, which he shared freely and graciously with me. In later years, we spent many evenings at the hostel transcribing and translating together taped conversations from the healing room. He knew the local resonances of many Urdu and Telugu words for which I may have initially known only a superficial or "standard" meaning. I thank him for his sense of humor, friendship, and assistance.

Lakshmi Narasamamba worked with me during my initial seven-week research with Amma and Abba in 1990–1991. We went to Amma's healing room together every day and spent our evenings transcribing and translating tapes. Lakshmi was responsible primarily for Telugu translations. She has remained an intellectual colleague in the following years. Durga Yeramilli, an anthropologist turned software computer engineer in Atlanta, spent one summer transcribing and translating Telugu transcriptions of healing-room interactions. My deepest thanks are offered to these two friends for assisting in this tedious work and for the friendships that developed from it.

Students in my "Women, Religion and Ethnography" classes at Emory University have been instrumental in the development of the style and tone of this book. Through class discussions and slides, many of these students got to know Amma on what they felt was a personal basis and continued to ask about her long after their graduation. I thank them for their engagement.

Many colleagues have responded to and supported my new direction of fieldwork in vernacular Islam; at various stages of the project they have been conversation partners, readers of conference papers and/or earlier versions of the book manuscript, and resources for translations of specialized Urdu phrases. I hope they will accept individual thanks and know what their presence has meant to me: Peter Claus, Paul Courtright, Carl Ernst, Dick Eaton, Ann Gold, Waqas Khwaja, Margaret Mills, Kirin Narayan, Vasudha Narayanan, Gordon Newby, Laurie Patton, Velcheru Narayana Rao, David Shulman, Devin Stewart, Susan Wadley, and an anonymous reader for the press. I also gratefully acknowledge the support I have received from Indiana University Press, particularly the careful reading and editing of Rebecca Tolen, and my copyeditor, Kate Babbitt's, love of language. I also want to acknowledge the institutional support without which this book would not have been possible: the Ford Foundation (sponsor of the workshop during which I first met Amma), American Institute of Indian Studies, Fulbright, Emory University Research Council and Faculty Development Award, and publication subventions from Emory College and the Graduate School of Arts and Sciences.

Finally, my family has been more than patient and supportive over all these years with my multiple trips to India and resulting absences. They went with me to India during the primary research with Amma, 1994–1995, when Rachel and Peter studied at Woodstock School and Mike left practicing in the emergency room to teach biology in the classroom. I lived primarily in Hyderabad, and Rachel wondered why "my Amma" couldn't live just down the valley in Mussoorie. That year, Peter began to understand at some intuitive level "what Mom does." For Mike, Peter, and Rachel's acceptance of me as a fieldworker and the impact this has had on their lives, I am deeply grateful. Amma and Abba have been woven into our family's lives in both tangible and imperceptible ways that will surely continue to resonate in coming years.

A Note on Transliteration

I have transliterated the Dakini Urdu language (a vernacular form of Urdu based in the Deccan region) Amma, Abba, and members of their healing community used according to a standard system for other South Asian languages (such as Hindi and Telugu). I have avoided transcription of Urdu and Arabic words according to their literary forms, preferring to provide their oral pronunciation in this sociolinguistic context of South India. So, for example, I have transcribed the word for "messenger" as *maukīl* rather than the standard Arabic transliteration of *mua'kkal*. One reason for this decision is to avoid (performatively, in my own writing) the Arab/Arabic-centeredness of Islam that is often assumed in scholarship about Islam even when it is practiced in other parts of the world, to avoid assuming connections between Arabic and South Asian traditions that may not actually be present in practice, and to see South Asian traditions as the primary context for Amma's practice and speech. Of course, Amma herself acknowledges the power of the Arabic written word of the Quran, but she reveals her own situatedness in South Asia by pronouncing Arabic as "Arabi."

Words in single quotation marks indicate that the English word has been used in an otherwise Urdu or Telugu conversation or narrative.

Dakini Urdu and Telugu do not indicate capitalization. In translation, I have capitalized the word "God" when it refers specifically to Allah or a Hindu deity. I have used lowercase when the word "god" refers to a generic category.

IN AMMA'S HEALING ROOM

INTRODUCTION: CALLED TO
AMMA'S COURTYARD

My heart pulled for you and you came.

In January 1989 I was quite literally called to Amma, the Muslim female healer who is the focus of this book, by the green flag that flies atop her courtyard.[1] Many years later now, another set of flags marks the gravesites of Amma and her husband, Abba, and brings some level of closure to this project. Flags fly above many small shrines of the green-painted graves of Muslim saints that mark the urban landscape of the South Indian city of Hyderabad;[2] some are actively attended to and others are crumbling and dusty. Other green flags fly above courtyards or are tied to trees, marking a site of current or past Islamic ritual activity. In the years since I first met Amma, I have slowly learned of the male lineages and authorities represented by these flags and have become keenly aware of how easily Amma's narrative, a woman's story, could get lost behind lineages of male saints represented by the flags. I wonder how many other narratives have been lost over the years, traces of strong women left perhaps only in a name, a miracle experienced under a flag, a dream not easily decipherable, or other traces with no name at all. This book seeks to tell some of the narratives of Amma's unusual position of authority, negotiation of gender, and practice of spiritual healing.

Amma's healing room represents a level of popular, non-institutionally based Islamic practice that has been underrepresented in religious studies on Islam in South Asia. One of the purposes of this book is to bring this level of practice and experience—what I have called "vernacular Islam"—to the study of Islam and, by writing ethnographically of a particular place, to remind us that "universal" Islam is lived locally. Here, on the ground, vernacular Islam is shaped and voiced by individuals in specific contexts and in specific relationships, individuals who change over time in social, economic, and political contexts that also shift. To study vernacular Islam—in this case, through the lens of a specific female healer in South India—is to identify sites of potential fluidity, flexibility, and innovation in a religious tradition that self-identifies as universal and is often perceived to be ideologically monolithic.

In linguistics, the term "vernacular" is associated with languages or dialects spoken in particular social and geographic locations; vernacular dialects or languages might be juxtaposed to "standard" forms of a language that cross social and geographic boundaries or locales. Thus, for Islam, the Five Pillars incumbent on all Muslims—declaration of faith, prayer five times a day, charity, fasting during Ramadan, and performing pilgrimage to Mecca—are examples of knowledge and practices that are "universal," or transnational, the equivalent of the "standard" form of a language (including its basic grammatical structures and vocabulary). Other universalistic characteristics of Islam are the authority of the Quran and the Prophet. Certain marriage customs and other life-cycle rituals, dress and forms of veiling, and devotional practices, on the other hand, often take local, vernacular forms while still being considered to be Islamic by those who practice them (Flueckiger 2003b, 723).

The healing tradition described in this book is one such vernacular expression as it has taken form in the South Indian city of Hyderabad in the 1990s. Amma sits in a healing room built off of her living quarters, where she meets forty to fifty patients a day—Hindus, Muslims, and Christians—writing amulets of various kinds, battling what she calls illnesses of the *śaitān* [lit., the devil], physical, social, and mental illnesses caused by spiritual disruption. Such spiritual illnesses, Amma asserts, can be countered only by spiritual healing, while purely physical illnesses can be healed only through allopathic (physical) treatments.

Most South Asian religious traditions share healing as an important vernacular religious idiom, and many religious healing sites in India draw patients from different religious traditions in the same way Amma's practice does; spiritual healing is effected across boundaries of religious difference. Most Hyderabadis with whom I have spoken about my own research over the last fifteen years can relate a story about their immediate or extended family of religious healing (and this crosses class and levels of literacy). Many of these stories involve visits to *pīrs* [Muslim spiritual teachers/healers] or *dargāhs* [shrines of Muslim saints], and many patients who end up at Amma's healing table have, as they say, "wandered" from healer to healer before finding healing success. Numerous spiritual healing alternatives are found within a mile of Amma's healing room. In one direction is a Hindu goddess shrine where, in hopes of gaining fertility, Hindu petitioners tie coconuts in the limbs of the trees that surround it and many Muslim petitioners offer *tāzziyā* [bamboo representations of the tomb of the Prophet's martyred grandson Hussein]. Down the road in the other direction is a *dargāh* where a Muslim *bābā* sells rings of precious stones that are said to protect the body and restore the balance of its elements. (Abba wears such rings on each of his fingers, each with a different kind of stone.) Farther into the neighborhood adjacent to the university one finds St. Anthony's Church, where a diverse array of patients line up on Thursday mornings to receive the blessing of healing from Saint Anthony. A charismatic Christian house church in the same neighborhood hangs a big banner across the entrance to its compound that reads "Jesus Heals" (rather than the perhaps more familiar evangelical Christian mantra "Jesus Saves"), and the church identifies itself as a "healing church."

Just days before I was to leave Hyderabad to return to the U.S. after my year's fieldwork in 1994–1995, I was invited for a farewell dinner to the home of a Hindu upper-class secondary school teacher. When I arrived, she unapologetically asked me if, before eating, I would accompany her to a goddess temple in fulfillment of a vow she had made to visit the temple for eleven consecutive Thursdays. She had made the vow to seek healing for her young servant girl, who had been diagnosed with leukemia.

The only allopathic treatment that had been offered the girl was a bone marrow transplant that was beyond the financial means of either the girl's family or that of my hostess. On the way to the temple, my hostess stopped to light candles as an offering at a small Catholic roadside shrine to the Virgin. When she heard the details of my fieldwork, she begged me to take her to Amma before I left Hyderabad, hoping that she would be able to target and "attack" the presumably spiritual causes behind the young girl's illness. Resorting to multiple religious healing systems/healers for a persistent illness or family trouble in this way is typical of many, even most, Hyderabadis. Spiritual healing characterizes vernacular religious traditions in India, creating a shared plane of experience and assumptions of spiritual powers that impact physical bodies across lines of educational, class, caste, and religious differences. But each healing site is uniquely created by who "sits" in it and the means through which they claim authority to be there. In the case of Amma's healing room, it is her gender that most uniquely characterizes her practice, and analyzing how she is able to negotiate authority to practice in a ritual role traditionally limited to men reveals other sites of creativity and flexibility in vernacular Islam.

Called to Amma's Courtyard

In the winter of 1989 I was in Hyderabad to codirect a three-week workshop called "Women, Folklore, and Fieldwork," held on Osmania University campus and sponsored by the Ford Foundation. My codirector was folklorist Margaret Mills, who had conducted her earlier fieldwork in Afghanistan. She was familiar with Islam and I was fluent in the Hindi/ Urdu spoken by Hyderabadi Muslims, so we decided that we would conduct the fieldwork for this workshop among Muslim women. Our intention was for workshop participants to collect women's life histories. We reasoned that this would also provide a unique opportunity for the nineteen Hindu workshop participants (women with master's degrees and doctorates in anthropology, English, and folklore) to work with a community not of their own linguistic and religious backgrounds. This would be the first time most of the workshop participants had entered a Muslim home, eaten with Muslims, and observed their rituals firsthand.

Before the workshop began, we had asked our university contacts to make some initial inquiries in the community to locate Muslim women with whom we could work. When we arrived in Hyderabad, we learned that no contacts had been located, and after three days of the 21-day workshop had passed, we realized that we would need to make these contacts ourselves. Because of periodic tensions between Hindus and Muslims in Hyderabad, there seemed to be some nervousness among the university personnel about a group of Hindu women working with Muslims, and they subtly tried to change our minds about having chosen a Muslim context for our fieldwork. Some of the workshop participants were housed in the Osmania University Guest House, which is perched up on a rocky hill overlooking a neighborhood of university housing for nonacademic employees (janitors, clerks, watchmen, etc.). From that distance I had noticed a green flag flying in the middle of the neighborhood, and I knew that under such a flag we would find some kind of Islamic ritual activity, a place where we could begin to find women with whom to work. It was with some nervousness that I walked with two of the workshop participants across the road and into the cluster of homes to see who or what was beneath the green flag.

There, in a shaded courtyard under the flag, sat several Muslim women in their black *burqās,* Hindu women in brightly colored saris, and a handful of men. Others were crowded around a small doorway, pressing to get in, straining to catch a glimpse of someone inside or hear a voice from within. We too stood at the periphery of that group and asked what was happening and who was inside. When Amma heard whispers of the presence of "some women from the outside," she called us into the healing room.[3] She was seated on the floor in front of a small wooden writing desk covered with slips of paper held down by paperweights. Ten to twelve people were seated on the ground around her. She asked them to move over to make space for the three of us, invited us to sit down, and soon called for tea.

Amma was a middle-aged woman (when I first met her in 1989, she was in her mid-fifties) who briefly identified herself as a *pirānimā* [wife of a *pīr*, a Sufi teacher/master] who meets patients here in the healing room and writes *tāvīz* for them [amulets with Quranic verses, numbers, and names of God written on them]. Her healing practice, she continued,

1. Patients waiting in the courtyard of Amma's healing room, 1989.

was based on the Quran, and its success was guaranteed for illness caused by spiritual forces. But she was curious about how we had found her. I explained that we were living across the street in the Guest House for three weeks while teaching/taking a course at the university, but we were restless staying inside and studying all day; we wanted to meet our neighbors. (Only much later did I learn what an appropriate term I had used for the context: restlessness/*becainī*. It is a symptom with which many of Amma's patients come to her for relief.) After all, I continued, "What's the use of staying only in the Guest House and classrooms?" The patients sitting around Amma laughed and confirmed our intuitions: " 'Correct, correct'."[4] I visited Amma nearly every day in the three weeks that followed, fascinated by her strong presence in a public ritual role that I would have expected to be traditionally closed to a Muslim woman. At the end of the workshop, during the course of which the participants had been welcomed, fed, and told many stories by the women of this neighborhood, I sadly took my leave of Amma, expecting that this would be my last visit.

However, through an unexpected unfolding of events, I was able to return to Amma's courtyard for seven weeks in 1990–1991. I worked with Amma again for nine months in 1994–1995, one month in 1996, in January 1999, and again in January 2000. Amma always assumed I would come back after my very first afternoon visit, first expecting a daily visit during the 1989 workshop, and then from across oceans that physically separated us. As she told me, in some variation, upon each return, "I knew you would come. My heart pulled for you; my heart pulled for you and you came." When I walked through her door in September 1994 unannounced after an absence of three years, she told me she had dreamed of me surrounded by water. I was wearing a black sari blouse. Her heart pulled, she said, and now I had come.[5] By the time I left Hyderabad in July 1995, after ten months of fieldwork with Amma, she assured me we need not be separated although oceans would be between us; all I needed to do was call to her in my dreams and she would come.

I first came to Amma with little firsthand fieldwork experience of Islam and only slightly more "book" knowledge. While I speak Hindi fluently and am able to communicate with Amma orally with little problem (gradually learning Urdu words specific to the context of her practice), I do not read Arabic. Thus, I often felt like I came to her as do most of her patients, who also do not read Arabic; in fact, I never saw a patient read an amulet or ask Amma about what was written on it. Had I come to Amma's healing room with a fluency in reading Arabic, classically trained in Islamic studies in a university context or one of traditional Islamic scholarship, I might have focused more on the written word—what was written on the amulets; the connection between these texts and the Quran, *hadith*, and other Islamic texts; the relationship between Indo-Persian Islamic traditions of Hyderabad and Arabic traditions—rather than oral communication and performance in the healing room, and the questions and focus of this study would have been very different.

Gender and Religious Identities at a Healing Crossroads

During the course of my first meeting with Amma, perhaps in an effort to make me and my two Hindu colleagues feel at ease—and I later heard similar statements in several other contexts—Amma asserted, "There are only two castes [*jāti*, species; true distinctions]: men and women. Muslims, Christians, Hindus—they're all the same." *Jāti* literally means "birth" and is the Indian-language term for regional endogamous caste groups—the religious, social group into which one is born. It is also the word for species; so that in Indian-language translations of the story of Noah and the ark, the animals go up into the ark two by two, "*jāti* by *jāti*." When I met Amma again in January 1991, right after the Gulf War had broken out, she added to a repetition of her earlier assertion, "After all, don't all mothers cry when their sons are killed in war?" Her statements imply that motherhood crosscuts and supersedes boundaries of religious difference and that gender, not religion, is the ultimate boundary of distinction between human beings.

Amma's assertion about gender and religious identities directs us to two significant features of vernacular Islam as performed in Amma's healing room—a site where Islamic religious practice is negotiable, creative, and flexible: 1) the articulation of an Islamic cosmology that encompasses difference and a religious practice that depends on a worldview shared across religious boundaries represented by its participants—Amma even declares these boundaries to be nonexistent—and 2) the potential flexibility of gender roles in domestic and ritual contexts of Islam in practice. Concerns about gender and religious identities carry differential weight in the healing room itself, however. Amma and her patients often talk about gendered experience and negotiations of gendered roles and authority—these are of immediate concern to them as well as to the fieldworker who notices Amma's unusual public position of authority in a traditionally male ritual role of public healer. Female patients, in particular, frequently comment that they come to Amma from great distances because of her uniqueness as a *female* healer. However, rarely do patients say they are coming to her specifically because she is a *Muslim* healer; religious identities, cosmologies, and theologies are not openly articulated or debated in this healing context.

During my fieldwork with Amma over the years, I was often asked by her patients what I was doing there at her healing table. I told them that I was planning to write a book about Amma so that Americans, more particularly my students, would know that there are powerful articulate women in India such as Amma. (Abba once proudly interjected, "Yes, Amma is going to appear on exams in America!") I sometimes tried to explain the stereotypes of Muslim women that often appear in the American press and conversations: the woman in a black *burqā* with no life (agency) behind the veiling. I elaborated that I knew a lot about Hindu women's lives and practices and now I wanted to learn more about the ways and practices [*niyam*] of Muslim women because books about Islam often do not include much about women's everyday lives. One of Amma's age-mates who often sits with her in the healing room explained in more colloquial terms, which I myself began to use, "She wants to know about women's things [*zanāne kī bāt*]." Many patients and disciples were surprised that there could be such a level of ignorance of their lives and customs in America,[6] and they often enthusiastically encouraged me to continue my work. Because of the structural and personal inequality these women often experience, "women's things," or gender, is a named category and an indigenous concern in this community. As the Personal Narratives Group asserts in its introduction to *Interpreting Women's Lives*, "For men, gender has been an unmarked category. For a woman, however, the story is rarely told without reference to the dynamics of gender" (1989, 5).

While my engagement with issues of gender was immediately understandable to Amma's healing community, my interest in the dynamics of religious identities and elements of worldview shared across these boundaries was more difficult to explain. Why and how religious healing works across religious boundaries is implicitly assumed and understood by patients; these issues are of more concern to scholars and students outside this local context than to the Muslim and Hindu participants who interact with Amma.

Amma and her patients, however, have no question about who is a Hindu and who is a Muslim when they meet and speak with each other in the healing room. Visually, Hindu and Muslim identities in Amma's healing room and courtyard are marked in several ways. The most obvious marker for women is whether or not they are veiled (which, for Muslims, might range from covering one's head with the end of a sari to wearing the full black *burqā*). But not all Muslim women veil. Among unveiled women, Hindus can be identified by the vermilion powder forehead marker called, in Telugu, a *boṭṭu*. Most Hindu women in Hyderabad apply such a vermilion mark on their foreheads daily, and Hindu men may apply it after worshipping in temples or their home shrines. Further, sari styles and colors and types of jewelry may also differ according to caste and religious identities. It is difficult to visually determine whether the majority of men who come into the healing room are Muslim or Hindu unless they have just attended a Hindu ritual and have the forehead marking on or if they are highly observant and committed disciples of a Muslim *pīr*. Circumcision, the external sign of a Muslim male, is not visible, of course, at the healing table. Male disciples' commitment to both their *pīr* and Islamic identity is marked by shoulder-length hair, beards, *surmā* [eyeliner], and embroidered or white crocheted skullcaps/head coverings.

But at this place, in the healing room, religious distinctions and identities are not those that matter most. Patients know, understand, and accept the contours of the religious landscape and identities encoded in practice and performance at this site of vernacular practice. The patients who come to Amma for healing, whether they are Muslim, Christian, or

2. Muslim family seated at Amma's healing table, 1995.

10

3. Hindu couple listening to Amma's diagnoses, 1995.

Hindu, recognize in her a charismatic woman who controls spiritual forces that cross religious boundaries and have impinged upon their lives in negative ways. This much they share, although the ways they identify and interpret these forces and their understanding of the means through which Amma controls them might vary significantly. However, when I described my work to individuals outside the context of Amma's healing room in Hyderabad and later presented numerous papers about her practice at academic conferences in the United States, the issue of religious identity, difference, and propriety was often of primary concern to Muslim members of those audiences. Several Muslim audience members over the years have raised vigorous objections to my research of what may be identified as "Sufi" practices, telling me that "all this" was not "true Islam" but was rather influenced by Hindu culture. I was asked what the purpose of such research was, of what "good" it was, and I was often admonished that to sit at Amma's healing table was not an appropriate way to learn about

Islam. These comments distinguish between something these critics perceive to be "real" (standard, universal) Islam and vernacular expressions of Islam.

Several scholars, including Katherine Ewing (1997), Peter van der Veer (1992), and Claudia Liebeskind (1998), have observed that many nineteenth-century and contemporary South Asian Muslim reformists criticized the public display of particular Sufi practices such as veneration of the saint at his/her gravesite shrine [*dargāh*] even as they themselves n still accepted Sufi identity and historical Sufi saints to be important Muslim scholars. Indian Deobandi reformists in the nineteenth century, for example, self-identified as Sufis but argued that Sufi practice should be internalized; they objected, in particular, to what looked like worship of the saint (Metcalf 1982, 158). Many reformists have criticized this veneration of saints as an infiltration of Hindu practice and ideology into Muslim communities. Spiritual healing such as that practiced by Amma, one that calls upon angels and other powerful messengers to intervene in the physical and social world, is, according to the critical Muslim voices that I heard, only a small step from what is perceived to be "heretical" saint veneration that belies the crucial Muslim concept of *tawhīd* [the unity of God].

Internalizing this critique, my first working title for this book was *Healing at the Boundaries.* Even as I argued that my purpose in writing the book was to analyze vernacular Islam as *practiced* and not to be prescriptive about what was "true" or "false" Islam, I was subconsciously persuaded that Amma's practice was, nevertheless, on the periphery of some "true (monolithic) Islam." I returned to Hyderabad to sit at Amma's table for a month in 1996 with an uneasy question of how to frame this book in such a way as to protect her (and myself) from the incessant critique that "this isn't Islam." Perhaps, I thought, this kind of healing practice really *was* peripheral to Hyderabadi Muslim culture, a perspective I might have missed by centering my work with a single individual and physically situating my fieldwork primarily in her healing room and contexts related to it.

However, when I returned to Amma's healing table with this question of marginality (and, therefore, legitimacy with relationship to Islam) troubling me, I was immediately struck by the fact that Amma herself (and her patients and disciples) did not see her practice or her healing space as marginal at all. During the month I lived in Hyderabad on this visit, I asked most everyone with whom I spoke outside the healing room, Hindu, Muslim, or Christian, whether s/he or anyone in their family had been to a spiritual healer like Amma. I came across only a handful of people, regardless of educational level or religious background, who had not had any experience with religious healing. Some of the Muslim re-spondents were the same people who had earlier voiced objection to my research; but now when asked specifically about their own experiences, they admitted that when a child had been chronically or critically ill or a woman in the extended family had had problems of infertility, for ex-ample, someone in their family had visited a *pīr* [Sufi teacher/saint] or *dargāh* for healing.

Indian Muslims are not alone in their participation in vernacular Is-lamic healing practices, particularly as they are associated with saint ven-eration. Similar traditions are found in Muslim cultures from Indonesia and China to Morocco and Egypt (for examples outside India, see Bowen 1993; Crapanzano 1973; Ewing 1997; Hoffman 1995; Morsy 1993). Un-der the strong hand of the Wahhabi reform movements, the absence of saint veneration and associated practices in the Saudi kingdom is an ex-ception rather than the norm. Nevertheless, many critical voices that have emerged from, or been influenced by, this movement are loud and artic-ulate in international media and transnational contexts.[7] Amma is surely aware of the critiques of the kinds of practices in which she engages,[8] but this debate entered her healing room only once during all the months I worked with her. One of Amma's close disciples and his three brothers were absent from the healing room when I returned in 1999. This disciple had been a regular at Amma's healing table, so I asked where he was. Another disciple told me the four brothers had found a new guru who had told them that "all these things" that Amma did were wrong; he said the disciple had "become a Wahabbi." Amma did not engage in this conversation except to mutter, "Let him go." Amma sees herself and her practices not as peripheral but at the very center, a center through which multiple axes of religious identities meet and cross at what I have called a "crossroads," *caurāstā* in Hindi and Urdu. I take seriously Amma's self-identification as Muslim and seek to understand how and when

13

this identity is shaped, enacted, and articulated at this site of vernacular Islam.

Amma's Healing Room as a Crossroads: *Caurāstā*

A crossroads in Indian contexts is conceptualized as a center, but only one of many centers in a network of multiple roads with numerous crossings. In traditional Indian cities, towns, and local neighborhoods, *caurāstās* are meetingplaces where roads and people are experienced as coming together as well as going out. I have not heard the term *"caurāstā"* used in the sense that "crossroads" is often used in English—as a place in one's travels or life where a decision must be made to turn one direction or another, such as is implied in Robert Frost's "The Road Not Taken," a poem that has helped to shape American English connotations of "crossroads." Another more recent image of crossroads in American popular culture is the final image in the 2000 Hollywood film *Castaway*, in which the main character (played by Tom Hanks) stands at a crossroads in the middle of Midwestern American cornfields, making a decision to go one way or the other, a decision that will forever determine the direction of his life. Indian urban crossroads are not these kinds of forlorn or lonely places of personal decision; their corners are bustling with tea stalls, bus stands, and movie theaters, filled with crowds and conversation. When someone answers a request for directions in traditional neighborhoods of Indian cities, s/he is often given the response: "Go to X *caurāstās* [X often being marked by some identifiable building such as a hospital, theater, government building, etc.], then turn left," and so forth. Even though *caurāstās* serve as important identity markers for particular neighborhoods, very few people who pass through them actually live there or even stay there for very long; they are *public* gathering places and social spaces, not domestic spaces. Finally, *caurāstā* may also be experienced as dangerous places, in part because they are spaces through which any kind of person can pass; a person does not have the kind of control here that s/he might have over her/his domestic space. Many Indian crossroads are marked with protective shrines; others are sites at which dangerous "leftovers" from a particular ritual are left at a distance from the ritual site itself. It is with these many connotations that Amma's healing room serves as a crossroads, a *caurāstā*: a public social space uniquely created by the particular roads and travelers who cross through it.[9]

Amma's healing room is a physical locale where patients of many different religious and social identities meet for a common cause, creating a shared identity between them—as Amma emphasizes, they are not Hindus or Muslims in this place but patients with troubles and/or disciples who have entered a relationship with Amma and Abba. But this is not a space where they dwell; it is a *caurāstā*. When they go home and arrange the marriages of their children or conduct death rituals for their parents, it matters very much whether or not they are Muslim or Hindu.

Healing sites are only one of several kinds of crossroads where Hindu and Muslim traditions have traditionally and still do intersect and/or share space. Other similar *caurāstās* include shared genres of music (for example, outside of its Muslim ritual context, *qavvālī* is a genre of popular music on the radio and in music competitions in North India), traditionally Hindu dance genres such as Bharata Natyam performed by both Hindu and Muslim dancers, festivals during which members of different religious traditions invite each other to their homes or during which they participate on other levels, shared linguistic and literary traditions (see Narayanan 2000 for a Tamil example), marriage and other life-cycle ritual customs (including turmeric "baths" for brides and application of henna on their hands), shrines of Muslim saints where both Hindus and Muslims come to worship, and the relationships between living gurus and disciples of different religious identities. Once axes of difference cross through the *caurāstā*, where they might be said to collapse or be overlooked in favor of the common "task" or performance at hand, they reassert themselves in different contexts (at the far ends of the axes) and help create boundaries of difference. Examples of these axes are endogamous marriage customs, death rituals, and attitudes toward image worship; the farther the axes move out from the *caurāstā*, the more it matters who is Hindu and Muslim.

Relationships Shaping This Project

During my first extended fieldwork with Amma in 1990–1991, she invited me to sit next to her in a chair where her disciples often sat when

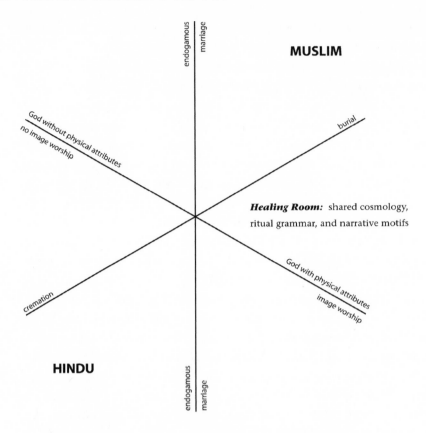

endogamous marriage

MUSLIM

God without physical attributes
no image worship

burial

Healing Room: shared cosmology,
ritual grammar, and narrative motifs

God with physical attributes
image worship

cremation

HINDU

endogamous marriage

4. *Caurāstā* of Amma's healing room. Intersecting axes of identity and context: marriage (endogamy by religious tradition and caste), death (burial/cremation), image worship/no images.

they came to visit her. It was a preexisting seat for learning and an easy place for an ethnographer to slip into. This is what disciples do: they sit with Amma to learn, both through conscious teaching and simply by being in a space permeated by her *barkat* [spiritual blessing/power]. When I returned to Hyderabad for long-term fieldwork in 1994, after several months of sitting in a chair by her side, Amma asked me to move to a rickety folding chair across the table from her. From this space, she asked me to help her fold amulets which she had prescribed to patients and upon which she had written their names. (Each kind of amulet is folded or rolled differently, and I was not equally efficient in all the different modes—a matter of considerable amusement to other disciples.) Sometimes there were two or three of us sitting on that side of the table helping her; Amma laughed and commented that this was just like a school, with a teacher and her students. Many patients assumed I was simply another disciple; if they asked directly, Amma often answered with some variant of, "She doesn't need to be a disciple [*murīd*]; she loves God and I love God, so we have a connection [*nisbat*]." As the years progressed, Amma drew other parallels between our personalities: that we were both inquisitive, loved learning, and had the freedom to "move about" (in public). She interpreted these connections as having been desired by God. Once when I brought her a miniature china tea set from the United States, she looked at it carefully and then said, "You brought these little things because of your great love for me. This was His [God's] order. He put the love in your heart. Why? Because I love Him, He sent love to your heart. And because I love you [lit., want you] and you love me, you brought these things." Her comments reflect the common belief in Sufi mystical traditions that the relationship between *pīrs* [teachers] and disciples are preordained, that the *pīr* calls out to his disciple (often through dreams), and that disciples might wander for months or years, from *pīr* to *pīr*, before finding the one who is ordained for them (see, for example, Liebeskind 1998 and Ewing 1997).

Sometimes patients and visitors to the healing room assumed that I was sitting at Amma's healing table in order to learn her practice so that one day I, too, might practice, as was the case with several of her male disciples. I tried to explain that I simply wanted to understand, but not practice, what Amma does. Amma teased one inquisitive patient, "No, no. I'll teach Jo-ice how to deal with *śaitān* [devils] and then she can open a store in America." Another time, she laughed and said, "Jo-ice's husband is a doctor of *insān* [people]; Jo-ice and I are doctors of *śaitān* [the devil; i.e., illnesses caused by the devil]." The patient asked if there were healers like Amma in America. On that occasion I said, "No, people in the U.S. may have *śaitānī* [negative spiritual forces impacting their lives], but they usually don't understand it to be such, so they don't have practices like this. As a result, however, perhaps some of their illnesses don't get better." Amma agreed: "If the problem is caused by *śaitān*, then no other kinds of treatments will work." On other occasions, particularly in private conversations with Amma, I tried to explain how psychotherapists practiced in the United States, what kinds of illnesses they treated, and suggested that they were perhaps the practitioners who were the closest equivalent to her. (Only later I realized that I had left out several more explicitly religious healing traditions, such as those practiced in several charismatic Christian denominations, Seventh-day Adventists, and Christian Science.) Amma often teased me that she would come to the United States, then, and set up business in my house.

Although I often figuratively, culturally, and spatially filled the role of a disciple, Amma and Abba never asked me to become a formal disciple [*murīd*]. Initially, I did not know quite what being a disciple would imply and what initiation rituals were required. At the end of my first seven-week period of intensive fieldwork with Amma in 1990–1991, on the day I was saying goodbye, Amma gave me a set of prayer beads [*tasbī*] and said, with a somewhat amused tone, "Now you're my *murīd*." At the time I had not yet seen an initiation and thought that this minimal gesture might be it. I returned home that afternoon a little confused as to what my obligations now were, since I was leaving India the next day to return to the United States. I told my fieldwork associate, with whom I had been working the last several weeks, about the prayer beads. She reacted unexpectedly strongly, even angrily, "She's just taking advantage of you! Now she can tell everyone she has a foreign disciple!" However, I thought to myself of all I had been given and of which I had taken advantage: I had sat every day for seven weeks at Amma's right hand, had been served tea and lunch with her day after day, asked what might have seemed like intrusive questions over and over, taped numerous hours of conversation and narrative performance, and would return to the United States to present conference papers about Amma. If her reputation increased slightly due to my presence, of which, at the time, I was doubtful, I was certain the relationship was not one-sided.

When I returned to Hyderabad for a year in 1994–1995, patients again frequently asked Amma if I was her disciple. She never said yes, but, as mentioned above, often answered that there was no need for me to be, because "she loves God and I love God." On other occasions she would say I spent more time with her than her disciples did, so I was like a disciple. Amma explained to one patient, "She's come from America. We have an old friendship, with love from the heart. She's been coming from America for ten years now." And when disciples worried about my safety in the face of the negative spiritual forces with which Amma was dealing, Amma quickly asserted that there was no reason to fear because she and our close relationship would protect me.

It was not until the winter of 1995 that I first witnessed a formal initiation, an elaborate ritual that only Abba, and not Amma, formally participates in as spiritual guide/teacher [*pīr*]. I realized that the presentation of prayer beads was not an equivalent of this formal ritual, but it was perhaps the closest Amma could "legitimately" do, since women do not formally make disciples in traditional Sufi lineages. In retrospect, I realize that Amma and Abba may not have asked me to become a disciple because of their own wisdom and insight—they knew I would not likely be able to fulfill the obligations of a disciple in such a relationship and that such a formalized relationship might have put me in some awkward situations. For example, close disciples are expected to visit Amma and Abba on a regular basis (some daily, others weekly), and they always wait to leave the healing room until Amma gives them permission to do so; sometimes they are late for work or miss an appointment as they sit with her, waiting. The disciple is expected to be totally obedient to the *pīr*. With the intervention of oceans, differences in cultures, the pressures of time in fieldwork, and the requirements of intellectual inquiry in an American academic context, it was not clear what such total obedience and subservience on my part would have implied or whether it would have been possible.

Nevertheless, I did fulfill *some* obligations, as I could, of a daughter and disciple. I visited Amma almost every day I spent in Hyderabad, and if I did not come, she always asked where I had been and whom I had visited, showing her approval or disapproval at the end of my story. I made no direct payments for the time and hospitality she offered me, but I did give her, upon my arrivals from and departures to the United States, gifts of a nature appropriate for a disciple: saris, fruits and nuts, small American knickknacks (good scissors were a favorite, since she used them every day to cut paper strips for amulets). Toward the end of my year-long fieldwork in 1995, I gave some slightly larger gifts of money (also appropriate for a disciple of some financial means) to put toward train tickets to make pilgrimage and to buy an elaborate *cādar* [embroidered velvet cloth] to offer on my behalf at the tomb of the saint Muinaddin Chishti at Ajmer. Finally, after Abba's death in 1998, I contributed money to help build up Abba's newly constructed gravesite. Amma and Abba often treated me as a disciple in their consciously framed teachings about how a disciple should live: about love, patience, human nature, and God. But I was also a fictive daughter. I ate with the family and went on family outings and shopping trips, and Amma included me in her gifting of new saris (with slip and blouse as well as matching glitzy glass bangles) to her daughters on the occasion of their biggest annual festival of Gyarwin Sharif (observing the death anniversary of their spiritual lineage's founding saint in Baghdad).

My relationship with Amma intensified and shifted over the years, and this relationship shaped my work in many ways. First, she gave her permission to me to sit at her side in the healing room with my tape recorder and notebook day after day, to enter her home at will, and to accompany her on pilgrimage and to patients' homes. Because I entered this fieldwork context knowing little about this level of vernacular Muslim practice, with its specialized vocabulary and ritual, initially I asked what must have seemed like many naive questions. Amma patiently answered these questions both directly and indirectly, ultimately determining what it was she wanted me to know. Several times when I asked for an explanation of something, she would say, "Ah, Jo-ice, this is a heavy matter [*bahut bhārī bāt hai*]," and that would end the conversation. That is, Amma implied that the question at hand was a matter only for those of a certain spiritual development, which presumably I had not yet reached; that it was beyond my understanding for other reasons; or that this was not the time and place for such explanations. Sometimes she would answer, "I'll explain everything sometime when we have time," but the explanation often would not be forthcoming, either because she forgot about it or because extended time alone was rarely available. Once she explicitly told me that there were some things she could not tell me, as she had not been given permission [*ijāzat*] to do so by her own *pīr*. Here, too, Amma's wisdom helped shape some of the knowledge represented in this book: that is, there are some "secret" things about this spiritual path that

I would not be able to write about if I knew them. Therefore, ethically, it may be easier for me not to know them, since that specific esoteric knowledge is not crucial to answering the questions that became central to my work.

Near the end of my year with Amma in 1994–1995, I was about to leave her room to attend a Hindu ritual being conducted to bless the home of a dear friend of both of ours when Amma stopped me to say, "Now that you've sat with me so long and we have developed such a close connection/relationship [*nisbat*], you shouldn't accept *prasād* [food offered to Hindu deities] anymore. You should certainly go, but don't eat *prasād*." This injunction was an indication of having reached still another level of deepening personal and spiritual relationship with Amma. Another stage of the relationship was marked by Amma asking me to help fold amulets as I sat there at her table, as only disciples do this. Actually, her request came through a humorous reprimand: "Are you just going to sit there? Why don't you start folding *fālitā* with Hussein [a disciple]?" Shortly before I left Hyderabad in April 1995, Amma taught me some short *zikr* [recitations of the name of God]; Abba said that all I needed to do was recite these and he and Amma would come to me. Finally, an important marker of our relationship, particularly from Amma's perspective, came when I told her about Abba's appearance to me in a dream after he had died. She was comforted by this and told me it was an indication of his love for me. Amma set the pace of our developing relationship and frequently interpreted it both for those in her community (in ways I might not have thought to) and for me.

But Amma also determined the shape of my fieldwork on a much more practical level. Because I fit into fictive relationships with Amma of both mother/daughter and guru/disciple, she took authority in telling me "what I should do"; I complied when I could. As mentioned earlier, even from the beginning, during the three weeks in 1989 when I was teaching the folklore workshop, Amma quickly began to expect my presence in her room every day. When I returned to work with her in 1994, my initial research plan was to accompany patients home, to hear their stories outside of the presence of Amma, to find out more about other genres of healing they accessed, and so forth. But as I entered the healing room again after a prolonged absence, it became quite clear that I needed to make a choice: either I could align myself primarily with Amma and tell the story of this level of practice from the perspective of her healing room and courtyard (realizing the limitations of this perspective as well as its strengths) or I could conduct broader survey research, visiting numerous healers and meeting with patients in their homes to observe how their narratives changed outside Amma's presence and the context of the healing room. I realized that the latter research strategy would preclude the intimate relationship, loyalty, and access that I would eventually establish with Amma and Abba. I chose the former.

The Case for Case Studies

This book is a study of one woman's life and work rather than a panoramic view of South Asian religious healing traditions or of Muslim healing sites and healers. It is not a comprehensive study of South Asian Muslim women's ritual activities and/or oral performance genres. A study of the practice of one female Muslim healer in South India cannot make all-encompassing generalizations about Islam, about women in Islam or women in India, or even about practices of healing in vernacular Islam in South Asia. It might, however, suggest possible parameters of these categories and point to directions for further research in all these areas. More important, this case study suggests the possibility for agency and action, flexibility and creativity within these religious and cultural contexts. By working with a single individual over time and in different stages of life, this study analyzes sites and processes of negotiation available to an individual, examining how Amma articulates and negotiates gender, authority, and religious identities and how these shift over time. The possibilities for the flexibility inherent in vernacular practice are not unique to Amma, but they are often observable only by working with specific individuals over time. Analyzing these possibilities helps us be aware of and look for similar possibilities in other contexts.[10]

While the experience of every individual is worthy of documentation and study, not all individuals are equally articulate, observant, interpretive, or dramatic in relating their own and others' experiences. Ethnographic studies of single individuals (including through the genre of life history) have generally been about individuals who are particularly articulate and good storytellers, which also means that they might not be "typical" on many levels (see for example Abu-Lughod 1993; Behar 1993; Kendall 1988; Shostak 1981). Marjorie Shostak tells us that she interviewed many !Kung women before she settled in long-term work with Nisa, who seemed to understand in ways that the other women had not what it was that Shostak was most interested in and, perhaps more important, what it would take to teach her these things so that she would understand (Shostak 1981, 39). Amma has all these characteristics. Because she is a professional healer (defined here, in part, as someone who meets the 'public', rather than just family members), she comes into contact with and hears the personal narratives of a wide range of people—Hindus and Muslims, men and women—from a variety of economic and religious backgrounds. This is in contrast to many of her age-mates who do not work outside the home or to men whose employment limits their interactions with persons from many economic, religious, and social backgrounds. Amma is a particularly keen observer of human nature, since part of her role as healer is to frame human experiences of illness and suffering in ways that are meaningful to both the individuals and the communities in which they live. Amma's unusual breadth of knowledge and interest in learning, heightened abilities of observation, and dramatic storytelling style are accentuated when compared to many other women in whose courtyards and kitchens I drank innumerable cups of tea and with whom I conversed.

A common critique of the case study approach is that it is simply anecdotal. Many of my academic colleagues in India, in particular, questioned the validity of this kind of fieldwork for this reason. They encouraged me to conduct a representative sampling, not only within Hyderabad among Muslim healers but also in other parts of the country, or to include healing practitioners of other religious traditions; many had specific healers in mind whom they thought I should include in such a survey. I was frequently asked something like, "So do you really learn something new every day, day after day, sitting with your Amma? Isn't this a waste of time, especially if Amma is so unusual and not like other Muslim women?"

Judith Okely offers some responses to this question in her article "Defiant Moments: Gender, Resistance and Individuals" (1991), arguing that it is only by looking at culture at the level of individual lives that "cracks of resistance" to dominant ideologies are revealed. Further, she continues, these cracks are often more visible when we look at the lives of and listen to the stories of unusual individuals. While such individuals might be dismissed as eccentric, their very idiosyncrasies are defined as such by the dominant structures within which they live. As Margaret Mills has made the case for studies of unusual individuals, "The *telling* case may seldom be the *typical* case" (1995; emphasis in original). The fact that Amma is so unusual as a Muslim woman in a public healing practice in Hyderabad suggests the parameters of what is stereotyped as "usual" in gendered roles and positions in Islam in South Asia (stereotyped by the community itself as well as by outsiders). The case study provides a window into the ways individuals interact with, and their experiences feed back into, the social construction of gender and dominant ideologies and models for action. Finally, as Lila Abu-Lughod argues, "focusing on individuals encourages familiarity rather than distance and helps to break down 'otherness'" (1993, 29). An individual such as Amma works and lives in networks of relationships with family, patients, and disciples as well as within the contexts of wider religious and cultural traditions; to focus on Amma as an individual is also to look through an expanding lens at wider communities and contexts.

Abu-Lughod takes the argument for the benefits of focusing on in-dividuals one step further in "Writing Against Culture," her introduction to *Writing Women's Worlds: Bedouin Stories,* where she argues that the "typical" often exists more in the imagination and scholarship of the an-thropologist than in practice. Experimenting with a range of narrative forms (including "stories of everyday life, arguments, reminiscences, folk-tales, poems, songs, and even a written letter and an essay with oral com-mentary" [32]), Abu-Lughod demonstrates the ways individuals subvert typification, homogeneity, and coherence. She further argues that the nar-rative ethnography she employs is necessarily situated or positioned, leav-ing traces of the performer/teller and audiences, and thus is a genre that inherently dispenses with the pretense of "objectivity."[11] Similarly, in her study of the trope and personhood of the Sufi *pīr* in Pakistan, *Arguing Sainthood: Modernity, Psychoanalysis, and Islam,* Katherine Ewing looks for sites of individual agency and subjectivity within what is frequently assumed to be a hegemonic force of modernity (4). Individual negotiations and alternative constructions of culture are, she finds, most visible in "everyday interpersonal arguments and [in] the telling of personal narratives" (5). *In Amma's Healing Room* is situated in the traditions of narrative ethnography that Abu-Lughod and Ewing advocate.

My focus on specific interactions and rituals as performed by given individuals at specific moments is also influenced by performance studies. Scholars such as Charles Briggs (1988), Richard Bauman (1992, 1977), and Catherine Bell (1998) characterize performance as an "emergent" phenomenon that shifts at each occurrence according to the shifting contexts in which it occurs. Sometimes these shifts make little difference in the experience and creative potential of the performance, but other times they do directly affect what is created through the performance and/or how it is received or experienced by participants and audiences. After they establish a grammar of performance of a particular genre or repertoire of genres, performance studies scholars are interested in specific ethnographic instances of that genre in performance rather than in generalized descriptions or an idealized abstract of a ritual or oral performance genre. To analyze specific instances is to foreground individual agency, observe the ways individuals manipulate and negotiate with tradition to create meaning of their own circumstances, and understand culture-making as a dynamic process (Bell 1998, 209).

Ethnographic fieldwork with individuals over time makes it readily apparent that individuals do not stay frozen in time and place. During the first months I sat in Amma's healing room, as we were getting to know each other, she often performed narratives that illustrated how different she was from other women and illustrated her successes as a healer. I heard very few personal narratives of pain and what she would call "troubles" [*pareśānī*], such as those her patients bring to her. However, as I became more integrated into her healing community and family, the nature of the narratives she performed began to change, particularly when we were not sitting at the healing table. They revealed cracks, difficulties, and continual re-creation and negotiation of the authority she displays at the healing table. Had I not worked with Amma over a period of time,

I might have only been told those narratives of exceptionalism and would not have learned of Amma's own personal pain and burdens and the ways she negotiates these with her professional role as healer.

In addition to the question of what an ethnographer can learn from a single individual and whether such study is representative, many of my academic colleagues in Hyderabad wondered how I would or could verify whether what Amma was telling me was really the "truth," especially in personal narratives of her childhood, her visions, and her healing miracles. Recent scholarship on life histories has focused less on historical verifiability of narratives than with their performative impact as representations that both reflect and construct social identities (Alter 2000, Kratz 2001, Lawless 1993, 1988). Katherine Ewing describes the constructive potential of such personal narratives:

> Narratives in which a subject accounts for its past activities, as in a life history, also display conflicts and inconsistencies as the individual as experiencing subject claims or denies identity with past positionings. Through narratives the subject works to cover the gaps created by these slippages, thereby indicating its presence while evading capture. (1997, 6)

One of my goals when I returned to Amma's healing room for a full year of fieldwork was to elicit her life history as an extended narrative. I soon realized that this genre of elicited narrative would be difficult to record during Amma's busy days; she simply did not have the time to sit with me alone for hour upon hour either before or after her long healing days. I did, however, tape many personal narratives in shorter segments, which were performed as part of Amma's healing rhetoric and in everyday conversations. I became interested in how and when they were performed and how their content shifted over time. Particularly regarding Amma's narratives of her early years and narratives of visions and dreams, I am less interested in their verifiable "fact" than in the ways Amma performs narratives as self-representations and the ways they create and sustain her identity and authority as healer. By reproducing and analyzing many of these narratives, I hope to reflect Amma's voice in the ways she chooses to represent herself.

Names and Anonymity

Conversations and narratives that I recorded at Amma's healing table or while sharing lunches are not in any sense "private" in their indigenous performance contexts. The healing room is filled with people and Amma encourages patients to pay attention to other cases that precede theirs;[12] it was rare that Amma and I were alone in her living quarters. Amma and her patients knew I was recording these interactions, and both Amma and Abba were proud that a book would eventually be published about them. I tried to explain what the book might look like and how it might used in university classes. I showed them a copy of the book I had written on Chhattisgarhi folklore of middle India (Flueckiger 1996) and explained that instead of the photograph of Chhattisgarhi women on the cover, I would put a picture of Amma on the cover—would that be all right? Abba laughingly pressed me, "Why only Amma? Why not me, too?" Then I showed a map of India that had been reproduced in my earlier book and asked if I had Amma's permission to reproduce one of her amulets in the same manner. She was puzzled about why this would even be a question—of course I could. In fact, she encouraged me, "Show two or three! Why just one?"

I have been periodically encouraged by scholars in the United States to use pseudonyms for Amma and Abba and not to reveal the site of Amma's practice or to fictionalize it in some way so that they could not be easily located or identified. One anthropologist even thought I should not show Amma's face but should use only photographs that were shot from the back or side. However, pseudonyms and anonymity would be a foreign concept to Amma and Abba, who are proud of her renown. I have decided to honor their decision to represent them by name, location, and photographs in this book, with the lingering reservation that although they gave their full permission and took pride in their identities being known "beyond the seven seas,"[13] they could not fully know what this might mean and who the readers of this book might be and how differently they might think from the audiences and patients Amma and Abba know.

Hyderabadi Cultural Contexts

Amma's healing practice is located in the South Indian city of Hyderabad, which is the capital city of the contemporary state of Andhra Pradesh and the fifth-largest metropolitan area in India. (Together with its twin city Secunderabad, the urban area has a population of close to five million.) It lays at an intersection of north-south and east-west geographic axes on the rocky dry landscape of the Deccan Plateau. Today it is known internationally as one of India's high-tech cities and is a major source of highly skilled software and computer engineers who have emigrated in high numbers to the United States. Several international companies, including Microsoft and General Electric, have also established branches in Hyderabad to take advantage of the highly skilled local workforce. While the city's landscape is changing rapidly with a burgeoning middle- and upper-class population and the proliferation of new highrise apartment buildings, Internet cafes, and widened streets lined with "modern" glitzy stores such as Nike, United Colors of Benetton, Levi's, and western-style multistoried department stores, most Hyderabadis have little access to these. Coexisting with these newly configured cityscapes are traditional neighborhoods intersected with narrow gulleys and streets through which fruit and vegetable vendors pull hand-drawn carts and the pace of traffic is set by pedestrians, bicycles, and motorcycle rickshaws (called "autos," short for "auto-rickshaw"). Perhaps the most startling contrasts to high-tech Hyderabad are the poorest neighborhoods of Old City, where there is no indoor plumbing or running water, open drains serve as sewers, and the majority of the population subsists on the wages of daily laborers. Many of Amma's patients are drawn from neighborhoods like these.

The ethos of what is considered to be unique "traditional" Hyderabadi culture, which is still palpable and visible today in architecture, music, dress and jewelry, and culinary offerings, is drawn from its Islamic past. Hyderabad's 400-year history begins with the Islamic Qutub Shahi dynasty (1512–1681). The Qutab Shahi rulers were Shii Muslims and great patrons of Persian arts, language, and culture—the impact of which can still be felt in Hyderabad today. The Qutab Shahis ruled until 1687, when Mughal emperor Aurangzeb's army captured Golconda after a long dramatic siege (which left a legacy of oral legends that still circulate today, including those of the saint Yusufayn, whose *dargāh* is one of the most important in Hyderabad).[14] But the Mughal Empire was already in decline and in 1724 the Mughal viceroy of the Deccan, Mir Qamaruddin, declared independence and established another Muslim dynasty, the Asaf Jah, whose sovereigns are called *nizams*. They ruled Hyderabad, the largest independent state in colonial India, until 1948.

When Indian independence was declared in 1947, the *nizam* announced that he would join neither India nor Pakistan but would remain independent until he saw how the political scene developed. But the new Indian government fully expected the princely states to accede to the union in matters of defense, foreign affairs, and communications (Smith 1988, 9–10). The *nizam* negotiated with the government for over a year and tensions rose. On September 13, 1948, the Indian army invaded the state of Hyderabad and quickly defeated the *nizam*'s forces. This date and what they call the Police Action are indelible in the memories of elderly Muslim men of Abba's generation, who in 1948 were young men seemingly sideswiped by forces of history beyond their control.[15] (Interestingly, I heard very few women speak of the Police Action.) Many Muslims from the city of Hyderabad migrated to Pakistan after the Action, and both Muslims and Hindus from the countryside migrated into the city.

In 1956, when the states of the Indian union were redrawn according to linguistic boundaries, the city of Hyderabad became the capital of Andhra Pradesh, whose official languages are Telugu and Urdu. While Telugu is the mother tongue of most Hindus in Hyderabad and Urdu the mother tongue of Muslims, many Hyderabadis understand and speak both Urdu and Telugu at a functional level. Amma and Abba also speak both, Telugu with their Hindu patients and Urdu with their Muslim patients. Since the 1970s, another factor that has influenced the Muslim experience in Hyderabad is the high percentage of workers going to Persian Gulf states; it means many families are separated for long periods of time, but it also has resulted in an influx of new money into the local economy.

Traditional Hyderabadi culture, for Amma, Abba, and their agemates in Amma's healing room, is characterized as more than simply "Islamic," however. Amma's publicly articulated memory, and that of many of her older Hindu and Muslim patients, is that "old" Hyderabad,

29

"in former days," was characterized by a peaceful, even familial, coexistence between religious communities, when Muslims and Hindus participated in each other's festivals and wedding and birth celebrations. I heard many narratives of these days in December 1990, immediately after the curfew was lifted that had been imposed after communal unrest and violent riots that had erupted around the Ram Janam Bhoomi/Babri Masjid issue.[16] The immediate precipitating act of violence in Hyderabad in 1990 was rumored to have been the killing of a Muslim 'auto' driver by two Hindus, although it was later found to be a dispute between local gangs over land and had little to do with religious difference (Kakar 1995, 64–65). The rioting lasted ten weeks, and both the violence and the resulting curfew affected residents of the Old City in particular, where many day laborers live without even a one- or two-day reserve of food in their homes.

I realize that contemporary contexts of unrest might generate narratives of nostalgia for a reality that may never have existed, and when the "old days" ended and the "new age" actually began is never very clear in these conversations. Nevertheless, Amma often articulates a deep sense of loss of those days when Hindu and Muslim communities and families lived peacefully side by side and interacted regularly. She observes that Hindus and Muslims are becoming more and more segregated in residential housing patterns and in social interaction, and she regrets that her own children know much less about Hindu culture than she does. The common Hyderabadi perception of tolerance and easy coexistence between communities contradicts the historical record of what Javeed Alam has called "endemic violence" in Hyderabad since 1979 (Alam 1993, 150) and evidence of tensions between Hindus and Muslims (in Indian English, "communal" tension) in what he identifies as "thirty-one years of relative but uneasy coexistence" prior to 1979 (156). Before 1990, the last riot had been in 1984, but between 1979 and 1984, communal riots were an annual occurrence. The occasions for communal tension, if not actual unrest or violence, are often religious processions and festival celebrations in the city, such as the Hindu processions of Ganesh images on the final day of Ganesh Caturthi and Muslim Muharram processions.[17] Even in the days of the *nizam*, there had been heightened communal consciousness due to factors such as the discrepancy between the percentage of

Hindus who lived in Hyderabad State and the percentage of Hindus who held positions in the government bureaucracy and in other spheres of employment (Alam 1993, 163). Today the Muslim population is approximately 40 percent of the city of Hyderabad (10 percent of which is Shii) and the highest concentration is in the Old City, whereas in the newer areas of the city (Secunderabad and north), Hindus are a clear majority. Osmania University, in whose employee quarters Amma lives, lies on the boundary between Hyderabad and Secunderabad; both Hindus and Muslim students attend the university and its professors and other employees are drawn from both communities as well.

The Context of Sufism

I identify Amma and Abba as Sufis, although I never heard that term used in Amma's healing room and courtyard, where the Muslim participants speak in Hyderabadi Dakani Urdu. (The term "Sufi" itself derives from the Arabic term for the wool [*suf*] that was worn by early Muslim ascetics, and the term "*tasawwuf*" came to be applied to their mystical practice; see Ernst 1997, 18 ff. for a discussion of the evolution of the terms "Sufi" and "Sufism.") The religious practices and rhetoric of Amma's healing room and Abba's teachings fall into a constellation of practices with what Carl Ernst calls a "family resemblance" (xvii) that is commonly associated with Sufism. These practices include honoring the founding saints of various established Sufi orders/lineages (*silsilā*, such as Qadiri, Chishti, etc.), celebration of the death anniversary of a founding lineage saint, the centrality of the master-disciple [*pīr-murīd*] relationship through which spiritual knowledge is transmitted, the absolute authority of the *pīr*, articulation of the importance of the distinction between inner and outer meanings of certain phenomena (esoteric and exoteric knowledge) and the importance of the interior life, the practice of *zikr*, participation in *samā* [musical assemblies of devotional singing], and acknowledgment of the spiritual significance of dreams and illness/healing.[18] In Hyderabad, one of the most productive questions to determine whether or not someone participates in Sufi practices is to ask if s/he has a *murśid/pīr*, or Muslim spiritual teacher/master. A person may answer yes to this question even if s/he condemns other kinds of Sufi practice, and an affirmative answer can also imply a range of commitment and relationship between master and disciple.

Abba is a *pīr*, meaning he is a religious teacher who has been given permission by his own *pīr* to teach and to initiate disciples. While Amma and Abba frequently assert that they and their disciples "immerse in the colors" of all of the major Sufi orders (*silsilās*, each one associated with a particular color), they specifically identify with the Qadiri and Chishti *silsilās* when speaking of their revered saints:[19] Ghaus-e-Azam Dastagir (also known as Sheikh Abdul Qadir Jilani,[20] d. 1166 and buried in Baghdad) and the Chishti saint of Ajmer, Gharib Nawaz Sarkar (Muinaddin Chishti, d. 1236). Abdul Qadir Jilani is specifically credited with being the founder of the Qadiri *silsilā*, but he is also honored as the patron saint of other South Asian Sufi orders; he is often called "*pīron kā pīr*" the "greatest *pīr* of all *pīrs*." In her teachings, Amma never mentions the names of the saints who would have been in the lineage between Gharib Nawaz Sarkar and her own *pīr*, Sayed Shah Mehamud Alam Husseini Sailik, or even of the importance of lineage per se. Instead, she poignantly describes the relationship between these two saints and their importance to contemporary Indian Muslims as follows:

When people remember Allah and when the tears fall down from their eyes, the angels gather these tears and take them to Gharib Nawaz Sarkar [Ajmer Baba, also called Khaja Baba]. He, in turn, carries them to Ghaus-e-Azam Dastagir of Baghdad, who in turn takes them to the Prophet. From the Prophet, the prayers are answered by Allah. This is why Allah says that He has made the day for work and the night for meditation.

On another occasion, Amma sighed with deep emotion and told me that "we love God better" here in India, on this very soil, because of the presence of Gharib Nawaz Sarkar. Abba's full name on the nameplate outside his house is written as Sheik Hussein Qadiri. However, after he died and his name was printed on the sign above his grave, Chishti was added: Sheikh Hussein Qadiri Chishti. As his son later explained to me, "We perform *samā*, right? That's what Chishtis do. So, we're Qadiris *and* Chishtis."

Western scholarship on Sufism in South Asia has been primarily historical and focused on Sufism as practiced at major shrines [*dargāhs*] and through associated textual and literary traditions (see Ernst and Lawrence 2002, Ernst 1992, Eaton 1978). Few studies have been made of contemporary Sufi practices in their multiple variations at institutional and non-institutional sites. An important exception is Katherine Ewing's study of Sufi practices in Pakistan. She points out that in a modern Islamic state such as Pakistan, historical Sufism and historical figures are often more "acceptable" than are contemporary Sufi practice and saints, which are highly debated due to the influence of reformists and Wahabbis who criticize worship at the tomb of saints *pīrs* as *shirk* [associating someone with God] and modernists who see these traditions as superstitious and backward. Ewing's work "examine[s] the way in which competing ideologies that have emerged in the process of nation-building in Pakistan are played out in individual experience among ordinary Pakistanis" (1997, 5). She focused her study around the Sufi saint as the "target of much . . . ideological conflict about the place of Islam in the Pakistani nation-state," as well as a "nodal point where . . . political and personal processes come together" (ibid.). The practitioners with whom Ewing worked seem to be much more self-conscious about the terms of such debate about what Islam is and should be, and whether sainthood is commensurable with modernity, than are Amma and her immediate community in the context of Hyderabad and the secular state of India. In *Muslims Through Discourse* (1993), John Bowen describes a similar debate about the "true" nature of Islam at local levels in Indonesia.

There are contexts in the Indian Muslim community in which Sufi practices are debated and condemned, but these debates are rarely brought to Amma's healing room, perhaps out of deference and respect for her or because patients present in the room are there not to discuss ideology but to be healed. Amma herself does not directly engage this discourse or seem bothered by it. Because they are not part of the discourse of the healing room, I have not enumerated or analyzed these debates except where they have been hinted at by the participants themselves. The aim of this book is to describe a particular site of vernacular Islam in the terms, frameworks, and debates its practitioners themselves employ, and these reveal that the discourses of reformist and/or modernist Islam are not as all pervasive and penetrating to every level of practice as scholars of postcolonial South Asia and Islam often assume (see Ewing 1997, 7–10 for a similar argument).

Organization of the Book

Expressions of vernacular Islam are practices that respond to and create local contexts, and so I begin this book by laying out the physical and social parameters of the healing room. Chapter 2 then moves to a detailed taxonomy of the specific spiritual healing system Amma practices in, including her diagnostic procedures and wide array of diagnoses and prescriptions. Amma's control over the breadth and detail of these help to create, performatively, her spiritual authority as a healer. But Amma maintains that "even a parrot" (albeit a literate and smart one) can perform the mathematically based diagnostic calculations. She claims it is her (spiritual) "understanding"—what we might call charisma—that sets her apart as a successful healer, and her patients agree; they come to her primarily because she is a female healer, who is known for her loving nature and patience. Through a series of patient narratives situated in the healing room, chapter 3 explores what her "understanding" adds to the diagnostic/prescriptive healing system. Amma provides a framework of understanding for many patient narratives of suffering and illness and ends them with a declaration that they will be successfully concluded: a lost child will be found, an infertile woman will have a child, a baby's fever will dissipate. Chapters 4 and 5 discuss the primary theoretical questions of the book: how and where is vernacular Islam, particularly as expressed through gender and religious identities, most responsive to local contexts? Where is there room for creativity and flexibility in Islam at a local level? How are identities of woman's *jāti* and religion constructed, experienced, and negotiated in Amma's healing room? Even as Amma maintains that gender is a boundary that cannot be crossed, how does she manage to do so herself when she sits in a traditionally male ritual role? And when boundaries of religious difference are so pronounced in much public political and media rhetoric, how are these differences collapsed at the healing crossroads? Chapter 6 moves out from the healing room to a more self-consciously constructed Muslim space of the *samā* ritual, where Muslim identities are consolidated and performed and where gender remains a salient factor. This is the space where Abba most visibly displays his spiritual authority as *sheikh/pīr*, nevertheless, just as Amma's authority in the healing room is dependent upon and framed by Abba's authority as *pīr*, so too his authority at the *samā* is dependent and framed by Amma's practice in the healing room (most of his disciples were first Amma's patients). Theirs is a symbiotic relationship in which the traditional roles of the *pīr*—teacher/healer—are shared between them, Amma the healer and Abba the teacher.

Abba died in 1998 and Amma died in 2001. However, to convey the immediacy of the healing room, I have used the ethnographic present to describe habitual practices and ritual performances at Amma's healing table as they existed over a ten-year period (most particularly during 1994–1995). One-time incidents or narrative performances are related in the past tense, as are those descriptions of events that took place after Abba's death. The epilogue describes Abba's death and the shifts in the healing room thereafter. Practices and expressions of vernacular Islam at this particular crossroads will continue to respond to changing local and transnational contexts and players long after the last page of this book is written, as authority and ritual roles are transmitted to the next generation.

SETTING THE STAGE: THE HEALING ROOM, ITS ACTORS, AND ITS RHYTHMS

1

Patients come by auto, foot, and bus—from villages, Bombay, and Pune. My *fālitā* are taken even as far as Dubai.

Amma's healing room is a small crowded bustling crossroads of domestic and public spaces, personae, and discourses, a crossroads of ritual and storytelling, social and economic exchange, and family disputes and negotiations. As one enters the courtyard outside the healing room, one often sees a crowd of patients leaning into the doorway of the room, straining to hear Amma's voice or slip in a personal request out of turn. Other patients sit in small familial groups conversing quietly among themselves, entertaining restless babies or children, exchanging gossip with groups from other parts of the city, and/or sharing with others in the courtyard their stories of suffering and Amma's healing (and periodically giving their own advice to each other). On busy days, they may sit for several hours awaiting their turn. Although every so often a patient or her family might complain about the long wait, especially if a baby is crying inconsolably or if Amma is about to take her hour (or more) lunch break, usually patients resign themselves to waiting for their turn. Many patients spend the greater part of a day simply getting to Amma's neighborhood due to long distances and the vagaries of public transportation.

For women in particular, the day is an important social outing, as patients rarely come by themselves. It may serve as an occasion for mothers and married daughters or sisters who live with their in-laws to get together outside the scrutiny of others and the pressure of childcare and meal preparation. For a woman who has recommended Amma to a neighbor and accompanied her, this may be a rare occasion for them to talk with each other beyond the few minutes spent standing at the neighborhood water tap or rounding up their children from their play in the street.

Amma's Neighborhood

Amma lives in a neighborhood of Osmania University's subsidized housing for nonacademic employees. Abba used to work as a clerk in the English Department, carrying books to and from the library, and so forth, a position from which he had retired before I met him in 1989.[1] (The family has stayed in university housing after Abba's retirement under the name of one of his brothers, who still works at the university.)

The location of Amma's healing room in a neighborhood on a university campus is significant; in many ways, the university is a kind of liminal social space. Amma's neighborhood is not traditionally Muslim or Hindu; its inhabitants are both. It does not carry a particularly elaborate history or caste/communal ethos, and no one has deep ancestral ties to the land or homes (although this does not make it easier for the university to evict families that no longer have direct employment connections to the university). The university location may provide a certain freedom of access and activity that does not hold true of more-traditional neighborhoods. However, Amma's ritual healing activity itself does not differ significantly from that of *pīrs* located throughout Hyderabad's Old City.

Amma's immediate neighborhood houses neither a mosque nor a Hindu temple, although both are found in the vicinity. There are two mosques within a five-minute walk from Amma's house in each direction. One mosque is a small older structure with the four minarets characteristic of traditional Hyderabadi architecture, and the other was more recently built in what is sometimes called the Saudi style with just a single minaret. Many of these new mosques have been built with monies from Indian Muslims working in the Gulf States and Saudi Arabia. Just a little farther down the road is a small *dargāh,* outside of which sits a Muslim *bābā* selling rings with semi-precious stones.

A small shrine to the Hindu goddesses Durga, Pochamma, and Mutyalamma has grown up across the road from Amma's neighborhood under a wide-spreading neem tree, and a much older and larger goddess shrine to the village goddess Yellamma lies at a major intersection in the middle of the university, a ten-minute walk down the road. The lower branches of trees around this shrine are filled with coconut "cradles" tied by couples making vows to the goddess for a cure for infertility.[2] Over the last fifteen years, both shrines have grown considerably larger and more permanent, with cement walls built around the images. The outside walls of the three-goddess shrine are painted with bright images of the goddess Durga, Yellamma carrying pots on her head, and the brother Pota Raju; the surrounding courtyard has been paved with stone. The second shrine has newly built cement walls around its large courtyard; they were added sometime between 1999 and 2003. Each shrine is the site of a major annual festival during which its courtyard is filled with celebrants, but usually they are quiet, with only one or two worshippers present at any given time.[3] Amma's neighborhood itself is also periodically sacralized when, for example, during the annual festival of Ganesh Caturthi, several temporary shrines to the elephant-headed deity are set up or when Islamic devotional *qavvālī* music wafts over the neighborhood throughout the night once every month during Abba's *samā* [devotional musical gatherings].

Into the Courtyard

Amma's courtyard can be accessed from two directions: one tiny footpath leads from a major road that borders the neighborhood, winding through an overgrown weed patch often used by children as an outdoor latrine (many of the homes do not have indoor latrines) and in between neighboring houses to Amma's healing room. This is the neighborhood/ private access road that might even be characterized as "domestic." Most patients come to the courtyard through the other, more public, path off the main road; it is wider and is accessible to 'autos', motorcycles, and the rare car. This side of the courtyard is open to a large open field crisscrossed by footpaths leading to another neighborhood; the open expanse is punctuated by palm trees and the field is overgrown with brush.

Amma and Abba have gradually built on to the living quarters they received from the university, which originally consisted of a single small sleeping room, a kitchen, a bathroom, and the courtyard. They built on another sleeping room for their middle son (Khalid, who is also a *pīr*) and his wife and four children; much later, they built a separate small kitchen for them. The first room they added to the original living quarters was the healing room itself.

The courtyard is approximately 15 by 8 feet, the floor of which is laid with stone slabs; it is roofed by corrugated tin. Two sides of the courtyard are walled with the outside walls of the healing room and a family sleeping room and small verandah; the other two sides are open. Against the outside wall of the healing room is a flagpole that is the site of ritual (the *cillā*). Both the walls behind the flagpole and its base are painted bright green, and an image of a tiger is painted on the base. Some years the tiger is depicted as springing toward the viewer, roaring, and other years it is standing with a still gaze, as the murals are repainted by different professional artists every year or two. The tiger is associated with the Prophet's son-in-law Ali, who is called "Tiger of God" [*sher-i-khudā*] and the "First among the Friends of God."[4] On the green-painted wall behind the flagpole are written the names of the founding saints of the Qadiri and Chishti *silsilās*: Ghaus-e Azam Dastagir and Khwaja Garib Nawaz (one year the artist added *cillā mubārak*, meaning "blessings on this place, the *cillā*"). On one wall next to the flagpole is painted the *burāq* [a winged white horse with the head of a woman, the wings variously painted as folded down or extended out] that carried the Prophet on his night journey and ascent from Jerusalem to heaven, and next to the door of the healing room is a depiction of a horse carrying an open human hand [the *panjā*] under the protection of a royal umbrella. Amma describes the *panjā* as a symbol for the family of the Prophet: Muhammad, his daughter Fatima, his son-in-law Ali, and his grandsons Hassan and Hussein.[5] These are all images common to vernacular Islam in India; they are painted on the walls of many *dargāhs*, shrines, and Muslim healing sites.

5. Outer wall of Amma's healing room, on which is painted a horse carrying the *panjā*, and the base of the flagpole, showing the Tiger of God, 1995.

The Healing Room

When they arrive at the courtyard, patients first go into Amma's healing room and for 50 paise (only pennies in American currency) receive from Abba (or whoever is tending the small dry-goods store that fills about one-third of the healing room) a little cardboard square with a number written on it, to hold a place in queue. Amma periodically instructs her patients on the importance of keeping order in this way. She instituted this number-queue system in 1990 to bring some order to the increasing numbers of patients that crowd the courtyard. She maintains, "I don't even take my daughter or the sultan without a number. In front of Allah, there is no privilege [*ristā*, lit., connection or relationship]." However, every so often both the cardboard squares and patients in queue get totally out of order ("ahead and behind," *āge-pīche*, as Amma says). People are usually quite patient about such mix-ups, but on some days, if they have been waiting for a particularly long time, tempers flare. Mothers with young babies might complain that they should be given preference; the rare wealthy patient who arrives in a car rather than by bus or in an 'auto' might send in an emissary to tell Amma that someone of status is waiting (expecting her to take them out of turn, which she usually does). Sometimes the patients themselves send someone into the healing room out of order if there is a particularly sick child, a feverish moaning woman, or patient who is possessed and not easily controlled. But Amma is rarely sympathetic to complaints about long waits except in the most dramatic of cases; as she responded to one angry patient, "When my work is so grave [*gambhīr*] and important, how do you expect me to do it quickly?"

When I met Amma in 1989, she was seated on the ground behind a low wooden school desk. When I returned to Hyderabad in 1991, she had "moved up" to a comfortable office chair and wooden table. This move coincided with an increase in patient flow and income, but she attributed it primarily to her arthritic knees, which prevented her from easily sitting down and getting up from the floor. Amma is constantly making small improvements to the healing room: one year adding a fluorescent bulb overhead, another year two floor fans, then a cassette player to play devotional *qavvālī* music. At the end of my year with Amma in 1995, I bought her, as a farewell gift, a desk with a linoleum top and drawers. She was particularly excited about the drawers, in which she kept her money, extra sheets of amulets (yet to be cut and folded), and her tins of *pān* ingredients [betel leaf that various spices are wrapped in and then chewed like tobacco].

Amma makes sure that every possible seating space in the healing room is filled (and she often sees room for another person to squeeze in where others might not); she says she gets restless [*becainī*] if she sees people standing outside or leaning in the door when there is an empty seat. There is little room for individual privacy in this context, and it is clear that listening to the stories of others who may share a particular patient's difficulty and to stories of Amma's healing success is part of the healing and teaching process.[6] However, when there is no more room for patients to sit and they still continue to crowd into the room, Amma might shout at them to get out of the doorway to let in a little light and

air. Without looking up from her work, she frequently cries out, "*Havā,
havā, havā* [air, air, air]! Go wait for your turn outside! Do you think I
can breathe in here?"

Amma sits on a large swivel chair with arms behind a desk, around
which are arranged a few folding chairs and a wooden bench for the
patients whose turns are coming. Stacks of paper slips filled with Arabic
writing are arranged across the front of Amma's desk, held down by colorful chipped glass paper weights: one stack will be made into amulets
[*tāvīz*] for general well-being and one will become specialized fever amulets, one each for morning and evening *fālitā* (the slips are rolled up to
use as wicks that are soaked in oil and burned). Amma writes all day
long: her diagnoses are based on a written mathematical calculation and
her prescriptions are written on paper amulets, unleavened bread, saucers,
or fresh gourds. As Amma says, "There would be no world without pen
and ink." A clipboard, an inkwell, scissors, and one or two ballpoint pens
complete the healing paraphernalia on the desktop. The visual impact of
the written word (particularly the Arabic written word, Arabi, as Amma
calls it) in the healing room is striking for someone familiar with Hindu
healing contexts in which the written word is most often absent altogether.[7] The dominance of the written word helps identify the healing
room as Muslim space. But as we will see, the written word exists performatively and within a wide oral tradition, and both oral and written
words have significance beyond their semantic content.

When I was present, my small black tape recorder sat unobtrusively
next to the stacks of amulets. I usually turned it on as soon as I walked
in the healing room and turned it off only when I left several hours later;
patients sometimes asked about it, but few seemed to care that their conversations were being recorded. Only a handful of patients confidentially
whisper their complaints to Amma, and then it is as much because of the
presence of other patients as it is because of my tape recorder. Amma was
sometimes amused that I would want to record such mundane conversation. But when I explained to her the kind of notes I took from the
tape recorder when I got home and that its presence kept me from fran-
tically writing the entire time I was sitting with her, she understood.

At least once an hour, Amma stops all healing activity, relaxes, and
pulls out a motley assortment of small tin boxes whose contents she uses

6. Amma sitting at her healing table, 1995.

to make herself *pān*. Amma said she developed the habit as a young girl, when a doctor gave her *pān* as she was recovering from a tonsillectomy (he said it would help to cut down the bleeding). Abba frequently reprimands Amma for taking time out to make *pān* when the room is filled with patients. However, these breaks from healing action are often occasion for a story. And the stories are not frivolous; they are carefully chosen to establish and reinforce Amma's healing authority, to construct the worldview within which such spiritual healing is possible, and to nurture her relationship with her patients, all elements that are crucial to her successful healing practice.

Amma's is not the only authoritative presence and voice in the healing room. One-third of the healing room is designated for a small provisions store, of which Abba, who was 70 years old when I first met him in 1989, is the storekeeper. His seat is in the middle of the store section, on the floor, and (when the store has been newly stocked) he is often literally obscured by a veil/curtain of snacks, candies, and toys that are tied to strings hanging down from the ceiling. Several such domestic stores, sometimes marked only by the addition of a single shelf on the wall, are sprinkled through the neighborhood; most are supervised by women. In fact, Amma says it was she who first set up the store as a young mother. Abba took over as primary shopkeeper only after his retirement from university employment. After his death and until the dissolution of the store a few years later, Amma's sixteen-year-old granddaughter sat in Abba's place.

Abba's shop stocks spices, soap, incense, single cigarettes, matches, oil, eggs, cheap candies and snacks, and tiny plastic toys. Neighborhood children run in and out of the room throughout the day on errands for their mothers to buy an egg, a cup of sugar, a couple of pinches of tea leaves. Abba sometimes jokes with them and lets them linger over a decision about which toy or piece of candy to buy with the five or ten paise change left to them; other times he impatiently yells at them to take their purchase and run home. He also sells ingredients needed for Amma's nonwritten prescriptions, such as black seeds, iron nails, incense, and lemons. Amma and Abba seem to keep their healing and shop accounts separate. When Amma periodically wants to offer a friend or visitor (fieldworker included) a snack from the shop, she takes money from her healing coffer and gives it to Abba to purchase the snack. In his seat as storekeeper, Abba's primary concern does not, however, seem to be actually selling supplies; in fact, the profit margin from the sales serves only as a small supplement to the family income. (In 1995, Abba told me that the profit margin for the store was Rs. 1 for every Rs. 10 worth of goods sold.)

More important than the store's economic significance is its social significance as a site from which Abba presides as an authoritative presence: meeting the 'public', giving periodic teachings to visiting disciples, monitoring the flow of patients to Amma's table, and serving as a spiritual, conversational, and business partner to Amma. His religious role is externalized in his shoulder-length gray hair, his long beard, the *surmā* [silver powdered antimony] lining his eyes, and his long *kurtā* and *lungī* [traditionally styled loose shirt and male sarong-type garment]. In 1996, Abba was recovering from a recent heart attack and had to sit in an easy chair to rest, which prevented him from sitting on his customary low wooden stool on the ground in the store. He spent most of the day sitting out on the verandah of the house, often with a young granddaughter or disciple by his side, but he told me he was restless and felt useless sitting there outside the store.

The walls behind and next to Amma's desk are filled with framed photographs and lithograph posters. To "read" these and notice their changes over the years is to begin to understand the dynamism of spiritual lineages and traditions from which Amma draws: her immediate *pīr* and his lineage, the sacred geography (marked by pilgrimage sites) within which Amma lives, and the fluidity between Sunni and Shii traditions in Hyderabad. One poster pictures one of the miracle stories of the founding *pīr* of the Qadiri *silsilā,* Abdul Qadir Jilani; he is pictured bringing back to life a wedding party that had drowned twelve years earlier while crossing a flooded river. Another shows him seated in a circle of other renowned saints, a lion lying at the great *pīr's* feet. A third lithograph depicts a South Indian *pīr* called Mustangwali, who is dressed only in a white loincloth, carrying two baskets over his shoulder in which are sitting a dog, a chicken, and a goat. The miracle for which he is known is as follows: one of his disciples had no ingredients to make curry for him, so she used the animals he was carrying in his baskets. Before eating the curry, he asked the woman where his disciples (animals) were and he called for them. They came to life from the curry, bones and all. "This was his miracle [*karāmat*]."[8]

Other colorful bazaar poster prints depict pilgrimage sites that Amma and Abba have visited in Bombay and Ajmer and the Great Mosque and Kaba in Mecca (which they have not visited). Finally, an evocative poster of two birds crying tears of blood at the sight of the massacre of the Prophet's grandson Hussein at Karbala hangs on the wall. I never heard Amma or Abba expound on the tragedy of Karbala so central to Shii identity; nevertheless, this is one of a handful of images chosen for the wall of their healing room, perhaps serving as a tangible reminder of compassion in a context of pain and suffering.

Next to the bazaar posters hang framed photographs of Amma and Abba's *pīr,* Sayed Shah Mehamud Alam Husseini Sailik from Nizambad, and his whitewashed *dargāh* built on a rocky mountainside and a large photograph of Abba as a young man before he had fully grown out his hair and beard. Abba's framed *khilāfat,* the paper certificate a *pīr* gives to

45

his *murīd* at the time he grants the latter permission to make his own disciples, is displayed beneath a photograph of Abba when he was about 40 years old. Interspersed between the photographs and poster pictures are various clocks whose purpose would seem to be decorative rather than functional, since all show different times. And right behind the desk, easily visible, is a large calendar that indicates both the Islamic lunar date and what Amma and her patients call the "official government [*sarkārī*]" date, both systems in which they live comfortably.

After Abba's death in 1998, the *khilāfat* and the picture of the young Abba were replaced by a large picture of Abba taken shortly before his death (featuring his long gray hair and beard), now hanging next to the poster of the "company of saints" and the photograph of Abba's own *pīr.* Another addition at this time was a picture of a saint dressed in green, riding a prancing white horse; Abba's face has been superimposed onto the figure. The figure is holding a sword and behind him is a landscape of stylized snow-capped mountains and rivers. Several of Abba's closest disciples had this picture hanging in their homes during the year following his death, but none of them was able to explain its significance to me, saying it was simply a 'scene'. Amma's son Khalid later explained that the sword and horse stood for the Prophet's son-in-law, Hazrat Ali, as he went into battle, the picture now directly associating Abba with Ali and placing him in his authoritative spiritual lineage.[9] My gift to Amma on the occasion of Abba's first death-anniversary celebration was a gilt-framed 16-by-20-inch photograph of Amma and Abba. Amma was delighted to receive it and hung it on the wall, not right above the desk with the other saints, but way over to the right side above the store section of the room and not easily visible. At the time I wondered whether she put it there simply because there was not room on the main part of the wall or if the prominence of a woman on a wall that pictured male authority and lineage might not have been considered quite appropriate. However, several years after Amma's death, both Amma and Abba's individual photographs hung in the line of male saints represented on the wall above the healing table, now presided over by Amma's son Khalid.

Above Amma's desk and crisscrossing in front of the framed posters and photographs are numerous electrical wires running from outlets to

7. The wall behind the healing table after the death of Abba and Amma. Their pictures have now joined the family of "saints." Pictured below are Khalid, who now presides over the healing table, and, to Khalid's right, Amma's youngest son, Muhammad, 2001.

two clattering floor fans, a large fluorescent overhead tube light, a small desk lamp, and a dusty tape recorder. During the hot season when there are several hours of electricity load-shedding every day, the maze of exposed wires to support light and moving air seems to mock the sauna-like heat and darkness of the healing room, where Amma strains to write by the light of a small oil lamp and the natural light from the single small doorway. The room has no ceiling and the exposed beams serve as pathways for resident mice; they also support various decorative hangings, including a woven plastic decoration made by one of Amma's close friends and an American wind chime I once gave Amma. There is no breeze in the room to stir the chimes, but Amma attached a thin string to it and pulls on it every so often, to remind her of me and call me to her, she says.

The Healing Room as Commercial Space

Even though it is Abba who sits in the store as shopkeeper, Amma has a greater interest in and inclination toward business and trade than Abba does. Amma's position as someone who meets the 'public' gives her ample opportunity and connections to experiment in trade and business, and she often weaves business discussions and transactions into her healing activity. One moneymaking venture Amma was involved in outside her healing practice for a few years was owning (and taking big loans to do so) three 'autos' (auto-rickshaw taxis), primarily to provide jobs for her son, a son-in-law, and various disciples who came and went. She learned a lot about the mechanics of an 'auto', but rarely was more than one in working order. Such business ventures are often a source of conflict between Amma and Abba. One morning when Abba tried to persuade Amma to have someone take one of the 'autos' to a mechanic for cleaning, she abruptly confronted him:

We can clean it ourselves. Now, I've already given the money [to someone to clean it there at the house]. The matter is finished! Let it go. Sit quietly now. Sit quietly and let the vehicle get fixed. Don't raise your tongue. Sit quietly!
Abba [quietly]: If I sit quietly, others eat off of us.
Amma: No one gets anything from us [unfairly]!
Abba: Okay, get back to work. Look at all the people coming and waiting. If you don't keep working, where will the money come from? Does it blow in with the wind? I'm the one who has to give money to get this vehicle fixed and to buy what we need.

In fact, Amma's healing practice and other business ventures bring in more income to the household than Abba's pension or the store business. And she is continually thinking of ways to supplement the family income in directions that are consistent with both her position and her personal inclinations. One afternoon I came upon Amma sitting in the family living quarters surrounded by stacks of saris that an itinerant trader had spread in front of her. For just a few minutes, she was considering taking up such a side business herself, thinking of all the women who entered her courtyard as potential customers. She commented, "There are so many ways to make money like this, just sitting in your house. I can do whatever I put my mind to doing." Abba teased her, though, that her interest in this particular business was really that it would provide her with a source of new and beautiful saris to wear herself.

Another brief business venture, inspired by Amma's love of animals, involved raising various animals for sale: rabbits, chickens, and then goats. It turned out that the rabbits required too much upkeep. Amma had built a cage under the large wooden bed in the sleeping room, and the floor of the cage had to be washed down every day. Even then, the smell was too strong for the human inhabitants of the room. She then shifted to chickens, but they meandered too far from the courtyard and were stolen. Finally, Amma settled on the desire to raise goats, not just any goats, but "*beautiful* goats, with eyes lined in black." Abba complained that she wanted everything to be beautiful, even a chicken or goat to be slaughtered. Amma associates her love of animals with her love of humans, and she speaks to and of them with great compassion. For several years, she kept a caged parrot, to whom she spoke periodically throughout the day (and unfortunately for my tapes from those years, the parrot often spoke back in loud screeches that overrode any human voice).

The Healing Room as Ritual Space

The first marker that the healing room and courtyard are ritual space are the flagpoles that fly the green and orange flags representing the Qadiri and Chishti spiritual lineages with which Abba and Amma are affiliated. The flagpoles are similar to Shii *ālams* [flag standards] that are topped by metal decorative shapes or various Shii symbols (including the *panjā*, or hand, representing the Prophet's family). Abba offers *fātiḥā*, prayers, and offerings (usually food items) of thanksgiving at the base of the flagpole on behalf of patients who have returned after being healed. Amma, Abba, and their disciples identify this ritual site as a *cillā*. *Cillā* can refer to both the ritual site where flags of saints are kept and the 40-day period of seclusion, meditation, and ascetic practice disciples observe prior to receiving a *pīr*'s *khilāfat* or in order to gain a particular ritual/ spiritual skill—such disciples would be the only ones authorized to set up a physical *cillā* in their own homes.[10]

A handful of Abba's disciples have *cillā* sites in their homes, but he cautions disciples against setting up a *cillā* without deep commitment and discipline, as it requires constant physical and spiritual maintenance. The way Abba speaks about the responsibilities of maintaining a *cillā* is reminiscent of ways Hindus often speak about the responsibilities of installing a *murti* [image] of a deity in one's home shrine: once the image has been installed, the householder is responsible for caring for it, feeding it, bathing it, and putting it to sleep. At Abba's *cillā* in the courtyard, a family member or disciple lights incense and a clay oil lamp every morning and evening. The *cillā* is also the site of intense ritual activity during the annual Gyarwin Sharif celebration of the death anniversary of Abdul Qadir Jilani; during this festival the flags are replaced with new ones.

The courtyard murals and green walls behind the flagpole further visually mark the space as a ritual space. The tiger painted on the base of the flagpole is associated with Ali, the Prophet Muhammad's son-in-law and the first imam for Shii Muslims. Ali is also considered to be the founder of Sufi lineages. Thus, while the tiger is commonly painted outside Shii *aśurkhānā* [shrines where Shii *ālams*, metal crests on poles suggestive of battle standards carried by the martyrs of Karbala, are stored], the presence of this image does not necessarily connote a Shii space, as one Indian scholar of Islamic who visited Amma's courtyard with me first assumed. When I questioned Amma about this apparent Shii association, she was amused at my ignorance and laughed, "No, no. We're Sunni. But we all respect Ali, don't we?" The presence of metal flag standards that look like *ālams* and the mural of the tiger of Ali are examples of a shared repertoire of symbols and narrative motifs across the Shii/Sunni lines of identity.

A strong performative indication for women that the healing room is sacred ritual space is the fact that menstruating and postpartum women should not enter it. Muslim and Hindu women traditionally share taboos against entering sacred/ritual space (temples, shrines, even kitchens), and postpartum women also observe these taboos for forty days after birth, during which time they are considered ritually impure from the birth process. It was several weeks before I noticed that some women did not enter the room but claimed their turn with Amma by leaning over the doorsill from the courtyard, carrying on full conversations and receiving diagnoses and prescriptions without ever entering the room itself. One newcomer directly asked Amma if her menstruating daughter could enter. Amma said no, but she could undergo the necessary treatments as long as she herself did not directly touch any of the ingredients (a pot filled with ingredients to be passed over the girl's body to draw away the evil eye).[11] Earlier Amma had told me what a burden menstruation had been to her practice when she was younger. She had had to sit out seven days at a time, and it was inconvenient for all concerned, including patients: "It was a big problem when people came from so far away, but what to do?" She continued, "I prayed to Allah every day to stop my period, and ten years ago, He complied." This occurred at a time when Amma would have been in her early fifties; nevertheless, she saw menopause as an act of God.[12]

Finally, the continual presence of religious persons helps create the healing room as religious space. From an indigenous perspective, the *bar-kat* of Amma and Abba as *pīr* and *pirānimā* permeates the healing room. For several years, there was also another spiritual figure whose elusive presence helped to mark the healing room as sacred ritual space, or perhaps he was willing to move here because it already *was* a marked sacred space. In 1995, after I had been coming to Amma's room for several months, it occurred to me to ask what ("who," as it turns out) was in a small unobtrusive lean-to structure made of woven mats and boards. It was several days before someone would answer me directly; behind the closed door lay a bedridden *bābā* (Muslim religious mendicant) to whom Amma had given permanent shelter after she met him living in the grave-yard at a famous Hyderabadi *dargāh*. She had recognized his powers (manifest in the fact that he did not eat anything but only smoked cigarettes) and persuaded him to come live next to her healing room. Very few people, including disciples, knew of his presence there and Amma's family members rarely spoke directly of or to this *bābā*. They said he was particularly *jalālī* [of an angry or ferocious nature] and that no one should enter his room unless he specifically called them. Although he never met the public, Amma's daughters told me he had powers greater than hers.

He did not have to blow prayers over water to empower it with healing qualities; it simply had to pass through his hands to be so empowered. Amma estimated that he lived with them twelve years before he died at about age 90. After he died (sometime between 1996 and 1999), no one in the family spoke of him to me again. His presence was a reminder of the people who flow in and out of Amma's life, to whom she has given protection and healing; it also served as an example of the serendipity of fieldwork that determines which lives we encounter. In the summer of 2003, after the deaths of Amma and Abba and after Amma's son had hung his own authoritative lineage photographs on the wall, this *bābā*'s photograph joined those of Amma, Abba, and their Nizambad *pīr*.

The Healing Room as Domestic Space

Performatively, physically, and conceptually Amma's room is an extension of domestic space, even though she meets (particularly male) patients there who would not normally enter her home. One of the indications that Amma's healing room is experienced as an extension of her domestic space is the absence of veiling (called "observing *parda*" in Urdu) by the women of her family. Amma, her daughters, and her daughters-in-law freely enter this room without wearing their *burqās* or covering their heads, even though male patients who are not family members are almost always present in the room. Indian Muslim women veil only in public places where male nonfamily members are present. In contrast, in North India, married Hindu women who veil (by covering their heads with the end of a sari or with a shawl) observe the strictest veiling in front of their fathers-in-law, older brothers-in-law, and other elder men who fall into this kinship category. (Due to differing marriage patterns and social and economic regional differences, Hindu women in South India do not generally observe veiling.) Even if physical veiling is not observed, new brides in middle-class urban Hindu families often still maintain some distance and propriety from their fathers-in-law. When Amma's youngest son Muhammad got married, I was surprised to see his young bride sitting openly next to Abba and laughing and talking with him while eating lunch, something that would be rare in North Indian Hindu homes.

Amma's graying hair is covered by the end of her sari when she is praying over a patient, but her *burqā* hangs in another room and is worn only when she leaves the neighborhood. Similarly, other neighborhood women put on their *burqās* only when they leave the neighborhood. Domestic space is expanded with permeable boundaries beyond the walls of the physical house, in similar ways that Indian nuclear and/or extended family boundaries are expanded to include neighbors and family friends.

The healing-room space is also domesticated by the presence of Amma's household's dry-goods supplies stored in big stainless-steel bins in the corner of the room. Amma's daughters or granddaughters often come into the room while patients are present to get the day's supply of rice, lentils, flour, oil, or tea leaves, pausing for conversation if one of the patients is a family friend or acquaintance. After Abba died in 1998, the ambience of the room became decidedly more female and domestic. For several months, one of Amma's teenage granddaughters took over the role of primary shopkeeper, and the conversations in the room often revolved around the details of cooking and food, clothing and jewelry. Amma loved to describe her favorite dishes and the recipes she wanted to cook for me. The tenor of the room became more relaxed and jovial; no one seemed in a hurry, particularly Amma, and the absence of Abba's voice urging her to keep working was noticeable. The supplies in the store gradually dwindled, and when I returned to Hyderabad for Abba's second death anniversary in January 2000, the store had been disbanded altogether. Amma said it was just too much work for the money it brought in.

Rhythms of the Healing Room

The rhythms of the healing room and courtyard shift, sometimes rather dramatically, with ritual and festival cycles and the changing seasons, the day of the week, and the time of day. They are further affected by local political activities (curfews and strikes), outbreaks of flu or conjunctivitis, family visits or life-cycle rituals, and the activity of the store. Amma's healing day starts out slowly at about nine in the morning, as it is difficult both for her and her patients to finish their household and familial tasks and responsibilities before then. As she takes her seat behind the desk, Amma relaxes with her *pān*-making and engages in easy conversation with several disciples who regularly come to her room before going to their own jobs. But by eleven, the crowd has usually picked up, and Amma is often still at her healing table until eight or nine at night, by which time she might have treated between forty and fifty patients.

The proportion of Muslim and Hindu patients in Amma's daily schedule is highly variable, depending on their respective festival seasons, fasting days, and the day of the week. However, my sense is that the numbers seem to average out about equally, and this is also Amma's perception. Her interactions with Muslim and Hindu patients differ primarily in the language in which they take place (she speaks Telugu with Hindus and Urdu with Muslims) and the fact that she shares more common acquaintances with Muslims, who might be friends of Amma and her family and thus might stay longer and engage in more personal conversations. Many more women come to Amma's healing room than do men, particularly among the Hindu patients, because women are primarily responsible for most problems or illnesses that concern family health and well-being. More men come on Sundays (when they are off work), and their problems often concern housing, business, and marriage alliances rather than the health of the physical body.

Some days the healing room is filled with palpable energy and other days the air is flat and lethargic, because Amma says simply, "My heart isn't in it today." On these days, when her high blood pressure or arthritis is bothering her, when she is feeling the burden of family disputes, or when she is simply tired, she spends more time talking with family members and disciples and does not move as quickly from patient to patient. During Ramadan, especially when the month of fasting falls in the hot season and it is difficult to fast and move about in the heat, the courtyard is empty and only a few Hindu patients sit at leisure at Amma's table. The Muslim wedding season follows Ramadan, and during those days patients come in large numbers to Amma to consult about wedding matches and the amount of dowry being demanded.

Sunday is the busiest day of the week, when more people are off work and are able to come to Amma's healing room. Another busy time of week is Thursday afternoons, since most patients know that Fridays are Amma's "day off" from the healing room, when she visits the homes of disciples or patients, makes periodic visits to a *dargāh*, or goes shopping for a wedding or festival occasion. She also uses Fridays to conduct house exorcisms; in 1994–1995 she often conducted three to four exorcisms a month (sometimes two in one day). Even in Amma's absence from the healing room on Fridays, however, there always seems to be a handful of patients awaiting her return, when she unbegrudgingly attends to them.

International and national politics also impact the rhythms of the room, and their effects are reminders of transnational currents crossing through and affecting locally grounded healing practices. For example, in December 1990 when a ten-week citywide curfew in Hyderabad was lifted, patients from across the city streamed back to Amma's courtyard, and the courtyard and healing room were filled with high energy, heated conversations, and predictions of when the next citywide strike would occur. Both Hindu and Muslim patients exchanged gossip and rumors from different parts of the city that had been cut off from each other over the previous weeks, and no one minded long waits for his/her turn at the healing table, since most of the conversations were centered on the current events rather than the patients' problems at hand. Their shared "problem" on this day was anxiety; perhaps more than anything else, they had come to take temporary refuge at a place where someone they trusted asserted authority and control. Again and again, Amma and her patients reiterated that the recent violence between Hindus and Muslims was not characteristic of the Hyderabad they knew (seemingly embodied here in the healing room) and that surely it had been instigated by troublemakers hired by "outside" politicians.

I happened to arrive in Hyderabad from the United States on the day the curfew was lifted in 1991, and I went immediately to Amma's room. The only visible sign in her neighborhood of the recent violence was large piles of stones guarding every doorway, both Muslim and Hindu—pathetically minimal protection were violence actually to strike. There had been no violence here on the university campus, but residents were afraid of outsiders coming in to incite local residents and feared that there might be student strikes and protests. As we sat together around Amma's table drinking tea and talking about the recent violence and the impact of the curfew, a poignant and humorous incident occurred (only later remembered as funny). In the lull of the afternoon, we suddenly heard shrieks and a stampeding sound. There was only one small exit from the room, and it led directly into the path of what sounded like a crowd on the run. Amma declared that we should all just stay put. But soon patients waiting in the courtyard started laughing, and three runaway buffalos pounded through the small gulley paralleling the courtyard; the shrieks belonged to both the children herding and trying to control the buffalos and other children trying to get out of their way. Amma laughed heartily and dramatically described and imitated the looks of panic that had passed over her patients' faces. She assured us that even if the stampeders had been rioters, "It is all the will of Allah." Later she added that nothing would have happened to those of us sitting with her because her presence and power would have protected us all.

Only a few weeks later, the first Gulf War broke out and again politics dominated the healing room. Many patients were concerned about the safety and future employment of relatives working in the Gulf; there was also fear about local gasoline shortages, and my presence elicited questions about the U.S. government's motivations in the war. Rumors and stories of war and television coverage were shared; once again, rhythms and conversations of the healing room were shaped by political forces far from the familiar localized setting of the healing room. The healing room became a crossroads of international policy and discourse and very personal narratives of trouble and pain.

Family and Regular Participants in the Healing Room

Family conversations, disputes, and decisions frequently enter the healing room, domesticizing, often feminizing, the space. Amma and Abba had fifteen children; four male babies died in infancy or at birth and an adult daughter died of heart failure during the time I was working with Amma. However, only two sons are consistently present in the healing room itself: her youngest son Muhammad and her second-oldest son Khalid. Three of Amma's daughters visit or live with her from time to time, but when they do, they only pass through the room and do not assist at the healing table. The oldest and youngest daughters, Khamar and Rehma, regularly visit her on the occasion of the monthly *samā* (a ritual devotional concert presided over by Abba) and often stay, with their children, for several days at a time. A middle daughter, Sultana, and her

56

husband and daughters have periodically lived with Amma for weeks or even months at a time when the family is shifting between residences or when the husband is unemployed.

One of Amma's two sons who help her at the healing table, Khalid, is Abba's spiritual heir designate, having been given Abba's *khilāfat* at the young age of 18. He asserted that he had been identified for this position at birth: "Tell me, how are babies born? With their heads first or their feet first? One in a thousand is born with his/her feet first, right? And I was one of these. These babies either become spiritually very powerful or *śaitānī* [serving the devil]." Khalid is the only one of Amma's children who has completed a high school education; he has also earned his master's degree and has a permanent good-paying position in the University of Hyderabad postal service. (Earlier he had worked as a manager at a 'hostel' for students living on campus.) After work hours and on weekends, Khalid frequently sits with Amma at her healing table, diagnosing and writing prescriptions. For a few months, he set up his own healing room, but according to Abba, he was not successful because he worked too quickly, he was not patient enough, and he does not have Amma's charisma.

When I first met Amma, Khalid and his wife and three young children were living and eating with Amma and Abba and only sleeping in a separate small room. In the mid-1990s, as their own family grew with the addition of a fourth child—and tensions between the nuclear and extended families were more openly expressed—they built a separate kitchen and began cooking separately. After Abba's death, there were strong disagreements between Amma and Khalid about property and how best to pay off debts Abba had left behind. Khalid moved out and set up an independent household about an hour's distance from Amma's house and much closer to his workplace. He still came to the healing room periodically to meet with other disciples and try to take care of family business. Since Amma's death, he has moved back, taken over the healing practice, and serves as the caretaker [*sajjāda-niśīn*] of Amma and Abba's graves and *dargāh*. Above the healing table now hang photographs of Abba and Amma, and Khalid depends on their authority to frame his own slowly developing authority as the head of both the family and the spiritual lineage.

On the days when Khalid assists Amma in the healing room, his presence changes the dynamics of the room rather dramatically; everything moves a little more quickly and efficiently but not quite as happily. Amma's youngest, and clearly favorite, son, Muhammad, who shares many of Amma's mannerisms and her open nature, is a more constant presence in the healing room than his older brother because he is otherwise unemployed. He has studied only through ninth grade, despite Amma's encouragement that he continue his education. When I first met Amma, Muhammad was the only child still not married; he got married at about age 18 and moved out of Amma's house the next year into a tiny rented room behind her quarters. Muhammad sits with Amma almost daily, but according to Amma, he is not dependable, and this is a source of tension with his parents. He does not meet patients independently of Amma (as Khalid may do) but helps her in the mathematical calculations she uses for diagnoses and folds amulets. Amma depends on him, both to help her with patients and, more important, for his companionship.

Amma's partiality toward her favorite son periodically causes vigorous disagreements between Amma and Abba, Abba thinking that Amma gives Muhammad too many chances and too much financial support. When Amma complains that her sons are disobedient, Abba often answers with some variation of "Of course they don't obey you. You give them everything they want, food and money, no matter what they do. I keep telling you not to give to them, but you, too, don't obey me!" Amma sometimes vows that she will not give money, saying it is abnormal [surprising; *tajjūb*] for a mother to support a grown son rather than the other way around. But when one of her sons asks for money, she almost always gives.

Amma's oldest son went off to Madras to try his luck in acting in the movies, leaving behind a wife and four children. I met him only twice over the ten-year period I visited Amma's healing room. His deserted family lives in a separate quarters in Amma's neighborhood, but she supports them financially and the young grandchildren run in and out of the healing room. Disagreements between Amma and Abba about parenting and family life are openly discussed in the healing room in front of patients, disciples, and customers. Amma does not try to hide from them her troubles of family relationship; hearing these gives many patients confidence that Amma truly understands their own experiences.

Soon after Muhammad's marriage, Amma and Abba thought that he must have been fed *davā* ["medicinal" food that causes a person to be under the "feeder's" control]. This, they thought, could explain why he was not "serving them" appropriately, as a son should (i.e., working and contributing financial resources to the family). When I returned to the healing room a year later, relationships seemed to have mended and there was no talk of the past strain. While Amma and Abba's relationship has been relatively stable over the years I have known them, other family dynamics have shifted rather dramatically between my various visits to Hyderabad, reminding us again of the advantages of longitudinal fieldwork in contexts such as these that encourage the ethnographer not to freeze dynamic relationships in time.

The configuration of nonfamily persons who come regularly to the healing room changes with seasons, employment conditions, and shifting health. Most regulars are disciples who stop by on their way to and from work or in between fulfilling various household responsibilities. But others choose to visit regularly simply to receive Amma's blessings. For example, one summer a Hindu woman who sold sugarcane juice by the roadside dropped by every morning to offer Amma a glass of her juice and in exchange to receive Amma's *duā* [prayer blessings]. But she moved on to a different site once the monsoons started. Other patients and disciples, too, come daily for months at a time and then drop from the scene.

For a period of two months, a young man named Yusuf came every morning to receive Amma's blessing before he went to his job as a ticket seller at a local movie theater. He would not leave the healing room until Amma gave him her explicit permission, which often caused him to be late for work. While he was not an initiated disciple and seemed to have little relationship with Abba, Yusuf was devoted to Amma. He helped her fold amulets and seemed particularly keen to understand certain healing techniques and possibilities for their application. He periodically asked Amma to write out a particular amulet or mix a particular combination of herbs, and if she resisted, he became angry and sullen. Then one day he suddenly disappeared. Amma seemed unconcerned with his absence

59

and explained that his motivations were not good, that he had been a little too interested in *kālā ilm* [black knowledge] that could be used to harm others.

Two persons have been regulars in Amma's healing room over all the years I have worked with her—a male disciple and son-like figure, Hussein, and Amma's best female friend, Munnapa. Hussein is unmarried and spends most of his days sitting in the healing room, either tending to the store in Abba's absence (and he is the primary buyer of store goods) or helping Amma fold amulets. He works the night shift at a dairy, goes home to sleep for a few hours, and then comes to the healing room. In 1996 his elderly mother, too, came daily and simply sat on the floor of the healing room, listening, observing, and saying very little—seemingly simply to be in the presence of Amma, absorbing her *barkat*. In 1999 she was no longer there; ill health prevented her daily visits. In addition to folding amulets and preparing other ritual ingredients, Hussein also regularly performs a healing ritual called *hazrat* (in which he is able to visualize persons and objects at a distance), for which he had to "sit *cillā*" for forty days in order to garner the spiritual strength and authority to practice.

Hussein's story is typical of how disciples find and stay with Amma. As a young man he was sick and weakly. For years, he wandered from *dargāh* to *dargāh* and doctor to doctor looking for relief; for five years he sat at Dargah Yusufayn in the Old City, waiting for some kind of healing or miracle. Then he heard about Amma through an auto driver who himself had been healed by her; the driver persuaded Hussein that it was useless to sit at the *dargāh* day after day and took him to Amma. She diagnosed his problem as particularly "heavy," and successful treatment took forty days. Thereafter, Amma told him to "come sit with her," and he has come daily ever since. Hussein's father had been a spiritual man who had learned a system of healing with herbs, and with Amma's permission, Hussein later brought this system into the healing room.[13]

Hussein's female counterpart as a constant presence in the healing room is Munnapa, who has set up an ironing business in a lean-to shack next to Amma's healing room. She draws a small income from ironing brought in by neighbors, but the primary benefit of her work is the continual access to Amma that it gives her. She first started coming to Amma when she was rejected by her brothers because of the jealousy they exhibited when her daughter got married before their (older) daughters—against the common social convention that the elder sister (cousins fill the slot of sisters here) should get married before younger ones. The brothers told Munnapa she was no longer welcomed in her natal house, where they lived with her mother. Although she was married and lived with her husband, Munnapa perceived herself to be in a state of homelessness: "Without a father or a brother, then who do you have?" At the time she had a small ironing stall in front of her house, but she neglected it and, according to her own account, she began to waste away. A neighbor introduced her to Amma, and Munnapa began to spend her days sitting with her. Finally she asked Amma if could bring her ironing business along with her.

When her ironing is finished (usually by 11 A.M.), Munnapa sits in the healing room chatting with Amma and making her *pān* (an addiction they share), periodically making her a cup of tea over the coals used to heat her iron. Every day she brings her lunch in a tiffin and shares her food with Amma, sitting around the red cloth spread out on the floor for the family's lunch. She returns to her own home to prepare dinner for her family by mid-afternoon. Munnapa knows all of Amma's disciples and attends Abba's monthly *samā* gatherings and the annual festival of Gyarwin Sharif, but she herself has not become a disciple, and there has not been any pressure for her to do so. Munnapa's Hindu identity is dramatized by the particularly big red *bottu* [vermilion forehead marking] she wears. Her husband and two young grandsons often come to the healing room in the late afternoons or on festival days, and they all wear protective amulets [*tāvīz*] Amma has given them. Munnapa has ritualized a brother-sister kinship with Abba by celebrating Raksha Bandhan with him, a Hindu festival during which a sister traditionally ties a decorated *rākhī* string on her brother's wrist. Munnapa told me that she has never become a formal disciple of Abba's because she does not want to give up her worship [*pūjā*] to Hindu deities or wearing her *bottu*. But this decision has caused no strain in her relationship with Amma and Abba. Munnapa frequently contributes to conversations in the healing room, periodically helping in cultural and linguistic translation between Urdu and Telugu in Amma's conversations with Hindu patients. Her presence in the healing

8. Amma and her best friend, Munnapa, 1996.

room embodies its characterization as a religious/cultural crossroads, a *caurāstā*.

Patients often say they have been drawn to Amma because of her uniqueness as a female healer, because of her "love and patience." These qualities are partially manifest in the domesticity and relatively relaxed pace of the healing room, in part created by the presence of family members and family-based conversations, and in part by the flow of disciples and friends through the healing room. Patients have opportunities to witness the maternal and friendship identities of Amma, and they can see that she understands their own problems as created by webs of kinship and relationships. Many of them say they are drawn to her because she takes time with them as if they are her children and/or family members. But Amma's healing table is lined with stacks of paper amulets held down by chipped glass paperweights, and it is her training and control over the elaborate healing system of diagnosis, prescription, and treatment externalized in the amulets that contributes to her professional authority. This system is the focus of the next chapter.

THE HEALING SYSTEM

2

The whole world depends on pen and paper.

Pareśānī: Troubles Brought to the Healing Room

Amma boldly states that she 'guarantees' (using the English word) her treatments for all troubles and illnesses that are caused by *śaitānī*, literally evil forces but more generally the impingement of spiritual forces on the physical world. (*Śaitān* literally means "satan," but *śaitānī* has a broader meaning of evil or devilish things; sometimes the meaning can be "naughty" if applied to the behavior of a child.) Amma specifically excludes cancer, heart troubles, typhoid, and polio from the classification of illnesses over which she has control (all diseases that have, incidentally, directly affected members of her own family).[1] Many patients come to Amma with very specific complaints: infertility, high fevers in children, disobedient children (including teenage sons who do not work but just "meander around all day"), colicky babies and stubborn young children, babies who are failing to thrive, abusive husbands, troubles making marriage arrangements for their daughters, stolen gold, runaway goats, interfering neighbors, or failing businesses. Other patients come with generalized complaints such as "I don't sleep well, my hands and feet are pulling," vague restlessness [*becainī*], or general trouble [*pareśānī*] in the house.

Looking at the list of complaints with which patients come to Amma, we might be tempted to classify them as psychologically based illnesses as opposed to physical ones. But this is not the distinction Amma draws. *Śaitānī* can manifest in mind, body, or spirit. Amma is adamant that many illnesses for which patients go to allopathic doctors are illnesses only she (or another religious practitioner) can control, and she bemoans the fact that while she is quite willing to refer patients to doctors for illnesses outside her range of expertise, it is rare that allopathic doctors admit that they have no control over particular kinds of illnesses and refer them to her. Amma often recommends specific doctors, from obstetricians to optometrists, by name and phone number; some she knows personally, others by reputation through her patients.

Centrality of the Written Word in Diagnosis and Prescriptions

The centrality of the written word is striking in the healing room. Amma's primary method of diagnosis is based on the written word, as are most of her prescriptions and treatments (called *ilāj*, the same word used for allopathic medical treatments). Amma writes all day long, opening the "mystery of numbers" [*abjad kā phāl kholnā*, hereafter called *abjad*] to diagnose the troubles of a patient and writing out prescriptions: slips of paper to be folded and worn around the neck, rolled and burned in oil, smashed with a sandal, or hung in a doorway to flutter in the wind. She also writes on unleavened bread, gourds, and saucers. Amma's fingers are ink-stained, and her desk is covered with slips of paper on which mathematical calculations have been made, stacks of amulets upon which magical squares and Arabic letters and numbers have been written, a clipboard, and an inkpot.

The importance of the written word in Amma's ritual healing activity helps identify her healing practice as Islamic,[2] although there are also Muslim healers who do not rely on the written word. Abba once told me,

Allah gave power to the pen and paper. To the pen. He gave strength to the pen. And the paper. *Tāqat*—'power'. He didn't give 'power' to the tongue. If someone gets angry, what happens? You take him and report him to the police, to the collector's office. Then they look at the petition. They don't listen to the word of tongue, only the written word. The 'judge' can send you to the gallows. And if he wants, he can bring you down from there with the stroke of a pen. . . . It's all in the pen, in the pen and paper. Only these two things.

The written word is like the written judgment in a court of law: indisputable, powerful, and final. On another occasion Abba elaborated on the power of the written word to activate:

It's like if I write a letter to you and tell you to come; it's 'urgent'—a telegram. You can't refuse. Like that, there's a mantra.[3] And on [your] name, like if we know the name of your mother. Reading that and reading your name, we make an 'attack'.

In one discussion about writing, a patient asked me if I was sitting there to learn so that I too could practice like this in the United States. I said I had no intention of treating the public like this and that in any case, I didn't know Arabic. Abba interrupted, "That doesn't matter; you can write in 'roman'." And he wrote out in 'roman' on a slip of paper *bismillāh e rahmān e rahīm* ["In the name of God, the Merciful, the Compassionate"].[4] But when I asked if this would be as powerful as writing in Arabic, he admitted that it would not: "English will have a small effect and Arabi a big effect."

Writing is traditionally a male healing practice among Muslims in Hyderabad; women read and recite the Quran and blow healing prayers upon family members, but they rarely write. Amma's act of ritual writing places her in a male role, as does her meeting the 'public'. Amma often criticized Muslim healers who did not write. For example, she ridiculed one famous *bābā*, "What does he give? Nothing! It is nothing! He doesn't give anything, does he? He only says *duā* [prayer] and touches the patient with the end of his scarf. He doesn't write anything, does he?" When I visited another *pirānimā* whose practice is based on her interpretation of dreams, Amma wondered why I was interested in her when she "didn't give anything"—that is, the written word. Abba confirmed that for him, too, the only treatment that counted was the written word. With some derision, he once commented about a particular *muršid* to whom one of his disciples had previously gone, saying, "All he gave was *zikr* [name of God repeated in meditation] and *namāz* [formal prayer], but not treatment. He thought *zikr* and *namāz* were enough, without treatment!"

Amma asserts that her healing power is based solely on the Quran, that everything she needs for her practice is found in what she calls the "Book of Service" [*khidmatwālī kitāb*]. Abba calls the Quran "powerful magic" [*baṛā jādū*]. The last two chapters of the Quran, numbers 113 and 114, are frequently cited as the source of this claim and are themselves often used as oral or written prayers for protection. These chapters read as follows:

> Say: I seek refuge in the Lord of Daybreak
> From the evil of that which He created;
> From the evil of the darkness when it is intense,
> And from the evil of malignant witchcraft,
> And from the evil of the envier when he envieth.
>
> Say: I seek refuge in the Lord of mankind,
> The King of mankind,
> The God of mankind,
> From the evil of the sneaking whisperer,
> Who whispereth in the hearts of mankind,
> Of the jinn and of mankind. (Suras 113 and 114; in Pickthall 1994, 737–739)

When Amma exclaims "There would be no world without paper and pen!" she is referring not only to the world of her healing practice but to Allah's revelation and the Islamic concept of an eternal primordial Quran and the pen with which it was written. Human actions are also believed to be written in a book of deeds, and the Quran describes God as he who "taught man with the Pen" (Sura 96:3–4; Schimel 1970, 1).

Amma's rhetoric and vocabulary for healing rituals are also dominated by images of the written word. She uses the Urdu word *paṛhnā* [lit., to read or recite, but with strong connotations of reciting something written] to describe *namāz* [ritual prayer], *duā* [intercessory prayer], *zikr* [meditation], the interpretation of dreams [*sapnā paṛhnā*] and visions (many of which are themselves images of written words sent by God), and the oral recitation of the Quran. For many of these ritual activities, Amma and other participants hold open their hands as if reading a book. This pose is also the typical pose for a photograph taken at a ritual/religious site such as the grave of a relative or saint. Although the Quran is read from directly only infrequently in the healing room, it is the base from which Amma derives her healing authority and is the basis for her diagnoses and treatments. Many of the written prescriptions include numbers that represent the names of Allah or particular verses from the Quran. Thus, the healing setting is, in Shirley Heath's words, a "literacy event . . . [an] occasion in which a piece of writing is integral to the nature of the participants' interactions and their interpretive processes" (1982, 100).

It would be a mistake, however, to think that participants experience the written word in this healing practice primarily through its semantic content. The written Arabic letters are themselves inherently powerful, filled with *barkat* [auspicious blessings]. As the channel through which the revelation was transmitted, they are experienced as the very word of God. Patients who wear, drink, burn, or bury the written word of God and written representations of his name and those of his messengers and angels on various kinds of amulets do not know specifically what is written on the paper, and I never heard anyone ask. The Quranic words, verses, and names and the number substitutes for these lose their semantic content when written on slips of paper as they are spatially manipulated within various diagrams or written in such haste as to be illegible. Likewise, Arabic calligraphy loses its semantic context when the written names of God or the Muslim confession of faith [*kalmā*] are manipulated and formed so as to make the image of a bird, mosque, and so forth.

The words on the amulets worn around the neck or waist are understood to physically deflect the evil eye. Other amulets are burned and the smoke of the words is inhaled by the patient or they are immersed in water—the ink that washes off and is drunk by the patient is itself the word of God, internalized and protective. The efficacy of the amulets does not depend primarily upon the semantic content of their words but upon the spiritual authority they represent and embody and the authority with which they are dispensed. Patients come to Amma because they have heard that her healing "works"; they care much less about *how* it works than they care that it *does* work.

Amma explained that through spiritual discipline and service she has garnered the authority to call upon a constellation of Allah's *maukīl* [Arabic *mu'akkal*; lit., deputy, vice-regent, someone to whom power has been delegated] to come to her service and carry out her commands to facilitate healing. The Pakistani Sufi *pīr* that Katherine Ewing worked with used the term in ways similar to Amma; that is, to identify agents of God who serve the practitioner of *nūrī ilm* [luminous knowledge] (Ewing 1997, 132–138).[5] As Amma uses the word, "*maukīl*" usually references the four archangels, Israfil, Jibrail, Mikail, and Izrail; but the word may also refer to other lower angels and *jinn* [beings made of fire, usually invisible, who can be helpful or harmful to humans], all of whom are creations of and subordinate to Allah. Amma's *pīr* son, Khalid, once called the *maukīl* "*śaitān's* [lit., Satan's] brothers"; he said that there are both good and bad ones who "do this work for us—yes, like *jinn*." Some *maukīl* have generalized power (the four archangels, for example) and others have power over specific problems (such as fever, arguing neighbors, lost children). Khalid further explained that *maukīl* are present to do Amma's bidding as soon as she sits at her healing table; writing their names on amulets simply tells them what it is that they should do.

Diagnosis: Opening the Mystery of Numbers

Amma's primary method of diagnosing a patient's problem is *abjad kā phāl kholnā*, in which the Arabic letters of patients' names are given numerical values that are then mathematically manipulated. Islamic mystical traditions have long assigned mystical significance and symbolism to individual letters of the Arabic alphabet, for these are the very letters through which the Quran was revealed (Schimmel 1975, 411). Annemarie Schimmel has identified three characteristics that are shared between number mysticisms developed from Pythagorean and Platonic ideas; these also characterize the *abjad* system:

1. Numbers influence the character of things that are ordered by them.
2. Thus, the number becomes a mediator between the Divine and the created world.

3. It follows that if one performs operations with numbers, these operations also work upon the things connected with the numbers used. (Schimmel 1993, 16)

The Islamic tradition has added to these numerical principles the power of the letter, a principle shared with the Jewish tradition of *gematriya*. Carl Ernst suggests that "this kind of numerological analysis of Arabic formulae . . . goes back to the enigmatic isolated letters that preface a number of *surās* of the Quran," to which many different explanations have been given over the centuries (1997, 91; see also Schimmel 1993, 411). All of these systems agree that only the spiritually adept can truly decipher and manipulate these hidden meanings of numbers and letters.

The relationship between name and object is also filled with spiritual significance; that is, a name is never "simply" a name but affects and/or reflects the nature of the person assigned a particular name. Amma once insisted that a baby's name should be changed in order to change her ill health; she had been given the wrong name, according to Amma, which had resulted in her failure to thrive. Valerie Hoffman similarly reports that in Egyptian *zikr* [Arabic, *dhikr*] recitation practices, while each recited name of God unlocks a particular spiritual secret, "There should also be a correspondence between the numerical value attached to the sum of the letters in the name recited and the numerical value of the sum of the letters of the name of the person doing *dhikr* [zikr]" (1995, 132). Amma often answered my questions about the mystical or symbolic significance of names, numbers, and letters she had written on her healing amulets with something like, "These are very heavy [*bhārī*] matters," too heavy to be openly spoken of or revealed to the general public.

The tradition of *abjad* assigns each letter of the Arabic alphabet a numerical value.[6] So, for example, when one adds up the values of the letters forming the word "Allah," the total numerical value for the word is sixty-six. Amma asks each patient his/her name and that of his/her mother and writes out the name of each in the Arabic script; she adds up the numerical value totals for each name and then adds to them the value for the lunar day of the week.[7] She divides the total by three or four (depending on what gives a whole quotient), and the final quotient identifies the cause of the patient's illness and determines its appropriate prescription. Amma and her two sons, Khalid and Muhammad, gave several different explanations for the symbolic value of dividing by three or four. Amma initially told me that four signifies the four corners of the earth; Khalid explained four signified the elements of which humans are made: earth, air, water, and fire; while Muhammad said four was the number of *maukīl* upon whom Amma called. Similarly with three: Amma said three signified the three levels of the universe—heaven, earth, hell, but Khalid told me that three was taken from the three basic vowel sounds. The significance of these numbers was never expounded to patients and disciples in the healing room.

In 1990, Amma explained the system the diagnostic system this way:

It's like this. It's according to the stars. [She asks my fieldwork associate,] What's your name? Lakshmi: *lām* is 30, *kāph* is 20, *shīn* is 300, *mīm* is 40, and the last is 10. What's your mother's name? . . . What's today? Saturday is 357. Add these all up. Keep dividing by four. We're made of four elements, right? Earth, air, water, fire. If the remainder is zero there's nothing [wrong]; a remainder of one means it's *jismānī* [lit., having to do with the body; a physical problem]; two is *kartūt* [evil eye from a person]; three is *asrat* [evil eye from a supernatural being].

Four years later, she explained the system using my name:

Like your name is Jo-ice: *jinn* is 3; *nīm* is 40, *i* is 10, *sīm* is 7. Then, what's your mother's name? Ramoth: *re* is 200; *he* is 8; *ma* is 40; *t* is 400;[8] these two you add. Then, what's today? Today is *pīr* [Monday]; *pīr* is 376. Add these three totals and then divide by four. What's left after this? If two is left, we say *kiyā huā* [lit., something's been done to you]; if three is left, then it's *asrat*; if two or one is left, then we say it's *girā*, *balā girā* [an evil spirit has fallen on you]. If there's nothing left, then we say it's nothing. Then what do we say? We take the total of your name, that of the mother of all humans, Hava [Eve], is 12, and today is 376; add those three, and then again divide by four or divide by three; doing this, you get a number. If you don't get it one way, then you get it this way. There are three levels to the world; there are four corners of the earth. You get the result of two or one, etc.[9]

On another lazy Friday afternoon with no patients waiting in the courtyard and plenty of time to talk, Muhammad explained *abjad* this way:

You divide by three the total under the patient's name [because of the three totals added together, the arithmetic value of the patient's name, the mother's name, and that of the lunar day] and by four the total under the mother's name [because there are four archangel *maukīl*]. Then you compare the two remainders. If the difference is one or two, the diagnosis is *kartūt* or *asrat*. If the remainder is one or two, an outsider has done it. If the remainder is three or four, [the evil eye has been caused by] a relative.

The last time I met Amma, in 2000, she explained that one should add the totals of a patient's name, the mother's name (and now she was using the number for Hava's name rather than individual mothers' names), and the day of week; then divide first by four and then by three. If the number remaining is two, the diagnosis is *kartūt*; if it is one, nothing is the matter; and if the remainder is three, the diagnosis is *asrat*.

While Amma is confident in her mathematical calculations of *abjad* and says that this part of the practice is very straightforward, over the years, no two explanations of the system given by her or her disciples were exactly the same, even though they followed the same basic "grammar." Above, we see that Amma divides the total of the three numerical values of the names and day of week by four, but her son first divides the individual numerical value of the patient's name by three and that of his/her mother by four and compares the remainders. Muhammad's explanation of the remainders differs from those given by Amma (and on another occasion, by the same ones articulated by Khalid), but he has not been formally trained in the system and he does not practice independently of Amma (and thus does not name the diagnoses). I periodically collected the scraps of paper upon which Amma made her calculations (with her permission and causing her to laugh at my confusion) to see if I could figure them out and duplicate the method. Did she actually divide by three or four, for example? However, I became even more confused when I discovered on these scraps of paper that several of her actual arithmetic calculations (simple adding or dividing) were incorrect. When

I first discovered these miscalculations, I felt like I had been put into an ethical dilemma: What did this say, and what could I then say, about her confident proclamation of diagnoses and prescriptions based upon these calculations? I never mentioned this problem to Amma, because she had also declared with full confidence that to make these mathematical calculations was the easy part; it was the spiritual power behind the written prescriptions, not the mathematical calculations themselves, that effected healing.

One day as I was listening to Amma's explanation of *abjad,* it occurred to me that if a patient came to Amma on the same lunar day every year, and if that person kept his or her name, the mathematically diagnosed problem would be the same. When I asked her about this, she looked puzzled for a few seconds and then laughed and said she had never thought of this, but yes, that would be the case. Another dilemma arose when Amma asked me to help her write the names of patients on various amulets. I told her that I could write them in Hindi but that I did not know the Arabic/Urdu script. She told me that it was no problem writing names in 'roman' script. Knowing the importance of names and the significance of their mathematical value, I hesitated to comply with Amma's request: I was not sure that I always heard the names correctly (I was not familiar with some of them) and I realized that there would be several ways to transcribe a given name into English. I whispered my concern to a disciple sitting next to Amma. He too, found it disturbing that there could be various relationships between sound and letter in English. He exclaimed, "But if the word is wrong, the meaning, too, will change!" Amma overheard us and told me that it would not matter; it was the intention that mattered and that with good intention, the name would be "heard" correctly (by the spiritual beings who were being called by the amulet).

As Amma's eyesight deteriorated in her later years (a problem for which no doctor diagnosed a cause), she began to use more and more photocopies of *tāvīz* and *fālitā* rather than her own handwritten copies. On my last visit to Amma's healing table, the color of the paper for her prescriptions had changed from white to bright pink, which Khalid told me was simply because this color was available most cheaply at the photocopy store. Another adjustment made after Amma's eyesight had deteriorated seemed of greater significance. In 1996 I noticed that Amma rarely asked anymore for the names of patients' mothers, only for their own names. When I asked her about this, Amma told me that she used the name Hava (Eve) for all patients, since Hava is the mother of all of us. This kept her from having to make so many calculations on paper, which were becoming more and more difficult for her to read.

This part of the healing practice is mathematical and on the surface appears to be relatively objective, although it requires specialized training with a guru, and several of Amma's close disciples help her with this part of the diagnosis. But, as Amma says, "Anyone can *read*, even a parrot. It's understanding [that's difficult]." (What she means by "understanding" will become more clear when we examine individual narratives of healing.) The manipulation of numbers is, according to Amma, purely mechanical, and to produce an end quotient alone will not enable the healer to correctly diagnose and prescribe. To do the latter, a healer needs to know the weight (strength) and context of the diagnosed problem. In fact, only four general classes of diagnoses are generated and named mathematically; Amma brings to the numbers a spiritual "understanding" that identifies further gradations within each mathematically generated diagnoses. Interestingly, Amma often does not usually conduct *abjad* for children; rather, often she simply looks at them, taps their stomachs, and pronounces the diagnosis. She is able to name these childhood illnesses and further distinguish and gradate the arithmetically determined diagnoses because of her understanding of human nature and the webs of problems brought to her table and, more important, because of her spiritual wisdom and strength garnered through spiritual practices. These have created in her the authority to call upon spiritual forces to carry out her orders and then to declare the healing effected.

Naming the Problem

One of the ways through which Amma is recognized as a professional authority, and through which she performatively establishes and maintains that authority, is the range and finely calibrated differences of diagnoses (beyond the four generated mathematically) she has available to her with which to name the problem with which a patient comes and the wide range and numbers of prescriptions she offers.[10] This elaborate taxonomy distinguishes Amma from many other healers, especially women. Every patient walks out with handfuls of slips of papers folded in various ways and an oral list of detailed directions for their use. For example, a layperson might simply suspect a problem to be the result of a generalized "evil eye" [Urdu *nazar* or Telugu *diṣṭi*], but Amma rarely uses these general words. Rather, she is able to distinguish whether a spiritual force or a human has cast the eye, whether it was done knowingly or unknowingly, and what the "weight" of that evil eye is. The more specifically the problem is identified, the more specific the prescription can be, and a misdiagnosis can have severe consequences. So although the numerical range of the results of *abjad kā phāl kholnā* is simply from zero to four, the numbers of named diagnoses resulting from these numbers is more expansive.

Many *pīrs* are trained in the basic system of system of *abjad*, but each has a different range of diagnoses and prescriptions, depending on who their teachers are, their own levels of training, and levels of their spiritual understanding. Other *pīrs* work within other kinds of healing systems. Each healer is known for something unique, something that distinguishes him/her from others; for Amma, of course, one of these factors is that she is the rare woman who meets the public. One *pīr* who sits under a tree once a week by a remote *dargāh* at the edge of Osmania University campus is particularly know for his *jamālī* [easygoing] character and the fact that he heals in a "*junglī*" [uninhabited, forest] place. He diagnoses by cutting lemons in half and throwing them on the ground to see how many land face up and face down. While he himself makes a diagnosis, he does not identify particular problems out loud, and he has only one standard set of prescriptions: he throws water in the faces of the patients when they least expect it as they sit in front of the *pīr*, he gives all the patients the same amulets to soak in water and drink, he wraps up a pinch of sand in a slip of paper to sprinkle around the house, and he gives the injunction that patients should regularly perform *namāz*. Patients sit in front of him for only seconds before he brushes them away to make space for the next person. Another *pīranimā* who is married to the caretaker of a *dargāh* near the Secunderabad railway station also does not name diagnosed illnesses. Patients come before her with a problem and she "sleeps on it" in order to dream what its prescription should be. She gives a single type of prescription to all patients—to stay overnight at the *dargāh*—the only difference being the number of nights prescribed for each patient.

Below I provide a sample of the range of diagnoses and prescriptions available in the system within which Amma works that help create her authority and persona as healer.

Kartūt: evil eye purposefully caused by a person; deed; trickery. Amma identifies *kartūt* with the Telugu *bāṇāmati*, which itself has direct associations with sorcery. She explained, "We call it *kartūt* if you're sitting there and I do something to you; if someone does something to you. Having read various books, they do "crooked-straight" actions. It is when someone does something to you purposefully, someone you know, like a family member." Abba elaborated:

Kartūt is caused by humans [rather than a supernatural force, such as a *śaitān*]. If someone wants to cause some trouble or finish someone off, then s/he will read or say [*paṛh ke*] something in the other person's name. S/he might take a piece of hair from the person's head and say some words over it. Do you understand? A person does this. And *asrat* works like this: you see a car on the road and you like it or there's some food and you like it [you're attracted to it], what happens to the soul [lit., breath, *rūh*] of the dead person? It's just wandering around. Do you understand? And for those who have weak constitutions [lit., stars, *sitārā*; i.e., fate], when someone looks good [i.e., this soul sees something attractive], it comes on them. It's like that.

Karosā: a subclassification of *kartūt*. One of Amma's closest disciples who often helps her in the healing room gave this example of *karosā*. It can occur when a man dies and they bring his ashes[11] into the house and his spirit causes problems: "The entire house becomes restless, restless, restless, agitated" and requires exorcism. On another occasion Amma told me that *karosā* is a type of *kartūt* that results from enmity between people who know each other.

Asrat: [also called *balāyat*; lit., that caused by an evil spirit], Amma described *asrat* as the result of some *śaitān* or *malāmat* [evil spirit] catching hold of you. To make sure I understood, like Abba had earlier, Amma distinguished *asrat* from *kartūt*:

[*Asrat*] is caused by *śaitān*, it's the play [*khel*] of *śaitān*, and if a person does something to you . . . we call that *kartūt*. Humans do *kartūt*, but *asrat* is the hold of *śaitān*; it's also called *balāyat*. Like if someone receives a blow and dies and his/her spirit [*rūh*] gets loose or if someone falls from a building and dies or if someone dies and becomes a *śaitān* [and] his spirit is bad [lit., dirty, *gandā*], then it becomes a *śaitān* and gets hold of people; we call this *asrat*.

On another occasion, Amma distinguished *kartūt* and *asrat* by saying *kartūt* was caused purposefully by the evil eye of someone you know and *asrat* was caused unknowingly by someone you do not know, a passerby. In this case, the person may have an inherent evil eye that affects whatever is good and valuable that comes in his/her path of vision, whether or not s/he is envious of it or wants to destroy it. A Hyderabadi Christian friend told me that she had a sister-in-law who had such an eye. It seemed that no matter where this woman went, there was an accident of some kind; saris caught on fire, scooters were in accidents, jewelry was lost. The woman assured me her sister-in-law meant no harm, it was simply in her eye. Thus, the implications of *asrat* may extend beyond that caused by an evil spirit to include evil eye caused unintentionally by a human.

Davā: literally, medicine; when someone has fed you something to cause you to be under his/her control; the expression used is "you're in the service [*sevā*]" of the person who has fed you *davā*. Amma makes this diagnosis by looking at the lines on a patient's palms. As Amma's eyes became weak and she had difficulty making out the fine lines in the palm of a hand, she began to ask her son Muhammad or another disciple to "read" the lines to determine whether or not *davā* is present. Once Amma has determined that *davā* is present, she gives the prescription to the family member accompanying the patient or who has come to report the problem without the afflicted family member (in which case Amma "sees" the diagnosis in her mind rather than in the lines of the palm). She sends the patient to a bridge in the Old City, where, she instructs, "You'll find an elderly Hindu woman selling medicines [crushed and mixed herbs]. Buy medicines from her. These should be dissolved in warm milk and drunk by the patient; they will cause the patient to throw up the *davā*. The patient him/herself may not realize or want to admit s/he is under the influence of someone else and thus not want to take the medicine. In this case, put the medicine in the patient's food secretly. And finally, don't tell anyone!" When I expressed my surprise that Amma did not have the antidotes in her own healing room, she assured me she *could* make the medicines (and periodically does so for close family members or disciples), but that it is time consuming and there is no reason to do it when she knows where it is easily available.

After Abba died, Amma began to prepare the herbal *davā* antidote herself; coincidentally, I noticed, *davā* was now much more commonly prescribed than it had been in previous years. Amma explained that it had become inconvenient and a useless additional expense for patients to have to go all the way to the Old City, and so she had taken up the task of buying the herbs and grinding the antidote herself. Nevertheless, she did not keep these ready made, and patients always had to return the next day to pick up the prescription.

The work of Allah: Sometimes the *abjad* diagnosis reveals that "nothing" is wrong; that is, although the patient might have a complaint, there is no spiritual imbalance in the patient that can be treated through one of Amma's standard prescriptions. In this case, Amma may say, "It's nothing; it's the work [*karam*] of Allah," or "Allah *kā phasal* [the will of God]." In these cases, Amma listens to the patient's complaint and narrative but encourages the patient to endure it, as there is no treatment for something that is simply "the will of God." However, the patient, as patients in many biomedical contexts both in India and the United States do, often insists that Amma give her/him "something." So Amma sometimes complies by giving him/her amulets to be burned in oil [*dhuān*] or simply a generalized amulet of protection [*tāvīz*] to wear around the neck. Other times she insists that the patient should simply go home and endure the problem.

Ilāj: Treatments and Prescriptions

Written Prescriptions: *Tāvīz, Fālitā, Dhuān*

Amma's three primary prescriptions are based on the written word: words written on slips of paper folded into amulets to wear around the neck or waist or to put in one's purse or pocket [*tāvīz*]; amulets to burn, drink, hide under a rock or dresser, or smash [*fālitā*]; and amulets to burn over coals so the smoke can be inhaled [*dhuān*]. Almost every patient is given a general-protection *tāvīz, dhuān* to burn and inhale, and *fālitā* to immerse in water and drink. When a patient leaves the healing table, his or her hands are filled with pieces of paper folded in different ways to indicate how they should be used, enough to last five days. The number of prescriptions given to any given patient reminded me of all the tiny folded paper envelopes filled pills given to patients at many local Indian pharmacies—there is a certain power in numbers—as well as in the spectrum of different kinds of prescriptions. New patients are often confused about what each piece of paper is and how each should be manipulated differently, even as they assure Amma that they have understood her directions. I often heard returning patients laughing with new patients about their confusion over the differently folded paper prescriptions as the former explained again to the new patients "what was what." The confusion of one new male patient, who spoke Telugu, Urdu, and English, caused particular amusement in the room because otherwise he seemed so educated and competent. After numerous explanations by both Amma and the patients sitting around the table, Amma gave him leave, assuring him that he had provided the room with great entertainment [*manoranjan*] and that now he surely understood.

Tāvīz: the primary amulet for protection against all varieties of evil eye and other negative spiritual forces. Every patient leaves with at least a protective *tāvīz* if he or she does not already have one. It may be given for general protection or for a specific cause. A *tāvīz* is a slip of paper approximately 3 by 5 inches; Amma writes on both the front and back. It is folded widthwise into a narrow slip and again folded lengthwise until it is a small tightly folded square of approximately one-half inch. This square is wrapped tightly in strips of plastic cut from used plastic bags, and it is then tied closed with a black cotton string. Amma or one of her assistants cuts the string to a two-inch length if it is to be tied to a woman's wedding necklace [*mangalsūtra*]—perceived to be the external site of her auspiciousness and power and on which frequently are also attached her house keys and one or two safety pins. This piece of gold is not for beauty of adornment, as it is tucked underneath the sari and the actual pendant is rarely visible; rather, its primary significance is ritual. If a woman is unmarried or does not have a *mangalsūtra,* and in the case of children and many men, the string is cut long to approximate a necklace. "Modern" women and men keep the *tāvīz* in their purses and pants pockets.

To deflect the evil eye from a vulnerable breastfeeding baby, Amma ties a *tāvīz* around both the baby's neck and that of its mother. If Amma finds another healer's *tāvīz* on a woman's *mangalsūtra* or a child's neck, she first cuts it off before tying her own. She rarely comments on this sign of a visit to another healer, to which the present visit testifies as a "failure"; it is understood that in this healing system, the right relationship must be present for prescriptions or treatments to be effective and many patients have gone to many healers before coming to Amma. Every so often, Amma tells a patient that the *tāvīz* she has given earlier should be renewed, implying that it loses its efficacy or strength over time; she periodically checks the *tāvīz* of returning patients and cuts them off if she determines that they have become useless [*bekār*]. An old *tāvīz* should not be disposed of thoughtlessly or thrown in the trash but should be hung from a tree or immersed in a body of water, as is common for the disposal of other religious items across traditions in India (such as clay images of Hindu deities, for example).

The front side of the *tāvīz* is standard between patients and thus can be photocopied or written using carbon copies. Amma has stacks of these ready, although on Thursday afternoons and Sundays, when the crowd of patients is at its maximum, she often runs out and has to take time out to write or cut more. On this front side of the *tāvīz* are written the names of Allah, the primary *maukīl* and/or the numbers representing these names, and the *kalmā* [Muslim creed of faith], numbers representing certain powerful verses from the Quran, and magical number squares with the same powerful numbers written on them.[12] Amma always writes the

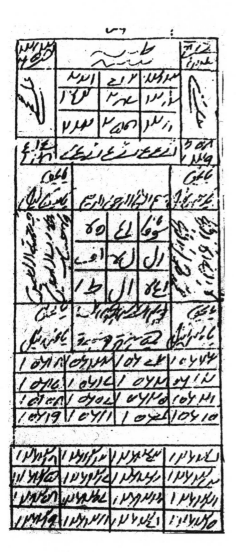

9. One of Amma's standard
tāvīz.

patient's name on the front side before turning the *tāvīz* over and writing
a specific request on the back side. Amma thus personalizes amulets,
something not true of many other Muslim healers who distribute similar
kinds of *tāvīz*.

In 1995, I noticed that Amma had added a small white-metal canister
tāvīz to her repertoire. Amma told me that these were "stronger" than

the paper *tāvīz* and that the cost was Rs. 51 instead of Rs. 15 for the paper one. I assumed that paper *tāvīz* were folded up inside the metal canister and the difference in cost was in the container, so when Amma gave one for each member of my family for me to take back to them in the United States, I did not open them. When I gave my teenage daughter Rachel her canister, though, she popped it open right away, and out came bits of leaves and stems. I had been asked numerous times at conferences at which I had presented papers about Amma if she used herbs in her practice and had confidently answered "no." Now I was in the United States with herbs scattered across the kitchen table and no explanation for what they were or how they were used. That opportunity would not come for another year; we will return to what I learned when we consider innovation in Amma's practice.

Besides the standard *tāvīz*, there are specialized ones. One, called *havā tāvīz* [lit., air/wind amulet], is written on a tiny piece of paper to be hung from the doorway of the home of a missing child. The child's name is written on the amulet along with that of the *maukīl* who will find the child, and the *tāvīz* is believed to literally call the child home. Then there is a special fever *tāvīz*, again written on a small piece of paper that is folded into a very tiny square; the patient should hit the amulet three times with his/her sandal and say, "Fever, go away, go away, go away" [*bukhār utro*; lit., fever, get up and leave]. Another specialized *tāvīz* is made from a large copper square and should be hung in doorways as a protection to the home; the cost of one of these in 1996 was Rs. 25.

Fālitā: distinguished from *tāvīz* in that they are paper amulets that are not worn on the person; rather, they are to be burned or soaked in water and the ink is drunk by the patient. *Fālitā* have less writing on them than *tāvīz* and call upon a specific *maukīl* associated with a specific problem. The *maukīl*'s name is written on the top half of the *fālitā* and on the bottom half is written the name/s of the offenders or the exact action/cure requested, such as "may an adversary's mouth be shut."

Abdul Jinn is the name of a *maukīl* who engages in specialized services regarding human relationships; one disciple called him the "chief minister" of all the *maukīl*. The *fālitā* that calls upon his services is soaked in coconut oil, having been folded around a hair of an adversary or the person upon whom Abdul Jinn's force should work. The patient should declare what goal s/he wants to be accomplished as the *fālitā* is burning, such as "may his mouth be closed" or "may he [husband or son, generally] stay at home instead of wandering around" or, regarding a husband who has been greedy with family money, "Listen to my words: give me money." Another *fālitā* calls upon the *maukīl* Badru, also called the "big *maukīl*," whose specialty it is to call people back home (for example, a married son who has moved out with his new wife). His name is also written on one of the drinking *fālitā* on which numbers are written. Other lesser *maukīl* are named Shafil, Jabbar, Khahar, and Dafe Balad. Amma says, "We call the *maukīl* to be present and they do our work. We write the names and they do the work."

Fālitā slips of paper are folded in several different ways, depending upon how one should burn them. If they are rolled like wicks (and it is important that they be rolled in a certain direction and burned only from the end that is marked with ink), they are burned in either "sweet" or "bitter" oil (coconut or sesame or rapeseed oil), depending on the diagnosis. If they are folded accordion style, they should be burned in coals in the evening. When they are simply left in flat form, they should be burned on coals in the morning; the patient should inhale the smoke of these both morning and evening. The two most commonly used *fālitā* are named *nās kā sūra* [lit., the form of man] and Abdul Jinn *fālitā*. The *nās kā surā fālitā* has a stick image (called a *putlā*, a doll, image, or effigy) of a man, with a head, two hands, and two feet drawn on it. Amma's youngest son, Muhammad, says that this one "finishes off all kinds of *śaitānī kartūt* [evil eye caused by evil forces] for the entire spectrum of afflictions it causes."

Upon another *fālitā* Amma draws a fish shape and writes numbers wherever lines intersect in the drawing. The patient takes a hair of either the person who is causing problems or the person who has the problem, folds it into the *fālitā*, and burns it as an oil wick. Other *fālitā* are filled with magic number squares. One of Amma's close disciples explained the number squares to be "*naqśā* Quran" [lit., diagrammatic Quran]. When Amma is writing numbers in the magic number squares, she does not write them in each square consecutively but does it diagonally and periodically skips squares, indicating the importance of placement and order in which the numbers are written; again, the semantic value of the num-

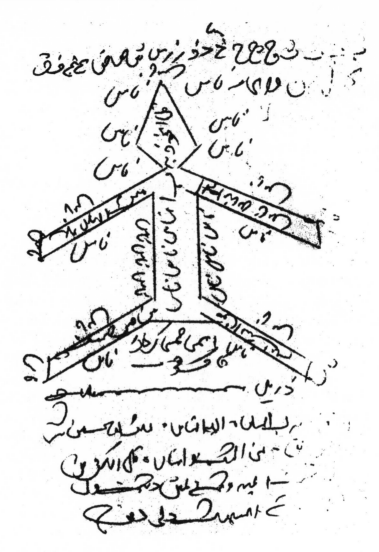

10. *Nās kā sūra falitā.*

bers and the Quranic verses and/or names they represent is less important than their ritual manipulation and physical value. I asked Amma several times what the numbers stood for and how they were ordered as she filled them in; each time she replied with some variation of "Jo-ice, these are heavy deep matters. I'll teach you one day when we're 'free'." But the day to learn the esoteric knowledge of this particular practice never came.

Dhuān: a subset of *falitā*; these are soaked in oil and burned in the morning and evening. Amma sometimes refers to them as *dhuān ke falitā*. Hussein, the disciple who assists Abba in the store, distinguished *falitā* and *dhuān* this way: burning Abdul Jinn *falitā* affects the behavior of *other* people; burning *dhuān* and breathing in the smoke takes out negative forces from within oneself. *Dhuān* are also burned and inhaled after a patient has completed the *utārā* ritual that physically absorbs the evil eye out of the patient and into a clay pot filled with various ingredients. After the evil eye has been removed in this way, the patient should go home; wash his/her hands, feet, and face; and breathe in the smoke of the *dhuān* as a final cleansing and protective act.

Drinking *falitā* and saucers: a prescription for general protection rather than an "attack" against a specific problem. Amma writes drinking *falitā* with an ink pen on tissue paper. She writes ten lines and then cuts each into a separate strip. Patients are instructed to dip the *falitā* into a glass of water, wash off the ink, and drink the inked water. Upon each strip is written the first half of the *kalmā*, *lā ilāha illā allah* [There is no god but God], followed by the words "*azizul jabbār*." Amma explained, "*Lā ilāha* is 'There is one God,' and *azizul jabbār* means that 'He is a great general.' If you write this and give it to someone, there's some efficacy from drinking it." Amma also writes protective Quranic verses and magical number squares on sets of saucers (which the patients bring from home); the patient should fill the saucers with tea or hot water, wash off the words, and drink the water for general preventative health and protection. Amma says the saucer prescription is stronger than the drinking *falitā*, as more words and numbers are written on them than on the paper ones.

Phulkā/capātī: unleavened bread. Amma writes Quranic verses, the names of God, number squares, and the name/s of the offending party on each bread. The particular trouble for which Amma prescribes this treatment is that of unfaithfulness of a husband toward his wife. The wife should feed the unleavened bread to a dog, and in the same way a dog is faithful to whoever feeds it, the errant husband will be faithful to his wife. Of course, there is a problem if the dog is not interested in eating the plain *capātī*. In this case, Amma instructs the patient to put some egg or ground-meat curry on it to make it more tempting. Once the dog has eaten the bread, the patient should come back to Amma, who then writes the husband's name on eleven neem leaves, which are known for their medicinal and antiseptic properties. Amma says that in her healing practice, she most often uses the numbers eleven, twenty-one, and seven: "These are the numbers we prescribe. We have to reckon with *śaitānī* [evil forces] with these numbers." The patient should place the neem leaves on burning coals, then add the rock salt over which Amma has prayed *duā*. Amma explained that the *capātī* reinforces and strengthens the relationship between a patient and her husband and the neem leaves (which are very sour) will sour the threatening relationship between the husband and the other woman.

Khādū: green gourd. The *khādū* prescription is used to strengthen and fatten up babies who fail to thrive. Abba explained that this happens because the mother's milk has been drunk by demons [*rakṣas*] and thus does not go into the baby's blood; the baby becomes weak and dies. Amma writes on a long light-green gourd and then hands it to Abba or the disciple who might be minding the shop, who anoints it with 'scent' (oil-based perfume) and wraps it up in a new white cloth. This "body" should be laid next to the baby for forty days; the life of the gourd will go into the baby as it dries out and shrivels up. At the end of the forty days, the lifeless gourd should be immersed in a body of water. I heard one mother complain to Amma that the *khādū* treatment had made little difference in her baby's health, but when Amma pressed her to describe exactly what she had done, the mother admitted she had laid the gourd next to her baby for only twenty days rather than the prescribed forty. Amma gently reprimanded her, "Do you eat meat when it's only half cooked? Then how do you expect this treatment to work when it's only half completed? Go back now and start again, for a full forty days." Amma used this case as a public example to all present of the importance of following all of her directions. Another treatment for babies is prescribed for a bloated stom-

11. Amma writing on *capātī* as a prescription for patient whose
husband has been unfaithful, 1991.

ach. Amma, or Abba if she is too busy, draws a large knife across the
child's stomach three times. After each of the three swipes, Amma (or
Abba) "cleans off" the edge of the knife on the earthen floor, seeming to
transfer the trouble from the stomach to the earth.

Often, once the primary patient is treated, others who have accompanied the patient will ask Amma for their *abjad* to be opened or will
present Amma with other family problems. Amma's practice is a "family
systems" practice; if there is trouble one place in the family, she assumes
that there is generally trouble somewhere else in the household and usually
complies with requests to follow the narrative of trouble from one manifestation to another, one family member to another. For example, one
morning a Hindu mother brought in three teenage daughters and a niece,
initially to consult about a problem with the oldest daughter's marriage
negotiations. Amma diagnosed her with *asrat* and prescribed the whole
array of treatments, *tāvīz*, *dhuān*, *utārā*, and a special *tāvīz* for marriage
to put under a heavy rock. But after Amma had dealt with this girl, the

mother asked for the *abjad* of the other daughters to be opened. One was diagnosed with *bālā girā*, which one of Amma's disciples explained is a diagnosis indicative of a difficult marriage. Another daughter had *asrat*; the third had *karesu* (a type of *kartūt*). And finally the mother was diagnosed with "only a little *asrat*." The treatments for all totaled Rs. 106.

On another occasion, three Muslim married sisters came together and between the three of them, Amma spent an hour diagnosing, prescribing, and listening to their individual narratives of "trouble." While several of their complaints were interrelated, they also brought in their own unique cycle of problems, one complaint leading to another. This time the narratives were meandering and seemed generated simply to be able to sit in Amma's *barkat*, and this time Amma became impatient, declaring, "It's enough; there are others waiting!" Abba or one of his sons often complains when too many family members sneak in under a single queue number (paying for only one cardboard number square, which was 50 paise in 1995 and was increased to Rs. 1 in 1999) and take up the temporal space of several patients.

Stronger, Periodic Prescriptions: *Utārā, Nahāvan, Bandiś*

Utārā: literally, to take off, remove, discard. *Utārā* is one of the few prescriptions that does not rely on the written word in any way, and it is also the prescription often identified by educated Muslims to be "Hindu"—that is, it is a shared prescription that might be given by both Hindu and Muslim religious practitioners and is not uniquely "Muslim." The purpose of this prescription is to rid the patient of one or another kind of evil eye by attracting it into other physical substances that are then carried away from the patient. Depending on what the diagnosis is (and specifically its "weight"), the ingredients of the *utārā* vary, but a primary ritual structure remains stable: a clay pot holding cooked rice (white or yellow, depending on the diagnosis), 100 grams uncut raw liver, seven *bhilāvan* seeds (*semecarpus anacardium*) stuck onto iron nails that are stuck into lemons, a prescribed number and color of flowers (the number and color vary with the diagnosis—seven or eleven, white or colored flowers),[13] and a coconut. *Bhilāvan* are hard-shelled small flat smooth nuts whose black indelible juices are used for permanent marking, such as on laundry. Taking the patient outside the house, a relative should circle the pot full of ingredients three times around the patient's head and three times the length of his/her body and leave it at a crossroads without looking back. The patient should then return home, wash his/her hands and face, change clothes, and inhale *dhuān*. *Utārā* is most efficacious when performed on Sundays, Tuesdays, or Thursdays. When the rare patient returns to complain that the *utārā* has not worked, Amma usually finds some step of the ritual that she had orally prescribed that has not been correctly followed: the patient has done *utārā* on the wrong day, has not used the exact ingredients prescribed, has used cut instead of uncut liver, has looked back at the pot left on the crossroads, has not washed correctly upon returning home, or has not inhaled *dhuān*.

Amma explained that the ingredients are determined by what will be pleasing to the person or *śaitān* who has cast the evil eye; the evil eye is physically drawn away from the afflicted person and into the clay pot, which can then be carried away and left at a crossroads. According to Abba, if the diagnosis is *havā*, the *utārā* ingredients are three *bhilāvan* and lemons impaled on nails and seven white flowers; for *asrat* the prescription is seven *bhilāvan* and lemons and eleven or nine flowers; *kartūt* requires three or seven *bhilāvan* and lemons and three colors of flowers. The stronger the *kartūt*, the more flowers or *bhilāvan* are required. Amma emphasized the *śakti* [or spiritual power] of the *bhilāvan*, and Abba elaborated: they look like eyes and to impale their hard shell is to penetrate the evil eye, or the eye of the being that has cast the evil eye. In many South Asian traditions the liver is considered to be a locus of emotion (as the heart is in the United States); hence this is the part of the animal (the cut of meat) chosen to attract the evil eye away from the patient's body. Abba explained the use of lemons: "Lemons are in place of chickens, in the same way that a coconut is a substitute for a goat. Lemons are the main things. The flowers, rice, and liver are those things that please a person. Like me, for instance, I like chutney [he laughs], so I would be given chutney."

When I asked Amma whether or not the evil eye carried to a crossroads would stick to someone who might stumble across the earthen pot, she nodded her head. I nervously laughed and told her that I had stumbled across such a pot the first time I had come to her house at night, in the winter of 1989, before I knew to look for such things and before I would have recognized what it was. She assured me that even then (before we had ever met), her protective power had been with me and that neither I nor any of her disciples nor anyone wearing or carrying her protective *tāvīz* had anything to worry about from a discarded *utārā*. (This simple comment reminds us again of the strong belief in Sufi tradition of the preexisting or fated bond between *pīr* and disciple; that is, the *pirānimā* is protecting her disciples before they ever meet her.) New patients sometimes expressed some ambivalence about putting out the *utārā* at the crossroads, accepting this theory of transference. One Christian male patient who was new to the healing room asked nervously, "Won't the police stop me?" Amma laughed, "Do you think that the police catch all these people sitting here who leave *utārā*?" She then said, "Okay, then, put it in a plastic bag and leave it," so it would not be recognizable. Another patient sitting at the table suggested that the patient wait until after dark to leave the *utārā* so no one would see him.

Periodically, when the evil eye to be drawn off of a patient is particularly stubborn or strong, Amma prescribes that a chicken be added to the ingredients of an *utārā*. After the clay pot has been circled over the patient, the live chicken is also circled (to absorb the remaining evil eye) and is then left in a graveyard to wander at will. This ingredient is added at Amma's discretion and is not determined by the numbers of *abjad*. Once Amma prescribed a live chicken for the *utārā* of her guru-brother (the man who was also a disciple of her guru and was thus fictive kin to her); but she took one look at his reaction and knew that he would not fulfill this prescription. Laughing at his lack of courage (whether courage to enter a graveyard or courage to deal with the live chicken is unclear), she substituted liver for the *utārā*. Liver is a difficult ingredient for Brahmins and other vegetarian high-caste Hindus to want to purchase personally and bring into their homes for the *utārā*. However, when some of them beg for an alternative vegetarian ingredient, Amma insists that the treatment is not effective without the liver (or chicken). One highly educated Brahmin friend told me that when her family performed *utārā* on a teenage daughter, they sent out their lower-caste servant girl to purchase the liver and, for the first time in family memory, meat was brought into their home. But, they told me, the illness for which the ritual was performed (which had been diagnosed as obsessive-compulsive disorder by a western psychiatrist) was alleviated, so they did not mind what would have otherwise been the pollution of their home.

Nahāvan: literally, bath. *Nahāvan* is a special subset of *utārā* to rid a patient of especially strong evil eye [*asrat* and *kartūt*]. The ritual involves a series of "baths" (three or five), which are really more akin to anointing with water and prayers than actual baths. They are prescribed only when regular *utārā* has already been performed correctly (after at least two attempts, since one failure is interpreted as a failure to perform the original ritual correctly) and the problem has persisted. *Nahāvan* take place after hours in the evening in Amma's healing room with the doors locked and only the patient, his/her relative or companion, and Amma and Abba present. The price for this ritual is substantial compared to most of Amma's other prescriptions, primarily because it involves Amma's personal services and many physical items and must be performed several times (on Sunday, Tuesday, and Thursday nights, like *utārā*). Amma often tells patients who complain about the price, "Well, it's a heavy problem that requires heavy treatment. The choice is yours." Abba answers such protests by citing the cost of all the various ingredients required for the ritual and by assuring the patient that Amma does not make any money on these rituals. Although Abba always insists in a "fixed price" ("If you come with Rs. 5 less than the total, I'll send you back!"), Amma is often willing to negotiate with a patient. In one case, the patient's father simply stuck Rs. 400 into Amma's hand after Abba refused to lower the Rs. 475 charge, saying, "Well, it's up to you. Understand that my daughter is like your granddaughter [appealing to fictive kinship]." Amma quietly put the paper notes into the drawer of her desk and gave the patient a slight nod, so as not to attract Abba's attention.

Particular cases of Nahāvan: When I first started sitting at Amma's healing table in 1994 and heard about *nahāvan*, I asked Amma if I might be able to observe it sometime. At that time, she told me, "Jo-ice, this is a very heavy thing. I do it behind closed doors and no one should see it." But one Sunday almost a year later, she prescribed *nahāvan* to a patient and I asked again if I could see this ritual before I returned to the United

States. She said, "Why not? You can take pictures, too." Since the ritual would take place after dark, I wanted to make sure that I could spend the night at Amma's after it was over and asked Abba's permission. He gave quite a different reply than Amma had, thinking that I should not stay for the ritual because the *asrat* [evil eye] might be too strong and affect me. In any case, he told me, "Only Amma and the patient can be inside the room, so you wouldn't see anything anyhow." He continued, "What if the *asrat* attaches to you and you go back to America? There would be no one there to heal it. Then you would have to come back to India." Laughing, he told me I should stay for Amma's "reading" but not what he called the *utārā* itself. Overhearing our conversation, Amma argued with Abba that her presence and my relationship with her would protect me and that there was no reason for me not to observe the entire ritual. Only when she cut lemons over the patient would she ask me to leave. But as it turned out, when the time came for me to leave the room after Amma's "reading," Amma and Abba did not ask me to leave; instead, they told me where to stand so that I would be able to see and yet not get splashed with water.

I attended this ritual on a Tuesday evening when three patients were scheduled to receive *nahāvan*. When I arrived at Amma's healing room at 7:30 in the evening, she was still meeting the last of her regular patients, having begun her long public day at 9 A.M. The three *nahāvan* patients waiting with me in the courtyard that evening were Hindus, a middle-aged man, a nineteen-year-old newly married woman, and a middle-aged female librarian at the university. The male patient had come with his wife and mother. The women told me his story: three of his family members had died in the last few months, the last of which was his older brother, who had been killed in a road accident in the middle of the night about five weeks earlier. The brother's body had lain unclaimed at the morgue for several hours until the police could locate his relatives. Since then, the patient had been experiencing unusual "difficulties" [*paresānī*], which his family attributed to the dead brother's soul that had felt disrespected as the body lay unattended in the morgue. The patient's wife held up her index finger and shook it back and forth as she described the situation to me—a gesture Amma and her patients often used to indicate a patient's physical condition of restlessness [*becainī*], weakness, and weight loss that causes them to become thin as a reed, easily blown in the wind.

The second patient was the young bride who had come with her mother and father. The girl herself did not speak or answer my questions; instead, her mother spoke for her—and even then, described her problem only in the vaguest of terms: "She has health [*tabiyat*] problems." Amma told me later that the young woman had been unable to carry a pregnancy to term and that she had diagnosed the problem as *bālā girā*. Amma explained that this was the name of a malevolent being with many heads, hands, and feet who snatches and eats fetuses and young babies. Before the ritual began, the young woman was made to take off her *burqā*, which she did reluctantly (she was wearing a startlingly bright pink sari underneath) and loosen her hair in preparation for the *nahāvan*.[14] Loosened hair is considered in many Indian traditions to provide entry into an otherwise protected (closed) human body. Traditional Indian women bind up their hair to protect against unwanted entry by various spirits and prevent "release" of their own sexuality. Here, the healing power of the *nahāvan* is understood to enter the patient's body more easily if her hair is loosened, and the unbound hair also provides a pathway for any evil spirits to exit. While Amma was further preparing the *nahāvan*'s ritual ingredients, the young woman's father tried to present his own complaints, as patients' companions often do at the healing table, but in this case Amma paid no attention to him.

The final patient was a middle-aged woman who was a librarian at the university. She was surprised and embarrassed when she saw me waiting with the other two patients' families in Amma's courtyard. She quickly assured me that she did not have any *particular* problem or trouble but was coming to Amma only for general blessings—something the expensive and complicated *nahāvan* prescription belied. Amma told me later that she had *asrat*. The librarian spoke to me exclusively in English until Amma insisted that she speak Urdu so that she, too, could understand our conversation. The woman asked me, in an accusatory tone, a question no other patient ever had: "Do you do this kind of work [that is, ethnographic research] in your own country?" And it was the first time I had ever felt uncomfortable as an observer in the healing room. I sensed that the librarian felt she was on display; being an academic herself, she perhaps thought that I would judge her as being "backward" or superstitious for resorting to this type of healing practice, as she implied her own university colleagues and family members had already done. She emphasized to me that she had come for the evening ritual by herself and would leave by herself, without the knowledge of her husband, who "doesn't believe in these things and would be angry." I asked her how much she was paying for the series of *nahāvan*; she answered only when it became clear to her that I knew already. Then she laughed and implicitly admitted that she had come for a specific problem when she said, "Rs. 650 is a lot of money for just 'blessings' when there's nothing wrong with me, isn't it?"

After the three patients had waited nearly an hour for Amma to be freed from the long day's queue of patients, they were called in with their families, only to be told by Abba that it was getting too late now and that really they should come back the next week. But Amma intervened, acknowledging the distance the patients had come and the time they had waited for her. So Abba began his role in the ritual by giving detailed instructions about what the patients needed to do at home after the *nahāvan* ritual was completed. He explained that each patient should keep five lemons in his/her pillowcase. Every morning, one lemon should be cut over the patient's forehead (widthwise, not lengthwise; direction makes a difference) and the two halves placed again in the pillowcase. After the last lemon is cut, he instructed, all the halves should be thrown in a well or another body of water.

The second set of instructions Abba gave concerned the daily special baths the patients should take in their own homes over a period of five days. Abba had already prepared a concoction with which they should bathe: an earthen pot over which he had blown blessings, in which were lemons, 'scent' (perfume), and coconut water. He instructed them to fill the rest of the pot with hot water, put a piece of their old clothing into the water, pour the water mixture over themselves, and rinse off with clean water. Then, Abba continued, the patients should burn Amma's *fālitā* over hot coals sprinkled with resin and inhale the smoke. He warned the patients to be sure to throw out all the used water on the same day and not to go to any graveyard or other place where evil spirits may lurk.[15] Finally, he instructed, every night the patients should burn the long wicks he had made for them, *tavīz* made with full pages rather than cut-up strips of paper, rolled up and wrapped with cotton and thread. Just as I was wondering how the patients would remember all of these little details and their sequence without writing them down, Abba asked them several times, "Now do you understand this? Are you sure you understand what to do? If you don't remember, if you don't do it, it won't work." And he repeated the instructions.

After his preparation of ingredients and explanations, Abba proclaimed that his part of the work was finished. Amma blew prayers of protection on everyone present before she began her work. Abba had prepared three plates of offerings, each holding two coconuts and twenty-one lemons. Amma explained that the lemons and coconuts were being offered in place of goats. When I later asked if actual goats were offered in the old days, Amma screwed up her face in disgust, "No! Think of all that blood!" Amma then pulled out a book (whose name she did not want to show me, warning me that the misuse of these texts could be dangerous and that their use required specialized training)[16] and recited from it, periodically blowing her words over the platters of lemons and coconuts. She skimmed the pages quickly, saying only periodic phrases aloud and whispering the rest under her breath. Every so often she would rub her palm in a circular motion on the table, hit the table, and point her index finger up toward the sky—a gesture she explained is indicative of the phrase from the *kalmā*, "There is no god but God." She finished this phase of the ritual by writing Quranic verses on a set of twelve saucers for each patient, six to be drunk from on consecutive mornings and six in the evenings. Now all preliminaries were finished and it was time for each individual patient's *nahāvan*.

Amma sent everyone else out of the healing room except the patient, Abba, and myself. The first patient was the young bride; she showed little expression, either fear or apprehension, even though this was her first time to experience *nahāvan*. Amma's healing table had been moved back against the wall to make room for Abba and the patient to sit on floor. The young woman sat on a gunnysack with her knees bent up rather than cross-legged, and Amma stood behind her. She blew prayers [*duā*] on each lemon before Abba cut it over her head; the rest of the lemons were cut over each shoulder, neck, arm, knee, foot, and back. Amma would have generally cut these lemons herself, but on this night she had a broken finger that prevented her from doing so. Then Abba, with some difficulty, broke the first coconut and threw its water directly on the face and chest of the young woman. Amma teasingly showed him how best to crack the coconut while saving the water, saying she had much more practice in this ritual act than he did. He cracked the second coconut more easily and poured the water in his hand, from which the girl drank, and the first of three prescribed *nahāvan* for this patient was over. After having repeatedly heard Amma's description of the ritual as "heavy, for heavy problems," the *nahāvan* bath itself felt to me rather undramatic—especially in comparison with various daily interactions around the healing table that involved storytelling, possession, trance, and mental illness or in comparison to house exorcisms. In the context of *nahāvan,* the patients had little to say and were passive, sitting quietly to be acted upon by Amma's rituals.

Bandiś: literally, tying up or binding; house exorcism. Amma offers the prescription of house exorcism to patients whose households are experiencing chronic troubles [*pareśānī*], with many of its family members experiencing one bad thing after another and/or the actual structure of the house experiencing problems, such as flooding, cracked walls, and so forth. House exorcisms are expensive; in 1994–1995, Amma charged Rs. 25 per every corner of the house plus the cost of the primary ingredients, which included several lemons for each corner and a live chicken to be sacrificed at the doorway to the house. Most of Amma's patients live in small homes with only two or three rooms, and the cost of the *bandiś* ranges from Rs. 200 to Rs. 500, but a large middle-class home is much more expensive.

Amma performs *bandiś* only on Friday, the day she does not sit in her healing room. In 1994–1995, she performed one or two every Friday. *Bandiś* are often occasions for a day of social visiting as well, something Amma does not have time for during the week. She usually takes a daughter, a grandchild, Munnapa, and/or a disciple or two with her on the outing, often eating lunch at the home she has exorcised and/or visiting homes of disciples on her way home. In later years, the numbers of *bandiś* declined substantially because Amma's stamina was not sufficient for the physical exertion required by the ritual; her worsening arthritis made it difficult for her to get up and down from the squatting position she took in every corner.

The ritual of *bandiś* begins with Amma reading from the Quran and a book named *Hifaz-ul-Bahar*. Amma prepared me for what was to follow:

The *Hifaz-ul-Bahar* includes the Arabic *kalmā* [creed of faith] by which *kartūt, jinn, karāmat* [usually a miracle performed by a saint, but here a powerful action performed by someone against the patient], and *balāyat* [action by evil spirit] are cut. Reading this, we blow [pray over] on water, bathe the person [with that water], cause the person to drink it, and cut lemons. All these things are beneficial. *Lā ilāha illā allah muhammad-ur rasūllul lāhi* is the *kalmā* from which we are all made, you and me. It's a great mystery [*rāz*]; we can't reveal that mystery or we, too, will get burnt, like a moth in a flame. That's what would happen, wouldn't it, Jo-ice?

One *bandiś* I witnessed began with Amma sitting cross-legged on a cot and reading for close to half an hour. Then she moved from corner to corner of the house, first breaking up the cement floor in each corner with a crow bar,[17] then burying several lemons on which were written numbers and names of God and over which she had blown *duā* and sprinkled 'scent'. She had arrived with the lemons all prepared, a process she said took several hours late into the previous night. She covered the lemons with earth before moving on to the next corner. (The householder would cement over the open corner after Amma left.) After each corner had been exorcised, Amma moved to the doorway of the house, in front of which the householder's husband had already pulled up the slabs of stone in the entryway and had dug a large hole in the earth. Amma asked the householder if she had followed earlier instructions and purchased a black chicken. A young son brought the chicken to Amma, who wrapped it tightly in a white cloth soaked in perfume. The chicken was buried alive in front of the doorway, along with several lemons. This house had only one central room and a tiny kitchen, so the exorcism took only an hour and a half. After Amma buried the chicken, the ritual was over and we were served tea. There was no talk about what had instigated the problems of the house and the requisite exorcism. Amma leaned back and relaxed against the wall, pulled out her *pān*, and began conversing with the householder about her family, the neighbors, and others they knew in common.

Delegation and Innovation: *Hazrat, Hāzirī,* and *Jarī-būṭī*

Amma has been generous in teaching and delegating specific prescriptive rituals to individual disciples who sit regularly with her in the healing room or in giving disciples permission to practice a ritual they may have learned elsewhere, thus carving out their own little domains of healing specialties. It is important to note that all of these delegated prescriptions exclude the manipulation of the written word. Depending on who is telling the story, some of the disciples actually taught specific practices to Amma, but all agree that they cannot practice any form of healing practice without her permission and that it is only with her power that their rituals are successful. The three most prominent of this class of innovative/delegated rituals are *hazrat, hāzirī,* and *jarī-būṭī.*

Hazrat: literally, his excellency or honor. This ritual calls upon Suleman (Sulayman in Arabic) Baba to reveal things that are happening elsewhere, "even in America." Suleman Baba is identified with the biblical King Solomon and is said to have powers over the *jinn*, ruling over visible and invisible worlds. Only Amma and Abba's oldest disciple, Hussein, who often sits in Abba's shop when Abba is taking a nap or has gone out, perform this ritual. The ritual is used primarily to find goods that have disappeared in one manner or another: a stolen or runaway goat or lost or stolen money or jewelry. Amma prescribes this ritual treatment in cycles; sometimes she refers a patient to Hussein almost every day and other times weeks go by when she does not give this prescription. Of course, Hussein must be present for her to give the prescription. When he is absent or at her own discretion, Amma can gaze inwardly, close her eyes, and find lost objects or people without the ritual. So it seems particularly generous for her to let Hussein claim this as "his" ritual and to prescribe this ritual when she herself can fulfill its purpose another way.

The *hazrat* ritual begins with Hussein methodically mixing a paste of kohl, the crushed leaves of five kinds of plants, and sandalwood oil (the principal cost of the ritual, at Rs. 80 for a small bottle). He places the mixture either on a mirror or on his thumbnail. He then calls on the Hindu deity Hanuman to go and call Suleman Baba, who, upon arrival, produces the visions in the kohl mixture—although Hussein describes Hanuman as a spiritual messenger [*maukīl*] and does not consider him to be a deity [*bhagvān*]. This is an example of the hierarchy of spiritual powers that enables the existence of Hindu deities in a Muslim world, a point to which we will return. Hanuman, a monkey character from the Hindu epic Ramayana, serves as a logical messenger in this context because of his powers to fly through the air and change sizes both to avoid catastrophes and see without being seen. Hussein gazes into the black mixture and eventually "sees" where the missing object is. Another disciple explained that the practitioner of *hazrat* should stare into the kohl preparation and say "Open the door," and Hanuman will appear.

Hussein said that he had learned this *hazrat* skill from his father, who was a *hakīm* (practitioner of Unani medicine, a system of ancient Greek medicine that has evolved within the Muslim world) but that he (Hussein) performed it only with Amma's permission [*ijāzat*]. He described it as a mechanical skill that could be easily learned if a person simply had discipline: "You must sit [in meditation] for forty days; only then you'll receive the ability. This means that you stay in a room and see no one, especially women, and do your own cooking. Anyone can do this, but the forty days is difficult and takes great discipline."

Hāzirī: literally, presence; trance. *Hāzirī* is another ritual performed to find lost objects or persons, but it is more powerful than *hazrat*—indicated by the higher drama and cost of the former. Like *hazrat,* only one of Amma's close disciples practices this ritual. This disciple, Sati, works during the week as a carpenter, so Amma refers patients who are looking for a lost object whose location can be identified through *hāzirī* to come back on Sundays, the only day Sati is able to come to the healing room for the entire day. For this ritual Sati meets patients in Amma's living/sleeping room, not the healing room. There, he sits cross-legged on a mat, lights incense, cups his hands in front of his face, and begins to pray. He picks up his prayer beads and begins to recite as he sways his body in a circular motion from his waist up. The movement becomes more and more pronounced, with larger and more vigorous circular movements as Sati begins to go into trance. He yawns noisily, and these yawns, too, build up in frequency and vigor until they suddenly stop and Sati begins to gasp rapidly and noisily. Suddenly his arms become stiff and he holds them out in front of him. This gesture indicates that Mustang Baba, a saint about whom Sati could tell me nothing other than his name,[18] has arrived. Sati describes the arrival as *hāl* or *hāzirī*. Sati gets up on his knees, eyes shut, and shouts to the patient, "Tell me! Tell me! Tell me what you want to find!" And the saint then speaks through Sati, telling the patient where the lost objects are.

One Sunday, two women came to find out who had taken their half-*tolā* (a measure of weight equal to about thirteen grams) of gold. When Sati demanded that the women speak, this conversation took place between the female patient and Mustang Baba:

Patient: Tell us who has taken Gausiya Bi's things, her half-*tolā* of gold.
Mustang Baba, speaking through Sati: A woman.
Patient: What color is she?
Mustang Baba: She's light-skinned and thin. She lives in front of your house.
Patient: In front of the house? It's been missing since the week before Id. Is she a relative?
Mustang Baba: She's not a relative. She lives in front of the house and has a small child. [Sati begins to breathe heavily again, as if renewing the trance, often burping in between deep breaths.] She used to come before this, too.
Patient: No, no one has come earlier; nothing's been missing before this.
Mustang Baba: She's with a fat man.

The patients seemed to disagree with Mustang Baba's pronouncement that there is such a person living close to or in front of their house, expressing some doubt in the validity of the *hāzirī* itself.

Patient: There is no one with a young child. No one comes to the house, and anyway, the door over there is always kept closed.

Mustang Baba did not argue with the patient but was silent. Nor did the patients argue further with him; they told me later it would have been disrespectful to do so. Sati stretched his arms out in front of his body stiffly and then relaxed, covering his eyes with cupped hands, and returned to his present consciousness again. He was exhausted and sweating and asked for a glass of water. He took a ten-minute break before agreeing to see the next patient. When a third patient asked for Sati to once again induce *hāzirī* to locate his missing twelve-year-old son, Sati refused, saying that to induce *hāzirī* even twice in one morning is physically exhausting and difficult and that the second time he had had to rely on inhaling incense in order to maintain his trance. He argued that it would not come to him three times in a single morning. Although patients do not openly express doubt that a *bābā* is *present* through *hāzirī* and that he speaks through Sati, they periodically confront and argue with Sati himself, even questioning his state of trance if the answer he gives is not to their satisfaction. His word does not carry the same authority as Amma's does; very few patients argue with her about her diagnoses and prescriptions. Sati does not have an ongoing relationship with the patients like Amma does; he is not a healer in this ritual but a conduit only, serving at the behest of Amma.[19]

Jaṛī-būṭī: literally, roots and herbs, used medicinally. When I unexpectedly learned at my Atlanta kitchen table in the summer of 1995 that the metallic cylindrical *tāvīz* Amma had given my family contained crushed herbs, there was no way to ask Amma about them until I returned to Hyderabad in the fall of 1996. Amma laughed at the story of my surprise and chagrin over how I could have missed observing this practice over an entire year of fieldwork. She assured me she had only recently started using *jaṛī-būṭī* and that she keeps the herbs and roots hidden, filling the *tāvīz* late at night. She asserted that there is so much power/strength [*tāqat*] in jungle herbs and roots that "it can burn you, just standing there; and it can close someone's mouth. It can break your body into pieces and if you ask it to, it can put it back together again. This is the same kind of *jaṛī-būṭī* that Hanuman-ji used in the battle of Ram and Lakshman, when Ram was so severely wounded" (describing an episode from the epic Ramayana, in which Hanuman flies to a mountain to find life-restoring herbs for the dying warrior Lakshman—not Ram, as Amma said). Amma continued by giving me a short teaching on the importance of continuing to learn new things from wherever you can:

It's like this: learn everything. It's born in some people; you have the interest to learn and so do I. But there are some people who aren't smart. One should take [advantage of] Allah's power [*tāqat*] and the power of the trees, too [i.e., *jaṛī-būṭī*], the power of the saints and the power of the *pīrs* and *murśids*, too. Everything is useful. This is the way it is. There's power in books and also in trees.

Amma often displays a sense of personal pride in her own curiosity and willingness to try and learn new things. She sometimes compared our personalities and "work" in this way: "Just as you've come to learn, I, too, keep learning in my work."

As Amma went on to talk with the next patient, her youngest son Muhammad confirmed that Amma's use of *jaṛī-būṭī* was new and told me that she had learned about it from her disciple Hussein, who as a young boy had learned it from his *hakīm* father. Hussein said he had practiced some minimal *jaṛī-būṭī* outside the healing room over the years but had not given this knowledge to Amma or been given permission to use it until only recently. It was not clear what prompted this move. When I returned to Amma's healing room in October 2001, six weeks after she had died, the *jaṛī-būṭī* seemed to have quickly taken over; it was piled high in corners and on top of a newly acquired four-drawer file cabinet, whose drawers, too, were filled with bunches of dried plants and roots. At this time, Amma's youngest son Muhammad and the much older Hussein were the primary practitioners sitting at Amma's table—Khalid had not yet moved back. It made sense that they would rely primarily on the nonwritten prescriptions over which they felt they had the most authority.

When we were visiting at Sati's house one Friday afternoon, Amma asked him to show me the herbs and roots of *jaṛī-būṭī* and explain "what was what," but, she cautioned, "Tell only some things, not everything." He first showed me small clay pots that were filled with herbs and roots and had been readied to bury in the corners of houses for *bandiś*. He emptied one pot, naming the various herbs that were in it. I asked from whom he had learned this *jaṛī-būṭī*, and he nodded his head toward Amma—an appropriate gesture regardless of who had actually taught him the specifics. Her permission was necessary for him to pursue the learning.

Sati brought out a large root from another room and said this one was a particularly expensive root, costing more than Rs. 12,000. He broke off a tiny piece, added it to some other herbs on a piece of newspaper, gathered the newspaper together and began to rub the herbs inside until the crumpled newspaper broke into flames. Sati explained that this could be thrown into someone's courtyard if you wanted to harm them but then quickly assured me he never actually did this kind of black knowledge [*kālā ilm*]. He only wanted me to know that such action was possible and that many of Amma's treatments were designed to counteract this kind of action initiated by *kālā ilm* practitioners. I asked Amma which treatment is stronger, *jaṛī-būṭī* or *tāvīz*. Amma said they were equally strong, but Sati added that it is good to use both systems, because it is rare that someone who has opposing powers can contradict both.

Duā: Amma ends every patient interaction with *duā*, laying her hand on the patient's head (or sometimes another part of the body, such as the chest, where the illness lays) and whispering a personal prayer on behalf of the patient. She finishes by blowing the words onto the patient, words and breath that themselves are considered to be filled with *barkat* and healing power.

Fluidity of Practice and Prescriptions

While Amma's diagnostic method remained stable over the years (with the exception of the substitution of Hava's name for those of individual mothers of her patients), her choice of prescriptions varied considerably. First, there was the matter of technology: she began to rely on photocopied rather than handwritten copies of *tāvīz* and *fālitā* when the technology became cheap enough to balance the time spent hand-writing hundreds of amulets. The first time I met Amma, in 1990, she was hand-writing all *tāvīz* with carbon paper; in 1994–1995, the *tāvīz* were photocopied copies of her handwriting; in 1996, they were professionally printed and Amma wrote on the back of them. Had I not witnessed the shift from handwriting to carbon copies to photocopies over the years and Amma's ease with this adaptation, I might have attributed more to the power of the handwritten word itself than would have been warranted.

There were other forms of fluidity in the choices made in prescrip-

12. Amma blessing a patient with *duā* at the end of a healing session, 1991.

tions. It became apparent that several different prescriptions might effect the same cure and that Amma's choices sometimes depended on the number of patients waiting, her own energy levels, or, perhaps most important, her own intuitions about what would be most effective. In 1996, for example, Amma wrote fewer personalized *falitā* with the names of specific *maukīl* and persons upon whom they should act than she had in the summer of 1995, when such *falitā* seemed the treatment of choice. A year later her preferred treatment was primarily the morning and evening *dhuān*, which are not handwritten but photocopied. This shift may have been due to the pressure of the number of patients and her increasing age and difficulty with writing due to poor eyesight. But Amma was not apologetic about the shift; rather, she seemed to feel equally comfortable with using a variety of prescriptions for the same illnesses.

Amma's diagnostic and prescriptive healing systems are based on an assumption that spiritual illness is generated from outside forces intervening in the physical, social, and spiritual worlds/bodies of a patient.

Amma's prescriptions externalize and ritually manipulate these negative forces in order to distance or destroy the *śaitānī*. However, as Amma continually reminded me, her spiritual wisdom and authority were needed for *any* of the prescriptions to be effective; their actual physical manifestation was less important. The written word has inherent power and the whole world depends on it, she taught me, but here Amma's spoken word directs the written word and causes it to take effect. Verbal performatives by both Amma ("she *will* be healed; the missing child *will* return home") and the patient (who has to say out loud what it is s/he wants to be effected as s/he burns a *fālitā*) are instrumental in the effectiveness of the ritual manipulation of the written word.[20] Ultimately, patients are drawn to Amma's person, to her spiritual charisma, strength, and authority, rather than to the details of the system of diagnosis and prescription she employs.[21] Performative display of a wide spectrum of diagnoses and prescriptions, however, helps create Amma's authority in the healing room—and are an external manifestation of her spiritual knowledge and authority—and patients are reluctant to leave her table without tangible physical prescriptions. But the meaning of their details and how they actually work are a matter for specialists to learn, not for patients to understand.

PATIENT NARRATIVES IN THE HEALING ROOM

3

They come crying; they go away laughing.

Individual patients come to the healing table with unique circumstances and present their problems to Amma in narratives that give depth, character, and variation to the "same" diagnoses. Many patients say that they chose Amma over other healers because of her patience in listening to these narratives, and Amma herself says that "understanding" is what is most important, not the mathematical diagnosis. We can begin to explicate what this understanding might mean by examining a range of individual cases and patients who have come to Amma's healing table.[1] Most of these cases involve what readers might identify as psychological problems rather than purely physical illnesses, and these illnesses generate narratives. Illnesses such as children's high fevers do not generally generate extended narratives in the healing room beyond those that tell of a patient's resort to multiple healing systems or healers within a single system.

Long-Term Chronic Problems and Health Maintenance

Some patients come to Amma regularly to maintain good health or for treatment of long-term chronic problems. One such patient is Mary, a middle-aged Christian woman, who nonetheless wears the big red *bottu* that is often associated with Hindu women. She works at a "convent" school and has been coming to Amma regularly for eight years. Her head shakes uncontrollably with what from my lay perspective looks like Parkinson's disease, but I agree with her assertion that the shaking has lessened considerably over the months and years I have known her. She comes every two weeks for a new supply of *falita*. The *falita* Amma prepares for her are different than the little ones stacked on Amma's desk. Mary is given large *falita* made from full sheets of paper (8.5 by 14 inches), rolled with cotton and bound with thread; Abba says each of these is equivalent to lighting ten regular-sized smaller *falita*. Mary brings with her incense sticks, rock salt, and bottles of water over which Amma blows *dua* and which Mary uses daily in her home; on several occasions she also brought a plastic bag of soil for Amma to bless before she sprinkled it both in her home and at the school where she works. Sometimes she brings saucers on which Amma writes and from which she drinks. These are treatments for Mary's chronic head-shaking, but with each visit she usually has specific acute requests, too—such as asking for Abdul Jinn *falita* with specific co-workers' names written on them to stop their argumentation with her. She is an old friend of Amma's and often sits with her for up to two hours at a time, even after she has received her prescriptions, which themselves take a long time for Amma to write out.

Another regular patient is also a Christian woman, a schoolteacher with bachelor's and master's degrees in education. She was anxious to tell me her story: she has been coming to Amma periodically with chronic chest pain since her mother had first brought her with another (unnamed) serious problem when she was a girl. The patient's heart problem seems to have begun when, she reported, her maternal aunt sent the Hindu goddess Kali to possess her, hoping this would disrupt her marriage arrangements to a man that the aunt had wanted her own daughter to marry. The patient said that she had been admitted to the hospital ten or more times in the last three years for chest pain. She went to specialist after specialist, but the EKGs showed nothing, although the pain remained. The patient also regularly visited a Hyderabadi Christian Pentecostal female healer and, more recently, had attended a large Pentecostal rally led by a German evangelist. The evangelist had told audience members to put their hands on the part of their body they wanted to be healed, and the patient thought her chest pain had eased somewhat. But still, she said, "a little remains."

I asked the patient, "So why are you coming now to Amma if the Pentecostal healer and German evangelist's prayer treatments have been effective?" She responded that Amma's treatment was faster and sometimes people just did not have the patience to wait or could not bear the problem long enough for Christian prayer treatments to take effect (the implication being that the prayers are not immediately effective). She continued, "As Christians, we are forced to come here. Evil should be removed by evil. That's why we have to come here; we're forced to come here." I asked if this meant that she thought Amma and/or her treatments are evil. "No, no. But others are causing this evil and it's not easy to clear away. Even Amma says this." The patient's explanation is indicative of an ambivalence not commonly or openly expressed among Amma's patients; they might doubt the effectiveness of a particular treatment or some educated patients might be embarrassed to be seen by their peers while participating in "superstition," but I only rarely heard expressions about the moral quality of Amma's healing practice. The fact that this patient is highly educated and that she is a Christian might have contributed to her construction of less permeable boundaries between traditions than are commonly experienced at the healing *caurāstā*. She might also have been somewhat apologetic about her presence at the healing table because of her perception that I, as an educated American, might myself be judgmental of the healing practice.

Possession and *Śaitānī*

One day while Amma was in the middle of filling Mary's prescriptions, an eighteen-year-old Hindu girl was brought in by her parents and brother. She was moaning "Amma, Amma" (addressing her own mother in this case and not the healer Amma) and periodically crying out sharply.[2] The patients waiting in the courtyard sensed that this was a patient who should not have to wait in queue and made room for the girl's brother to carry her into the room. Amma took only a single glance at the girl before proclaiming, "She's been struck by *śaitān* [the devil]."[3] Her parents told

Amma that the girl had been this way for the last eight days but that today her condition had worsened. Prior to this day, she had been affected only at night, when she saw devils in her dreams and was afraid. Amma did not seem to feel the urgency about this case that the rest of us did and finished making her *pān*, wrote Mary's few remaining prescriptions, and got up to go to the bathroom before turning her full attention to the girl.

While Amma was out of the room, I asked the father what had happened to bring the girl to this state. He told all of us sitting at the healing table that a female neighbor with whom the girl had been very close, as close as with her own mother, had been stabbed to death and that the murderer had poured kerosene over her body and burned it.[4] The narrator's daughter had loved this woman and had run in and out of her house as if it were her own. Now that this had happened, the father continued, the soul [*rūh*] of this dead pregnant woman had come on this girl and was trying to take her with her to the afterlife. In this case, the father had come with his own diagnosis of what he thought had happened, although he never expressed this to Amma. When Amma returned to the room and the case at hand, without opening the *abjad* of the girl, she pulled out the printed book titled *Hifaz-ul-Bahar* from which she read in a muted voice (the words were indistinguishable to the rest of us; the only word I could make out periodically was "*śaitān*"). When Amma was finished reading, she rolled a lemon around and around in her hands while praying over it, then cut it in half over the girl's throat. She then splashed water over the girl's throat and face and made her drink water over which Amma had blown *duā*. The girl burped and gagged several times as if she was about to throw up. Amma simply watched her for a few minutes, then prayed over her and made her drink more water before telling the family to take her out of the room. When I left an hour later, the girl was sleeping peacefully on the narrow metal bench in the court-yard. Her relieved father said that they would sit there until she woke up and then take her home.

Possession cases are not daily occurrences, but they almost always involve dramatic narratives and sometimes dramatic action as well. These are the cases that Amma says most women do not have the courage or strength [*himmat*] to face, hence eliminating them from the possibility of filling the role of healer. In possession cases, Amma rarely performs the *abjad* diagnostic ritual but simply declares what she "sees" in front of her—"It's *śaitānī*"—and then proceeds directly to the treatment. Many possession treatments involve getting the patient to speak, either in her own voice or through the voice of the possessing entity. Speech is the sign of returning sense and identity if it is one's own voice and names the problem if it is that of the possessor.

One late afternoon in 1991, early in my fieldwork experience with Amma, I entered the courtyard to find Amma hitting a male Hindu patient repeatedly with a bamboo stick and demanding, "Tell me your name! Tell me your name!" The patient's face was expressionless through the drama and he remained silent. Amma went back and forth between the courtyard and healing room, interspersing this treatment with that of other less-severe cases. Finally, after several hours, the man whispered the name of a *jinn* and his body went limp. This naming was the beginning of a cure, although the patient was also prescribed *utārā* and prayed over by Amma. Similarly, a teenage girl who had not spoken in two weeks was brought in by her distraught parents. Amma blew *duā* over her and demanded that she tell Amma her name. When she sat mutely, Amma pried open her mouth and blew into it, over and over, until the girl finally weakly uttered her name.

Most possession or visionary cases involve adult or teenage patients, and it seems to be culturally/spiritually inappropriate for a child to be affected by these kinds of problems, as illustrated by the next case. A Muslim father brought in his young elementary school–aged son, who sat wide-eyed and silent throughout the interaction at Amma's table. The father explained that the boy saw bones dancing in the graveyard that he passed every day going and returning from school. Amma laughed at the improbability of it but let the father continue. The boy had had a fever for four or five days and yesterday had come home from school having seen the dancing bones. Without calculating *abjad,* Amma confidently declared that the problem was *asrat* [an evil eye cast by a supernatural being] and that if the father performed *utārā* [circling the clay pot of ingredients over the patient's body], everything would be fine.

Father: I just don't understand what's happening. He already has two *tāvīz* that you gave him fifteen or twenty days ago.

Amma: Take them off.

Father: I don't understand; he's become so weak. I worry day and night.

Amma: For the *utārā*, you'll need yellow rice, raw liver, one coconut, seven lemons, seven *bhilāven*, eleven white flowers; put them in a clay pot. Take all the *tāvīz* off; take off what doesn't work. [She also prescribed evening and morning *dhuān* and drinking *fālitā*.]

The father returned the next day without the young son. At that time, Amma scolded him for talking about *saitānī* and the possibility of visions such as dancing bones in front of the boy, saying, "This isn't the way [*tarīqā*] of children [i.e., it is not natural for children to have these kinds of visions], so this must mean that you or someone else has spoken about these things in front of the boy and suggested them to him. This isn't right." The chastised father did not respond but immediately brought up the new problem at hand: his newborn baby had milk coming out of his nose when he was breastfeeding. Amma smiled, saying this was natural, but she still asked whether or not the baby's mother had one of her *tāvīz*. When the father said no, she encouraged him to bring the entire family back to see her on Sunday to receive general protective *tāvīz*.

When a pubescent girl was brought in by her parents with a similar problem of "seeing things," however, Amma did not scold them. The girl's eyes were closed and she was moaning continually. The distraught father told Amma that the girl had been perfectly normal when she had gone to the neighborhood tap that morning to draw water, but she had returned in this state, crying out, "They're hitting me; they're hitting me. There are four of them; they have knives." Amma immediately put her hand on the girl's head and whispered *duā* over her before declaring, again without performing *abjad*, that the problem was *kartūt*. She prescribed an *utārā* that included a live non-egg-laying chicken (instead of the usual 100 grams of uncut raw liver); she also prescribed drinking *fālitā* and *dhuān*. In these unusual cases of children "seeing things," Amma directed most of her attention and conversation to the parents of the children, calming them, as if their own anxiety had contributed to the problem.

Pāgalpan: **Mental Illness**

Experientially close to, but distinctly outside of, the category of possession is what Amma calls *pāgalpan* [mental illness]. Amma says she has little control over this class of illnesses since they are not usually caused by spiritual forces, and she often refers such patients to allopathic doctors or a psychiatrist she knows. However, some family members of mentally ill patients are reluctant to follow the referral, insisting that surely Amma must be able to do something. One morning, an elderly Muslim woman accompanied by her married daughter forced her way into the healing room, refusing to take a queue number, and immediately began complaining that her daughter was experiencing dizziness every day, did not seem to remember anything, and was *pāgal*, not "right in the head." Without looking up from the prescriptions she was writing for another patient, Amma told the mother that she should take her daughter to a doctor whose name she would give. The woman kept complaining about all the manifestations of the symptoms when Amma interrupted sternly, "Are you listening or not? There's the Gandhi Hospital. I'll give you the address. Go there and tell them the problem; they'll give you medicine and it will make your daughter better. If not . . ." Amma got up in mid-sentence to go to the bathroom.

In Amma's absence, the old woman took the floor and continued to elaborate about her problem to the rest of the patients. She complained that her daughter had already gone to a famous doctor and taken a three-month course of strong medicines; they had made some difference, but she was still in bad shape. The old woman spoke with urgency and persistence, but the rest of the patients had little interest in her story. I wondered if they had heard it before or what made the difference between this story and others to which patients listened more sympathetically. One of the women listening told the mother, "Look, we all have our problems; you should just stay quiet for a while," upon which the old woman cried out, "But sometimes my heart comes right out."

When Amma returned to the healing table, the *pāgal* woman's mother again asked Amma to tell her what to do. And Amma repeated that she should take her daughter to Gandhi Hospital and that her daughter would surely get better. When the woman began to cry again, Amma gently reprimanded her,

Allah told us to smile in our troubles. Don't cry! Don't cry! Smile in times of trouble. When my daughter died, I came and sat here and met the 'public' after only three days—she was the daughter who was the mother of four children. After the third day, I came here and sat in the morning. What is the condition of the heart? People know what it is; why do you have to show what's in your heart? Show everyone your face [lit., sun, *sūraj*], but show your heart only to God. Isn't that true? What we say with our mouths, in our teaching, everyone hears that; but no one can hear the heart.

Amma finally went on to treat other patients, even as the old woman kept complaining and muttering to no one in particular. The next patient, who was there on behalf of her thirteen-year-old daughter, whose hair was falling out in clumps, was amazed that I was not afraid of this *pāgal* woman and remarked to Amma, "What a clear heart she has, that she's not afraid of anyone." Amma explained that our relationship went back many years, implying that this relationship was the source of my "clarity." She characterized our relationship as one of love from the heart, not only of words, and said that her heart had tugged the very first time she had met me and that it continues to do so when I'm away. She continued, "Whenever I want to see her, I see her in dreams, although she doesn't talk in dreams." Amma has crafted some of this eloquent narration of our relationship for performance, performance that helps create relationships and establish Amma's authority and spiritual power.

At this point, the old woman was still talking and patients were whispering to each other that it was *she* who was *pāgal,* when Amma reiterated firmly, "We all have our problems. Now look at me. When my daughter, mother of four children, died, I was back at work in three days. It's all in Allah's hands." Both spiritual and nonspiritual illnesses are ultimately fated and in the hands of God, but Amma has been given the authority and power to intervene only in cases caused by spiritual intervention in the physical world.

Another particularly poignant case of what Amma called *pāgalpan* involved an old Muslim woman who was brought in by her daughter-in-law, but this time Amma diagnosed it as having been caused by spiritual forces. As they waited for their queue number to be called up, the old woman mumbled to herself continually, seemingly picking off of her fingertips little invisible objects, which she later told us were bugs. She complained of dizziness, but worse, she said, were the bugs crawling on her scalp and fingertips; she picked one off her fingertip to show Amma. The daughter-in-law explained that this had been going on for the last six months, during which time the family had taken the old woman to three different hospitals for treatment, but to no avail. Amma agreed that of course a hospital treatment would not work; the cure for this spiritual problem, diagnosed as *kartūt*, would be found only in spiritual prescriptions. The old woman again rubbed her fingertips and picked out a bug to show Amma. When Amma told her that she saw nothing, the old woman responded, "Well, that's only because of Allah's mercy, but I see them!"—perhaps suggesting that it is only because of God's mercy that any of us are sane at all. Throughout this interaction, Amma seemed to be suppressing laughter and other patients were laughing out loud; but the chuckles were of love and sympathy, not derision. Amma's prescriptions for this *kartūt* were *utārā, dhuān,* and *falitā.*

In many cases that Amma referred out because they were not caused by spiritual forces, patients asserted that they were nevertheless cured by the attention and *dhuān* and *duā* Amma gave. A seventeen-year-old Muslim girl was brought in by her mother-in-law with headaches that had been plaguing her since childhood and had caused her to get "dark." The older woman sighed, "She used to be so fair and beautiful. Now look at her—headaches all the time!" This was particularly significant because she was of marriageable age and fair skin is considered to be an asset in arranging marriages for girls in India. Amma took one look at the patient and declared that her only problem was that she needed glasses, and she proceeded to write down the name of a recommended eye clinic, explaining the system of patient registration there. Only then did Amma perform *abjad*, which, as she had predicted at the beginning of the conversation, revealed nothing. She confidently declared, "It's only a weakness of the mind." Rather confused, the mother asked, "Are you telling us to go to the doctor?" Amma again gave the name of the doctor and clinic, saying this was the same doctor she went to for her own weak eyes. Then, for temporary relief, she recommended mixing egg whites with water and putting the mixture on her head for several minutes before washing it off. Finally she offered a *tāvīz*, asking the patient, "Will you wear it, my dear one [*beṭā*]?" She also gave her morning and evening *dhuān*.

Marital and Family Problems

Possession cases are the most dramatic performances of Amma's spiritual authority and healing success for all present in the courtyard to witness, right in front of them. However, most cases are not this dramatic; many patients come to Amma because they have heard of her successes in healing failed marriages, family strife, or misbehaving children. For these familial and marital problems, Amma sometimes opens *abjad* and other times simply talks with the patients. When a young married woman came to Amma (on behalf of her mother-in-law) to consult about two brothers-in-law who wanted to move out of the family home and live independently, Amma first asked the young woman what it was that *she* wanted, what *she* thought would be the best outcome. After narrativizing the family dynamics, the daughter-in-law admitted that she thought the best solution was for the two couples to move out. Only then did Amma give her *fālitā* to burn "to close their mouths" and stop the arguing but not to keep them from moving out. Amma said that the argumentation must be ended first, and then "we'll see if they move out or not."

Often patients come with a stated family problem, but as Amma talks with them—perhaps more important, listens to them—a fuller, more complicated story generally emerges. A young Hindu woman came with the complaint that her much older husband "would not look at her." She was a second wife to a widower whose first wife had died after nineteen years of marriage. Since the husband was so much older than this second wife, he had not demanded dowry; her relatives accepted the arrangement since she was an orphan and it would have been very difficult to provide any kind of dowry, which would have been necessary for a younger groom. The patient had been working as a typist but quit this employment when she got married. At first, she told Amma that she thought perhaps her husband was sleeping with other women. But her deeper fear was not articulated until she had sat with Amma for quite a while and had already been given a prescription of feeding *capātīs* [unleavened bread] to a dog, a prescription to bring back an errant husband. Only then the patient whispered that she thought the "other woman" was her husband's own nineteen-year-old daughter. This she could not bear, she said, since it was incest—a sin, and a sin that she believed reflected on her as a wife. She told Amma that she had not said anything about this to anyone else because she thought no one would believe her; they would simply think it was a complaint of a jealous stepmother. Who would believe that a father would have sex with his daughter? But, she continued, she knew that Amma would see directly into her heart, so she was telling her the truth. Amma listened sympathetically, then urged the patient to carry out the *capātī* treatment and return when it had been completed. Amma gave this young woman understanding, something tangible to "do," and a framework of hope for change and healing.

Although there were more women than men who presented problems of marriage and relationship (including physical abuse), men, too, were sometimes mistreated by wives and came to Amma in despair—a situation defying common stereotypes of gender relations in South Asia. For example, in a single Thursday morning, two men came in separately asking Amma what they should do about their wives who had run off with other men; one man was a Hindu and one was a Muslim. Amma gave both men treatments to call back their wives. To discern the case brought by the Muslim husband, Amma first "read" into her own hands, closing her eyes, and saw the wife. She gave the man two rusty locks, one to put in the local pond and one to lock on the house door. These, she assured him, would bring back his wife. She instructed him to come back in two or three days if his wife did not return.

One unusual marital case involved an elderly Muslim man who was brought in by his two younger Hindu female neighbors. They reported that he had been beaten by his much younger wife—which caused everyone in the room to laugh, but the man did not seem to notice. Amma looked at both of his hands and asked those of us sitting at the table if the three lines in the palms of each hand matched up, as she could not see clearly. When we said yes, she thought the marriage could survive and wrote the wife's name on a *tāvīz*. She instructed the patient to put the *tāvīz* under a rock while pronouncing his wishes: "May her mouth be closed; may she not fight with me." She clarified that the old man must put the amulet somewhere outside, not in the house where his wife might find it. Then, to my surprise, the patient's very elderly mother was called in from the courtyard by the two neighbors, and Amma instructed her to take her son's *tāvīz*, as if he might lose it like a young boy. Amma also wrote out *falitā* on which were written: "May [the wife's name] mouth be closed." Only then, after Amma had performed *duā* over the old man, did one of the Hindu neighbors confide that her own husband beat her too, and she asked for a *tāvīz* similar to the one Amma had written for the elderly man.

Another male patient, this time a young Hindu man, came with the complaint that his wife did not listen to him anymore: "She used to listen, but now she does as she pleases. She keeps saying she needs to go to her mother's, or to this relative's or that. She's ruining my mind [*dimāg*]!" Amma and the other women sitting around the healing table laughed, but he continued his narrative unfazed, "I'm asking that she obey me." Amma opened the wife's *abjad* and determined that this attitude change had been caused by another woman [*kartūt*]. The husband was sure that his wife would not wear a *tāvīz* if he brought one home, so Amma gave him one written in his wife's name to put in his own pocket. She gave a second *tāvīz* to tie to a rock and immerse in a body of water. Amma asked the husband if he would be able to burn *falitā* if she wrote some for him. He said that he was a night watchman and stays home during the day, so he thought he would be able to find opportunity to burn them. Six days later the same man returned and stood at the doorway with great impatience, calling out his complaints to Amma without taking a number or waiting for his turn in queue. Amma asked him to wait for his turn and sit down: "I can't talk to you when you're standing up like that." He huffed that he did not have time to sit down and would come back another time, but before leaving he let Amma know that her treatment had not worked. In fact, he said, "Things are worse than ever. My wife's gone to her mother's place in Khazipet, taking one child with her and leaving two at home." Amma was not very sympathetic, barely looking up at him, and counseled the other waiting patients that the man needed

117

to be patient and that he might well not have carried out the prescriptions correctly.

Some marital problems are simply fated and Amma can only listen, such as that of a teenaged married Hindu woman brought by her nervous mother. Amma opened the patient's *abjad* but made no pronouncement when she had obtained a final quotient; instead, she closed her eyes and "looked" to see what the prognosis of the diagnosed problem was. Then she made a pronouncement in Telugu. I asked Amma's son, who was seated at the table, what the problem was, and he told me that the young woman's husband had threatened to push her off a rooftop and then jump himself because he had no children. When I ask the girl's mother how long it had been since she had gotten married, she told me it had only been a month. The narrative was unclear: perhaps the husband had been married before without children and was now panicking about the new bride's fertility, or he might have simply had unrealistic expectations. In any case, Amma gave the girl *fālitā* and a *tāvīz*, but when the girl left, she sighed and said, "It's her fate [*kismat*]; that man is crazy." In this case, Amma told me, the *abjad* had revealed "nothing," meaning nothing caused by a spiritual intervention over which Amma had control. Amma tried to provide comfort but had "seen" ahead that the outcome was not going to be good.

As this young Hindu woman was waiting her turn, a middle-aged Muslim woman sat down in front of Amma, sobbing, eventually managing to say that her husband had been fighting with her and had been particularly stubborn for the last month. She told Amma that they have six children and that the husband does not speak to them either. Amma first tried to stop her crying, repeating over and over, "Why are you crying? Stop now." Amma asked the woman if she thought that her husband had another woman, to which the wife answered "No." Amma then opened *abjad* under the husband's name and diagnosed that he had been given *kartūt* [evil eye] by another man. She gave the wife a *tāvīz* to put under a cupboard or wardrobe, telling her to say as she did so, "Don't fight with me; keep your mouth shut." Amma asked her to come back after a week.

As I left Amma's healing room that day, another patient who had heard the previous case walked with me to the main road. On our short walk together, she told me that she used to have a terrible time getting along with her in-laws, who had instigated all kinds of problems between her and her husband, resulting in constant fighting and physical abuse by her husband. She added that the tension in their marriage was heightened by the financial constraints under which they lived. Her husband worked in a company that makes car springs and his salary was only Rs. 3,000 per month, barely enough to support a family of four daughters. But, the woman testified, since she had come to Amma, things had gotten much better; and now she comes periodically when things flare up again, when even little things come up, as a measure of preventative health.

In the cases of soured relationships, whether between husband and wife, between parents and children, or between neighbors, Amma almost always assumes the side of the complainant who has come to her when she writes *tāvīz* and *falitā* that command the offending party's mouth to be shut. It is possible (even probable), of course, that the person about whom a patient is complaining would have a different story to tell. Amma and others participating in Islamic spiritual healing practices (practitioners and patients alike) distinguish between "black" and "light" knowledge [*kālā* and *nūrī ilm*], knowledge that is used for healing and knowledge that is used for destruction. In narratives in the healing room, it becomes apparent that the same action/prescription might be experienced as *nūrī ilm* from one perspective and *kālā ilm* from another perspective, depending upon whether one is the actor or receiver of the knowledge. But Amma does not consider the prescription to burn a *falitā* in order to bring about some effect on another person to be a form of *kālā ilm*—she insists that while she knows the mechanics of "black knowledge," she never uses it.

In cases of marital and family relationships, Amma does not ask the complainant to psychologically analyze the dynamics of the relationship and the reasons they developed. Amma is very directive, confidently naming the spiritual cause of the failing relationship and telling the patient exactly what to do with various physical prescriptions. However, the patient often leaves the healing table with new confidence that something *can* actually be done about the problem because of Amma's pronouncements that healing will take place. Perhaps, then, the patient returns to the relationship a different person in that context, which has the potential to change its dynamics.

Infertility

Infertility is one of the many causes of marital strife. And for infertility, Amma declares that her treatments (which usually include *nahāvan*) are 'guaranteed'. In the following case, it was the wife who came to Amma with the problem, explaining that she had been married for five years and that she and her husband fought a lot, especially if the husband's sister was home. The patient said that both she and her husband had been medically checked for fertility problems and that the doctors had found no physical problem. However, after Amma opened the woman's *abjad*, as she began writing out prescriptions and telling the patient the procedures and costs of *nahāvan*, the patient admitted that her husband had been found to have a low sperm count. Amma chastised her, "What do you expect me to do when the problem is his and he doesn't come?" She recommended a particular infertility doctor and then felt the woman's pulse, declaring that the woman, too, "had too little blood." Amma prescribed *fālitā* and *tāvīz* to close the sister-in-law's mouth in the meantime, before the couple could come back together for *nahāvan*. She gave two *tāvīz*, one to be placed under a cupboard and the other under a rock. *Abjad* had revealed a spiritually caused problem that had manifested itself both physically and socially, but at the same time Amma acknowledged that there were also physical problems over which she had no control. She recommended both a spiritual and physical prescription (the latter to be given by the biomedical infertility specialist).

Childhood Illnesses

Childhood diseases are the most physically visible of the illnesses brought to Amma for treatment. Across religious traditions in India, children are thought to be particularly susceptible to the evil eye in any of its forms, as babies are almost inherently beautiful and valued by families. In Indian cultures, it is traditionally considered impolite and even dangerous to the health of a baby for someone to comment on how beautiful s/he is, as this might attract undue attention and draw someone's eye to it. To detract such dangerous/evil eyes, babies often wear amulets, black bangles with shiny reflective inset stones, or black spots made of kohl on the bottoms of their little bare feet or on the side of their foreheads. Since boy babies are generally preferred, they might be dressed like girls to detract the envious evil eye. Babies might also be given nicknames with negative connotations (such as "dark one" or "little donkey") to prevent notice. But when the evil eye is successfully cast, it can cause young babies to fail to thrive, have difficulty breastfeeding, and develop high fevers.

Many of Amma's infant or child patients have already been taken to allopathic doctors before being brought to Amma, especially if the cases involve high fevers. But the parents who come to her are covering all bases, unsure whether or not the fevers have been caused by spiritual or physical forces. Amma diagnoses these cases through *abjad,* and if the diagnosis reveals a particular kind of evil eye, she gives prescriptions of *utārā* and *fālitā* to work at the root cause of the symptoms. But she also knows that allopathic prescriptions may relieve the physical symptoms and she often refers parents to a doctor or pharmacy (giving specific names and directions) at the same time that she gives them her own prescriptions. In cases of children, there is usually little lingering discussion or storytelling around the healing table, since parents are anxious to get home with their sick child and the child is often crying and restless.

The following was one of the exceptions, since the newborn baby was not in a crisis of high fever, throwing up, or crying. A Muslim woman came in with her sister's two-week-old baby; the mother herself had not brought the baby because she was still considered impure from the birth process and would not have been permitted in the room. Amma asked for the baby's name in order to begin opening her *abjad.* When she heard it was Khairazbi (derived from *"khair,"* the Urdu word for well-being/good fortune), Amma exclaimed, "What kind of name is that?" The baby's aunt answered that this name must have been given because the baby was the first girl after four boys in the family. Amma declared that this was not the right name; she should be given the name Muhammadi or Ahmadi. She said she had given this name to several babies, and that by the grace of God and prayers of Muhammad, they had survived. Amma then asked what day of the week the baby was born; hearing the answer Wednesday, she reconfirmed, "Yes, then, give Muhammadi; one should give the name according to the day." The aunt timidly suggested the name Rahmatunnisa (gift or blessing from Allah). Amma agreed that it was a sweet name but reiterated that the name should be Muhammadi. This discussion of names and the confidence with which Amma declared the baby's initially given name as inappropriate is significant in the context of the diagnostic system of *abjad,* which depends on the mathematical values of the patient's name and the lunar day of the week.

Only after she had negotiated a new name did Amma open the baby's *abjad* under Khairazbi, since this was the name under which the baby had become ill. Amma explained what the problem was: the baby's legs were crossed, which had caused her to become thin, and she was not drinking her mother's milk because someone had cast *asrat* on the mother. Amma gave a six-day supply of *dhuān* and told the baby's aunt to come back for more *dhuān* after a week. At that time, she should also bring a green gourd [*khādū*] for the 40-day treatment for babies who fail to thrive.

These gourd treatments are causes for celebration and frustration for mothers. When treatments are successful, mothers often bring back their fattened babies to show off (as Amma asks them to do). They often bring *fātīhā,* offerings of thanksgiving over which Abba presides at the flagpole, and distribute sweets to those in attendance that day. But other mothers come back with weak, skinny babies, complaining that the treatment has not worked. In these cases, Amma usually finds some direction that the mothers have not followed in the prescription and tells them to carry it out again.

Another Muslim grandmother and father brought in a one-year-old baby who had been crying for days and not sleeping. They had brought him in earlier and Amma had prescribed *utārā,* but they complained that nothing had improved after the treatment. Amma answered them emphatically, "It *will* happen!" As Amma tapped the baby's stomach and began writing out more *dhuān* and *fālitā,* her son, Muhammad, asked if the couple had used the correct ingredients for the ritual. He walked them through the steps of the ritual again and found out that they had passed the clay pot over the baby's body, not only on its front side but also on its back side. "That," he declared, "is why it did not work: you are not

13. Abba performing *fātihā* on behalf of a patient returning with her
baby, whom Amma has healed, 1995.

supposed to pass the pot of ingredients over the back of the body." The
patients backtracked in their narrative and seemed to feel that they had
been tricked into saying that they had passed the pot on the back side
when, they assured Muhammad, they had not actually done so. Muhammad said that they must have done *something* incorrectly in the ritual
sequence or it would have worked; they would have to perform the *utārā*
again. He instructed them again: they must circle the pot three times
around the baby's head—perhaps that is what they had done incorrectly;
they needed to make sure not to turn around and look at the pot after
they had left it at the crossroads; they needed to go directly home after
leaving the clay pot and wash their hands and change their clothes in
order to rid themselves of any evil eye that might have stuck to them.
Parents are usually willing to keep trying Amma's prescriptions until a
sick child recovers, but given the stories they often tell when they arrive
at her healing table of having gone to other doctors and religious healers,
Amma realistically expects that they will probably continue consulting

123

other practitioners, and she sometimes teases them about this when she finds another healer's amulet on a baby.

Misbehaving and Missing Children

Misbehaving children, particularly sons, are a common complaint of parents who come to Amma. In these cases, parents usually come without the child, unless he is very young, in which case he comes with them. One young Muslim couple brought in their seven-year-old son who had been causing problems by biting both his mother and people at school. The parents seemed at their wits' end as they described their son's disobedience; all he did, they said, was wander around all day [*ghūmnā-phirnā*]—all this at such a young age (implying that one might expect such wandering of a teenage boy but not from one so young). Amma initially told the couple that they would have to undertake the expensive treatment of *nahāvan*. But after diagnosing *kartūt* through *abjad*, she told them that they could try *utārā* first—a special one that requires a live chicken to be circled around the patient's head and then left in a graveyard. On this visit she gave them *dhuān* and *fālitā*. Then Amma turned her attention directly to the boy and gave him a good talking-to, telling him that if he did not straighten up, he would have to come back and get her (Amma's) "full treatment," something she assured him he would not like. The little boy, meanwhile, smiled impishly throughout, seemingly amused by the whole situation.

Misbehavior for teenage sons is often described as talking back to one's parents, an unwillingness to work, and the apparently chronic problem for many young Hyderabadi men of simply "wandering around." A Hyderabadi man working in Dubai came in to see Amma almost every day for a week during the middle of his five-month leave of absence from his work abroad. He was a disciple and was coming to serve her, but he also had a complaint about his son, who had started to use abusive language to his mother in his father's absence. Further, his father lamented, the son refused to work and wanted a love marriage rather than one arranged by his parents. His father was coming to Amma for advice about whether or not, under these conditions, he should return to the Gulf. He wondered, "What good is anything I do there if I can't protect my wife against the abuses of my son?" His request for advice was part of a general conversation and tea-drinking; he did not ask for his or his son's *abjad* to be opened and no diagnoses of spiritual imbalance or evil eye were made. Amma only sighed wistfully and said, "This is a new age. Forget about the old times [*purānā zamānā*] when it comes to sons!" One of the great sorrows of her own life, which she did not try to hide from her patients, was her disappointment in her sons. But the disciple begged for some assurance of constancy in the world, "But the sun is still the sun, the moon is still the moon, and a mother is still a mother, isn't she?" Before he went to the Gulf, he said, the family had had little money but also only little problems. Now, with more money, relatives and friends around them had become jealous and were casting evil eyes on his success. He explained to me, "In India no one needs guns—not when they have these spiritual means to hurt people. This black knowledge [*kālā ilm*] is a vile, bad thing [*gandī burī bāt*], a very vile thing."

More often than one might imagine, patients come to Amma with stories (and pictures) of missing, runaway, or kidnapped children. One Hindu father of a nine-year-old daughter came with a male companion who told the story that the man's daughter had not returned home from school four days ago. She had just been transferred to a new school and (as reported to them by her classmates) was standing in line to enter the school at the beginning of the day when she saw friends from her old school across the street. She ran across the street and had not been seen since. Amma asked Hussein to look for her in *hāzirī*, but he said he did not have any of the necessary kohl on hand. So Amma closed her eyes and "looked." She confidently affirmed to the father, "She *will* be found." She gave the father a *tāvīz* to hang from the doorway—its fluttering would call the girl back—as well as one to sink in a pond and a third to burn. Then she commented, "But the girl must be very smart, so she'll be okay. She could have made it all the way to Rajahmundry [overnight by train] by herself." It was only at this point that the girl's father and his companion pulled out a photograph of the girl and told Amma that they had already contacted the police. The calm demeanor of the father made me wonder whether he knew more than he was telling about where his daughter might be, but Amma did not question him further—as if she, too, knew that this was not the whole story and that there was no

125

true cause for concern. Other parents of missing children are usually over-wrought, and Amma's primary role seems to be to first calm them down and then strategize with them about the best way to search for the child in addition to giving them the fluttering *tāvīz* that will call the child home.

People also come to Amma with cases of missing animals. She fre-quently refers them to Hussein for his *hāzirī* treatment, in which he might see in a vision where the animal is, or she might prescribe the fluttering *tāvīz* to call the animal back and *fālitā* to be burned commanding the thief to bring it back. But with animals, she is often resigned to the fact that such theft is a sign of the times. As she told one distraught Muslim woman whose goat had been stolen from her courtyard the night before, "There's a lot of theft these days. I too have had a goat stolen from me. So if it comes back [with the treatment of *fālitā* and *tāvīz*], it comes back. But if not, what to do?"

Restlessness and Weakness

Chronic problems for which patients come to Amma for relief include general restlessness [*becainī*]—experienced as "hands and feet pulling"—and weakness [*sustī*]. Restlessness might be at least temporarily resolved by the outing to Amma's courtyard and the exchange of one's own per-sonal narrative with others around the healing table who might share or understand one's problem. But *becainī* is rarely the only presenting symp-tom, and as the patient sits with Amma, other more specific symptoms often emerge in the conversation. *Becainī* is also often the presenting symptom when a person is searching for his/her *pīr*, wandering from place to place looking for that relationship that will be satisfying and is consid-ered to be preordained.[5] Sometimes this search takes place in the form of a search for healing from a specific illness and its cure is the sign that that particular *pīr*, or in the case of Amma, *pirānimā*, is the one for whom the person has been looking. Amma often teased me about my own *becainī* when, after having sat at her table for several hours at a time, I would begin to shift around in my chair, or she would attribute my visible rest-lessness to the absence of my family.

Weakness, on the other hand, is taken more seriously as an end symptom. At one healing session, a middle-aged Hindu man, accompanied by his wife, came to Amma with the complaint of weakness, saying he had not been able to eat anything except coconut milk for two or three months. He was too weak to engage in his profession of slaughtering goats. He said he had gone to the doctor several times but that the doctor just kept giving him "pills, pills, pills," none of which had made any difference. First the doctor had taken an X-ray of his pelvis and then his kidneys; the patient's wife pulled these out of her bag and showed them to Amma, who examined them carefully. And then the wife proceeded to do most of the talking while her husband slumped against the chair, sighing deeply. The wife knew of Amma's "strong" treatments and begged her to perform a *nahāvan* on her husband, "Do this, and I'll touch your feet."

Amma informed them that the *nahāvan* would cost Rs. 450; this price included all the ingredients necessary for the ritual as well as the requisite *utārā*, an oil lamp that should burn for eight days, and *dhuān*. The wife asked if her husband should continue to take the pills prescribed by the doctor while he was undergoing these rituals. Amma laughed, "It does no harm. I take pills [for high blood pressure], and I'm still sitting here, aren't I?" As Amma began to list the ingredients necessary for the *nahāvan*, the wife asked if Amma could lessen the total cost just a little. Amma retorted,

Just look at the cost of the lemons these days and how many lemons are required for both the *nahāvan* and *utārā*—at least fifty or sixty! I can't lessen it one paisā. I don't eat a single paisā of what you give [i.e., all the money goes toward costs]. I can't take any less. [When the wife continued to protest, she said] Do you think I'm telling a lie? Look, when you go to a doctor for treatment, do you ask him/her to lessen it? So why do you ask me? How can I do that? You can take it or leave it; all I can do is tell you what should be done.

Abba, overhearing this exchange, jumped into the discussion, warning, "But if you don't do the treatment or only fulfill part of it, you shouldn't say that Amma's treatments don't work. If the treatment worked only being half-fulfilled, only burning *fālitā*, let's say, then why do you think

127

Amma would prescribe the full *nahāvan*?" Having been so chastised, the couple said they would come back the next day with the full amount of money.

Failing Businesses and Problems with Houses and Neighbors

Cases of failing businesses seem to be brought exclusively by men. Sometimes the problem diagnosed is with the individual conducting the business and other times the problem lays in the place/building itself. One Muslim male who came to Amma for his failing business was sure that the problem of his business lay in the building. Yet opening his *abjad* revealed that the elements were unbalanced in his body and that he had too much air/*havā*. (Imbalance of the elements is a diagnosis I heard Abba describe once at length, but Amma rarely uses it at the healing table.) Amma asked him if he had had arguments with anyone in his family. When he said yes, she remembered that he had come to her before for the same problem but that he had not put the *tāvīz* she had written for him in the store, as she had instructed him to do. The patient reluctantly confirmed this was the case and that his business had not gotten any better. Amma chastised him, saying that her treatments had helped many similar cases, so there must be something wrong with him, didn't he agree? He suggested that perhaps the problem was some form of evil eye, but Amma disagreed and said that the problem originated from inside *him*, not from the outside. This time she gave the patient a *tāvīz* to wear on his person and *fālitā* to burn and drink. He asked for something to put in the store, but she told him to carry out these prescriptions on himself first and then come back for the business *tāvīz*.

While many cases of "trouble in the house" are vague and generalized, with one thing after another—illness, flooding, financial strain, arguing relatives, and so forth—going wrong over a period of months or years for no apparent reason (and these cases generally call for house exorcisms), other house troubles can be attributed to specific causes, of which the following case is an example. This case raised, for the first time in my presence, the possibility that Amma's spiritual knowledge could be used to cause harm beyond "shutting someone's mouth." During Muharram

1995, a Shii woman and her adult nephew came to Amma's room several days in a row, both of them wearing all black, the color of mourning worn by Shiis during these days commemorating the martyrdom of the Prophet Muhammad's grandson Hussein. The aunt was an old friend of Amma's and much of the time while she was in the healing room, she and Amma gossiped about mutual acquaintances from around the city.

The nephew brought an initial complaint about his Muslim neighbor whose house shares a wall with that of his own. This neighbor had opened up a commercial bakery in the house, and the oven against the wall shared between the two houses gave out such heat that the patient's five children were suffering greatly, literally "drying up," he said. The patient brought with him a file filled with letters of complaint written to both city and health officials, asking that they close down the bakery on the basis of both health and the illegality of running a business on private property. He had first written to the medical officer of health, with a copy to the minister of health.

Amma told the nephew right away that she could "give him something" if he could somehow get into the bakery, something to sprinkle inside. Amma told him it would be a mixture of ashes from a cremation ground, soil from the old house, and other ingredients that would cost Rs. 250. But, she warned, he must not put it in his own house, not even for a single minute, while he waited for an opportunity to enter the bakery. Amma became quite dramatic, "Even someone like me [someone who is spiritually powerful] can't leave this mixture in my house or it will do to my house what is intended for the bakery," the implication being that the mixture would destroy any structure in which it was placed. The nephew immediately pulled out the requisite money and paid Amma. She asked, "Should I make them [the offenders] go insane [*pāgal*]? Do the bakery owners eat or drink from your hand?" [No.] "Do they eat from anyone else you know?" [I.e., so as to be able to put the mixture in their food.] The patient answered, "No, they don't eat from anyone else." Amma pondered: "We'll have to think of another way to get it into their house, then."

As the days progressed during which the aunt and nephew sat daily at Amma's table, more and more family problems came out, including a suspicion that a younger sister-in-law was sleeping with a neighbor when her husband was out of town for work. The nephew said that he could not say anything to her because he is older—it would not be proper for him to speak of sex directly to a younger sister-in-law—but that surely the truth would come out in the end. (To which the other patients nodded and said, "Yes, yes.") The aunt and nephew returned the next day with a report that that very day, yesterday, upon their return from Amma's, a policeman had come to give warning to the bakery and another policeman had come this morning. Amma was pleased and punctuated the end of their story with, "See!"—that is, see how her treatments had already worked, although she had not yet given the dangerous mixture but only *fālitā* to burn. The pair returned yet again a third day, bringing with them this time *capātīs* and salt for treatment of the apparent infidelity of the sister-in-law.

Ten days later, on the fortieth day of Muharram, the nephew and aunt came back to report to Amma that the bakery neighbors had called in three different *muršids* to counteract Amma's powers. Such reports about competition between spiritual practitioners are not uncommon. Amma herself tells of sending back the evil eye thrown toward her by her first guru/*muršid*, who was jealous of her success after she had learned the healing system from *his* guru. Amma assured her patient that her powers were greater than those being called against her, and then she moved on to the practical advice of telling him to submit his written complaint to the police once again. The nephew then told Amma that he had found out that the bakery neighbors buy tea from a 'hotel' (small restaurant) every day and that he thought that he could manage to put something in that tea. Amma wanted to know how he could guarantee that no one else but the bakery owners would drink the tea on a given day, to make sure that no one else would be harmed by it. Then she asked, as she did the first day, "Do you really want to make him crazy?" He confirmed that this was his desire; but on this day, Amma's question seemed more rhetorical, as if she had no intention of using the dangerous substance on the adversary. The nephew moved on to presenting the case of his seven-year-old niece, whose father had been electrocuted a month earlier and died. Amma opened the girl's *abjad* but found nothing. This day's interaction with the nephew ended with his request for three white-metal *tāvīz,* extra-strong *tāvīz* for extra-strong protection, for which he paid Rs. 165.

This story tells of spiritual knowledge and practice capable of being used for good or harm and of the capacity to relieve one person's troubles by directly affecting someone else's life in negative ways. One can imagine the bakery owner himself coming to Amma with the complaint that his neighbor was trying to shut down his business by reporting him to the police. If this were the case, Amma would presumably take his side. While this much I understand, the next step of the potential of causing someone to become mentally unstable is more troubling, but I never felt free to ask Amma about this directly. I had already heard teachings by Amma about the potential misuse of spiritual power and knowledge [*ilm*]—and this potential is a frequently heard critique of *pīrs* and their healing/ritual practices, both by other *pīrs* who are trying to establish their own superior status and critics of the healing of *pīrs* altogether. I felt that Amma might interpret direct questioning as a criticism that betrayed her trust. And in the end I trusted her more than I suspected ill use of knowledge and remembered her admonition: "These are very heavy matters, Jo-ice."

A particularly poignant and more typical patient interaction—another case of trouble with a house—was brought to Amma by two young teen-age Muslim brothers. Amma told them that they were too young to deal with and fully understand such family problems, and yet they were trying to deal with them since there was no adult in the family to do so. They presented Amma with the problem of their father, who had been particularly restless and belligerent since the family had built on a second story to their house. Amma declared that the problem had been caused by *asrat.* When she did not explain what this meant (and it became clear that these young men had not encountered anything quite like this before and did not understand the vocabulary Amma was using), the older brother asked what they should do about it. Amma replied, "Well, you have to do something; it's because of the [new] floor on top. You'll have to light an oil lamp for three days and I'll give you things for *bandiś* [exorcism] to put on both floors."

One of the sons asked if there was a person behind this *asrat,* indicating his lack of familiarity with the term (remember that *asrat* is evil eye cast by some nonhuman spiritual force, not by a human). Amma explained that the problem had not been caused by *kartūt*, evil eye cast by a person, but by *asrat*. She assured them, "I've seen it [the result of the *abjad* calculations, *asrat*] now. It's the same diagnosis, whether done in your father's name, your mother's name, or your sister-in-law's name. The problem is from *asrat* in the house; it's not *kartūt*." Somehow the son could not accept or perhaps understand this diagnosis, and he asked again, "It's not caused by some bastard [*harāmkāpnan*, a term used in Hyderabadi slang]?" Amma reluctantly admitted that "there may be just a little of that; there's a little of that and a little of this. And then there's the problem with your father, his anger. What to do? That's just old age; sometimes you just have to sit quietly in the face of old age."

The younger brother asked about his mother and Amma answered, "It's in the house; everything is like this, it's all mixed up [*kiccaṛ-piccaṛ*, lit., muddied up, confused]; there's no *barkat* in the house." *Barkat*, Amma explained to me in an aside, means a state in which even if there is only a little money in the house, it gets spent in the right way and there is always enough; when there is no *barkat*, even if there is a lot of money, it is of no use. While this is a specific example of how *barkat* (or its absence) might be manifest, more generally, the word "*barkat*" implies auspiciousness, a state that results in prosperity and success. I was not the only one who did not fully understand the concept as Amma was using it here; the older son asked for clarification. I reproduce at length the conversation that followed, to give an example of a tone and cadence typical of many of Amma's interactions with patients:

Patient: There's no *barkat*?
Amma: Your household earnings are quite good, right?
Patient: Yes.
Amma: The money is coming in, but you don't see any of it, right?
Patient: That's right.
Amma: Earlier, your earnings were good, right?
Patient: They were good, and we had enough.
Amma: You always had a little money around, right? You were living well. These troubles started only after you built the upstairs of your house, right?

Patient: We built the upstairs because we were having a lot of difficulty downstairs. There wasn't enough room; thinking this, we built the second floor.

Amma: The same thing happened in the case of the Ahmad Bakery owner. He built an upstairs. As soon as he built it, a ghost gave them a slap. He caused one person in the family to go crazy [*pāgal*], the daughter-in-law. Oh-ho, oh-ho; then they came to me. I asked them, "Earlier, you were prosperous, you all were happy, there were always four paise [money] nearby, right?" Everyone else [exaggerating; lit., all the world's learned ones/*āmil*] said the problem was *kartūt*. I said it was *asrat*. And the two of us argued. They brought an *āmil* in from somewhere, their former *āmil* from Gulbargah. They went to him and he said the same [i.e., agreed with me], and then they realized [it was the right diagnosis]. There was pain in the liver, and the *āmil* said it wasn't the play of *kartūt*. But it took a lot of money [i.e., they could have listened to me first, without spending the extra money.]

Patient: He [the father] doesn't understand what's happened to mother.

Amma [continues Ahmad Bakery story]: The daughter-in-law is still crazy.

Patient: If she [the mother] speaks, he becomes angry with her; sometimes he won't speak for four days at a time.

Amma: Do as I've told you, son.

Patient: Okay.

Amma: Of course he'll improve.

Patient: Okay, it's *asrat*; what do we have to do for our mother?

Amma: We'll have to do treatment. Bring your mother one day and I'll speak with her. You're young men; there needs to be someone older and I'll speak with them. Bring your mother and come, what do you say?

Patient: Okay.

Amma [turning to the other brother]: How can you bring your father peacefully [i.e., without him causing problems], that's the question. If you were older men, that would be one thing; [you could say] this is the path [i.e., this is what we have to do], this is the path, we need do this in the house, do that in the house, right?

Patient: Yes.

Amma: But you're young.

Patient: Now things in our house are such that no one pays attention to these things, who's doing what. Like we've come here, but no one knows. I brought my brother and came without anyone knowing. Now we have to go back and speak calmly, saying we should do this.

Amma: Yes, meet with your mother and speak with her calmly; tell her everything about this and that [sort things out]. Explain how things have become in the house—that after you put on the upper roof, there's been *asrat* on the house. Tell her all these things. [Long pause.] Okay, it's Sunday tomorrow. Come at noon tomorrow; you'll get all the details during the *hāzirī*. Listen to the full explanation. Be here at twelve o'clock tomorrow, when he sees people [i.e., Sati, Amma's disciple who goes into trance to find things for patients or to "see" what the problem is]. He gets *hāzirī*; the cost is Rs. 15.

Patient: Okay.

Amma: Tomorrow you will be comforted and you will know everything [the details of the *asrat* and what to do about it].

Patient: The *tāvīz* is for under the cupboard, right?

[Amma talks with another disciple, and then tells him to show the brothers where to put the *tāvīz*.]

Amma: Here, take these [*fālitā*]. [When the brothers looked at the folded papers questioningly and did not pick them up, Amma continued jokingly] Do you think I am going to sit here and burn them for you? Here, take them. [Pause.] Since you two are brothers, you only need to pay for one [queue] ticket. Hussein, give them back a rupee. [They had been charged for two tickets, at Rs. 1 each.]

Patients: Okay, we're going, Ammi [the common Urdu term for Amma, mother].

Amma: Yes, *khudā hāfiz* [good-bye; lit., may God protect you]. Give your father my *salām* [greetings]. Tell your Ammi to bring your father here.

Patients: Yes, yes; we'll surely come, *inšāllah* [God willing].

This interaction between Amma and the two young patients, who were trying to take on the responsibilities of a family before they were really ready, is typical on several levels. First, through the use of a testimonial, Amma reassures the patients, who presumably have not come to her before (since they did not know the basic structures and vocabulary of the healing tradition), of her authority and successful past history. The narrative of her interactions with the owners of Ahmad Bakery assures the boys that theirs is not a unique case but one shared by many others and that her diagnosis was confirmed by other learned spiritual persons. The patients in the Ahmad Bakery narrative had spent money unnecessarily by going to several different learned persons and by not trusting Amma's diagnosis in the first place—an unspoken admonition to the boys not to do the same thing. But Amma is, more than anything, compassionate toward the boys, who seemed to have no idea what to do. She gives them practical advice, spiritually charged prescriptions, and then asks that they bring their mother and father, who are really the persons who should deal with this "heavy" matter, to her.

Some healing-room stories are traumatic and their treatments might be expensive and complicated—stories of infertility and possession. Others narratives are much simpler and are reminders of the human condition, all in a day's living, about which there is often little Amma can do (stolen goats, for example). Amma completes or reformulates many patient narratives by providing an alternative ending when she asserts successful healing. For other narratives, healing may be affected simply by finding a sympathetic and spiritually wise audience in Amma.

NEGOTIATING GENDER IN
THE HEALING ROOM

4

There are only two castes [*jāti*]: men and women.

Many of Amma's patients say they come to her specifically because she is a woman whom they experience to be more loving and understanding than male healers. It is, in fact, her gender that most distinguishes Amma as a spiritual healer and her public authority that most distinguishes her as a woman. Her commanding presence and articulate voice break commonly held stereotypes of the Muslim woman in Indian society—the veiled woman in *pardā*, the woman without a public voice, the woman without religious authority.[1] Even as Amma declares that there is only one ultimate difference among human beings—a difference based on sex—she has transgressed that very boundary to sit in a position of public ritual authority that in South Asian Muslim cultures is traditionally limited to male Sufi *sheikhs* or *pīrs* (see Eaton 1984; Ewing 1984; Jeffrey 1978). This position and her success in it have not been given easily, however, and Amma must (and is able to) continually reassert and recreate her authority to sit as a public healer, even as she mediates and negotiates the very gender boundaries she herself has drawn.

Characterizing Woman's *Jāti*

Amma's assertion that gender is the ultimate distinction between humans—"there are only two castes [*jāti*]: men and women—is frequently voiced in Hyderabad, and in other parts of India, although the assertion seems to be repeated primarily by women (for a male example, see Alter 2000, 143).[2] When Amma declared during the first Gulf War of 1991 "The only real differences are men and women. Don't all mothers cry when their sons are killed?" one of her patients added, "All of us are simply mothers trying to feed our children; really, there are only two castes: men and women." And a Muslim patient explained to the Hindu friend who had accompanied me to the healing room that day—using a common formulaic phrase—"We say 'Rahim' [one of the names of Allah, meaning Merciful One]; you say 'Ram, Ram' [the name of one of Vishnu's incarnations]. But there are no differences, just men and women."[3]

Amma and the women visiting her healing room often characterize the "caste of women" as one filled with suffering and troubles. Talking about a professional "working woman" who was sitting at Amma's table one morning, one of Amma's female disciples bemoaned,

For men, there's no limit to what they can do, is there, Amma? When women do anything [out of the ordinary], then it's considered bad [*gunāh*]; it's bad—it's *yazīm*. [Amma: Yes, *yazīm*.] If I do anything at all, I have to ask for forgiveness. 'Gents' can do anything. They're forgiven for anything.[4] Let 'gents' do whatever they have to; all the elders and neighbors will say, "It's okay." But if 'ladies' do anything, it's wrong [*galat*]; it's wrong. If a woman has to go out to work like this, all the relatives and everyone in the neighborhood say, "*Thu, thu!*" But they wouldn't say anything about the 'gents' doing the same thing. India's like this; it's not good.

Outside of the healing context, over which she exerts authoritative control and where she is doing just the kind of thing the disciple complained was identified as "bad"—stepping out of conventional gender roles—Amma often identifies with the pain that characterizes women's

137

jāti as her own. In a conversation with Muslim age-mates, Amma talked about her own daughter's marriage that ended tragically when the daughter's first husband, the owner of a small *pān* shop, was murdered in an altercation with a customer over money (the young widow later married her husband's younger brother).[5] One of the women listening expressed her surprise that Amma, as a *pirānimā*, faced the same kinds of troubles they did. Amma responded by describing the lack of control and power which women, including herself, have over dowry, husbands, and marriages, concluding, "The life of a woman is useless [*bekār*]. . . . If children turn out, then you'll be happy, but if they don't, then there's trouble. Like mine, they misbehave [*badmāśī karte*], and therefore I'm not content. What does it matter how much you earn [when your children don't turn out well]?"

Menstruation and childbirth are two factors that physically and socially mark the *jāti* of women. Menstruating and postpartum women are considered to be polluted and are prevented from participating fully in many ritual practices; they do not conduct *namāz*, observe Ramadan fasting, visit *dargāhs*, or participate (even as part of the audience) in Abba's monthly *samās* or the festival of Gyarwin Sharif that honors Abdul Qadir Jilani. Amma's youngest daughter's husband, who is religiously learned and has the title *āmil*, gave menstruation as the primary reason women should not practice like Amma does and why he will not let his wife, Amma's daughter Rehma, follow the path of her mother: "Because of the things that happen to their bodies that don't happen to men; furthermore, women should observe *pardā*." Rehma herself concurred, "I would have to get the permission of my husband to meet men, and he hasn't given it. . . . . It is the instruction [*hukum*] of the Quran that women stay inside. Here [at my mother's place], I am much freer."

When she was younger, Amma observed menstrual taboos by not "sitting in her room" for seven days a month. However, while she commented on the inconvenience of this practice, Amma did not give menstrual taboos as the primary reason why women did not traditionally practice healing in the public sphere.[6] Rather, according to Amma, very few women have the inclination, courage, or time to engage such practice. Soon after I met Amma, I asked her if she was teaching her healing skills and knowledge to her daughters or daughter-in-law, as she was to two of her sons. In a tone of voice suggesting surprise that I would even consider such a thing, she answered, "No, they don't have the heart [*dil*] for it. If a possessed patient came in front of my daughter-in-law, she would faint from fear. She has no strength/courage [*himmat*]."[7] Amma continued,

There are many problems doing this work. Look at all the problems Indira Gandhi and Rajiv Gandhi [former prime ministers of India who were both assassinated] had. I've had just that many [and big] troubles. This is why very few women do this work.

On another occasion, Amma explained,

God made woman to care for the house; He made man to earn. If a woman, if a woman heals like this [does *ilāj*], she really has to think about it. What is a husband, after all? He's a god, isn't he? Tell me. He looks after us. It's like your husband is there [in the United States] and you're here; isn't his mind with you and yours with him? Don't you think about your children and plan for them?

A female patient concurred, "Very few women can do this work. You have to take time to learn; you have to do *namāz* at two in the morning. You have to leave everything [family and household responsibilities] and do this."

If a woman takes up the position of public healer, she will have to have someone else in the house willing to take on these duties; the roles of homemaker and healer are perceived as mutually exclusive by many in the community. Amma's daughter-in-law, who has the requisite *pirānimā* title, gave this lack of time as her first reason for not practicing as a healer, but she also added lack of wisdom and authority gained through life experience as other reasons (i.e., she was not old enough yet). This daughter-in-law's mother (who is an age-mate of Amma) told me that she had once gone with Amma to her guru and had become a disciple. But she had not stayed long enough to receive the full teaching (which required days, not hours) because she had to come home and take care of her family and house. She also used her household duties as the reason she did not go on various local pilgrimages when opportunities arose and as the reason she had not spent the night at a *dargāh* when the caretaker's wife prescribed this treatment for her. Abba said that his own *pīr*'s wife had not been involved in her husband's healing practice because "she was busy raising children, cooking, and washing clothes. Our own Amma switched from the service of children to the service of Allah and started doing the work of distancing people's troubles."

Amma also wrestled with the conflicting roles. When I first met her in 1989, she told me that she had begun her healing career as a new mother in her late teens and that she had not taken care of her children: "Allah raised my children, and I took care of the 'public'." But in later visits, the story she told shifted slightly: she had begun healing at age 30 or so, she said, and had given birth to only one of her eleven children after she started to heal publicly.[8] By that time her oldest daughters were able to help in the house, and she soon had a daughter-in-law to take over management of the home.

A second characteristic of woman's *jāti* for many Muslim and (North Indian) Hindu women in South Asia and a reason for their lack of participation in public healing traditions is their observance of *pardā*, gender segregation and veiling. Shahida Lateef has observed that one of the impacts of *pardā* has been the prevention of women's open and free access to other women (Lateef 1990, 135). My observation of women in Amma's healing room, however, suggests that women in *pardā* often find "legitimate" ways to circumvent their isolation.[9] A visit to Amma often means an outing for an entire morning or afternoon and women come in pairs or families; they rarely come alone. They come to her from all over the city and exchange news and personal narratives of troubles, pain, and suffering, narratives that help give definition to the *jāti* of women.

In the early months when I sat at the healing table, I found myself hoping that Amma would characterize her unusual healing position as one that fulfilled the potential of her gender, difficult as that might be under current social structures, not as an exception to it. Yet what I heard her most consistently articulate was the impermeable (and often oppressive) boundary of gender and her own exceptionalism as a woman who has crossed the boundary, once saying, "I have the form [*nakal*] of a woman but the heart [*dil*] of a man." I have heard similar statements from other postmenopausal women to simply refer to the fact that they have reached menopause; most elder women have more mobility in public space once they reach this stage of life, and in this sense, they, too, enter male space. But Amma's assertion is made in a context in which she is declaring her strength/courage to be equivalent to a man's, something other women do not possess—a lack that disqualifies them from sitting in the male ritual role of healing *pīr*.

In *Writing a Woman's Life* (1988), Carolyn Heilbrun writes of the difficulty women have often experienced in writing authentically about their own or other women's lives since the models for biographies or autobiographies have historically been male, particularly in the nineteenth and early twentieth centuries. She illustrates the importance of models when she writes about T. S. Eliot's difficulty in his experimentation in *Samson Agonistes*. His biographer, Peter Ackroyd, writes that this was the result of there being "no literary context for such writing from which to draw energy or inspiration. . . . He always needed [such a] safety net, as it were, before he indulged in his own acrobatics" (1984, 147). Heilbrun concurs: "It is precisely such a safety net that is absent from women's lives, let alone their writings. How are they to imagine forms and language they have never heard? How are they to live to write, and to write that other women may live?"(1988, 39). Amma's life narratives and informal conversations suggest that she, too, lacks such a safety net, a previously articulated story or model for female religious authority and action in the public domain upon which she can base or to which she can connect her own innovative position and life story. Amma says that out of all her *pīr's* female disciples, only she and her (now dead) sister have engaged in this kind of healing practice, specifically one involving writing. Not even her own *pirānimā* knew this practice. Her only models of public spiritual authority within the Sufi contexts she lives in are male, and it is with these authorities and male traditions that she negotiates a position for herself as a female healer.

Interestingly, while Amma views her own role as a healer to be outside the bounds and possibilities of her gender, when I asked many of Amma's neighbors and patients whether other women could do what she was doing, the answer was almost always a variant of "Any woman can do this, provided she can read Arabi" or "if she is a *pirānimā*." I suggest that their vision of potentiality is possible, in part, because Amma's life as a healer articulates a new possibility or model. Although this model might not be directly available to most of Amma's patients because they are not married to a *pīr*, it expands their existing repertoire of *possible* female stories. This is the way of social transformation: the interaction of "individual agency and [the constraints of] social structure" (Personal Narratives Group 1989, 5).

Juxtaposing traditional expectations of a woman's life and *jāti* with Amma's public life of ritual action, authority, and economic independence suggests that she and other women in her community must continually negotiate the contradictions they experience between the models they are given to live by, the stories they hear and see enacted, and the lives they lead. Amma straddles what she perceives to be the boundaries of gender: she experiences and identifies with the troubles of "woman" but at the same time has developed a power and authority to heal that is traditionally positioned beyond the options available to her *jāti*.

Other Female Healers and Specialists

I often asked both Hindu and Muslim patients and neighbors whether they knew other female healers or *pirānimā* who practiced like Amma—meaning a woman who met both men and women, both Muslims and Hindus, and charged money. Most respondents first answered affirmatively but upon reflection could not name or direct me to any others. One of Amma's young male disciples said he had gone all around the city to all types of healers (looking for a cure for his chronic weakness) before he found Amma, but he had not met any other female healers— they were all *murśids*. I myself met only four other Muslim women who were professional religious specialists/healers during the decade I visited Amma regularly, although many laywomen practice some kind of healing recitations and prayers in their own homes. Of these four, two women began their practice only after they became widows at ages 50 and 60. A third is the daughter of a *pīr* and is married to someone who is not a religious specialist; the fourth is slightly younger than Amma and is also a *pirānimā*. All four women address problems similar to those brought to Amma: marriage proposals or lack thereof, infertility, misbehaving children, errant or abusive husbands, and "trouble" in the house. The scope of Amma's practice is wider, however, including ailments such as child-hood fever and spirit possession. Three of the four healers do not accept direct payment for their services and treat only female patients/clients—thus differing significantly from Amma. The fourth does meet the 'public' and charges money, but she does not give *written* prescriptions.

The first healer is a married to the *muršid* caretaker of a small *dargāh* behind the Secunderabad railway station. Although the primary tomb is that of a male saint, the shrine is called a "women's *dargāh*" because women in particular go there in order to have various problems solved. Because women so dominate the space, they are free to take off their *burqās* once inside; the space approximates the inside of their homes, much as Amma's healing room does (where most patients do not take off their *burqās*, however, because of the crowded space and the relatively short time they are in the room). A middle-aged Muslim friend told me she preferred the Secunderabad station *dargāh* to others because of this freedom and the community of women there. They take their complaints to the *pirānimā*, who prescribes that they spend a certain number of nights at the *dargāh*. Several of this *pirānimā*'s patients told me that the reason you have to sleep at the *dargāh* is that if you sleep there, the saint appears to the *pirānimā* in her dreams and tells her what the your problem is. The *pirānimā* herself explains that she talks with both the male saint and his wife (who is also buried at the *dargāh*) just like she talks to her patients in waking moments but that no one else can hear their response. However, she says she does not like to bother the *bābā* [saint] with such mundane things as the physical complaints her clients bring—in fact, the miracle of this *bābā* is that he never defecated or urinated, so he is not concerned with matters of the body. To keep from troubling him all day long, when he is focused on Allah, she sets a particular time in the late evening to talk with him. When I asked the friend who first took me to the shrine how women decide whether to go to a healer such as Amma or to the *dargāh*, she said that they go to Amma when they do not have time or money to spend nights at the *dargāh*. About ten women were staying at the *dargāh* when I first visited; they had been there from between two weeks and seven months.[10] The *pirānimā* of this *dargāh* does not take direct payment for her services but benefits from offerings made at the shrine, which her husband manages. This *pirānimā* and Amma know about each other (although they have never met) and there seemed to be a sense of competition between them when I talked about one to the other. The *dargāh pirānimā* criticizes Amma for "demanding" payment for her services, and Amma criticizes the *dargāh pirānimā* for "not giving anything" (i.e., amulets or something tangible for healing). The wives of many *dargāh* caretakers [*sajjāda-niśīn*] in Hyderabad serve as ritual specialists in one way or another; however, their services are usually accessible only to women.

The second female specialist is the evening attendant at a relatively minor tomb of a woman saint within the compound of one of the largest *dargāhs* (Dargah Yusufayn) in Hyderabad. During the day she frequently carries out a ritual in her home called *dastarkhān*. In this ritual, an individual or group recites the ninety-nine names of God and/or the *kalmā* by counting out seeds into piles on a large cloth spread out on the floor, one for each name or recited *kalmā*. (The term "*dastarkhān*" means "tablecloth" and is the term used for the cloth spread on the floor around which families sit and eat.) Women ask this female specialist to perform *dastarkhān* on their behalf when they are experiencing a particular problem. She then invites other women in her community to participate and assist her by counting out the piles of seeds; she receives no direct payment for her services. These services are rather mechanical or instrumental; that is, they require time but not necessarily spiritual power or wisdom. The patients themselves could perform the *dastarkhān* to the same effect, but since they do not have time to do so, they "cause it to be done" and receive the benefits. In the evenings, this same female practitioner sits at the grave of a minor female saint and blesses anyone who stops by tapping them on the shoulders with a peacock-feather broom and spreading their offerings of rose petals on the grave.

The third female healer I met is a widow in her late sixties who lives with her only son and his wife. Her particular skill is the ability to communicate directly with the *jinn* and receive answers to questions a client may pose. In a practice similar to Hussein's *hazrat*, she gazes into a black shiny stone and uses concentration and recitation of the names of God or certain verses from the Quran to call the *jinn* onto that surface. She performs this service on an irregular basis in her son's home or the homes of family, friends, and friends of friends. She told me she had always been interested in spiritual things and in learning this skill in particular because her father and uncle were specialists in this skill. She went to a guru only seven years ago to learn how to communicate with the *jinn*. Her guru is a *murśid* who writes amulets and practices other healing techniques similar to those of Amma; however, while he was willing to teach this woman *ḥazrat*, he has specifically forbidden her from writing.

In contrast to Amma, the female practitioners described above have an exclusively female Muslim clientele and they do not receive direct payment for their services. Amma's mixed-gender clientele that is affiliated with multiple religious traditions and the direct economic relationship she establishes with them place her in the public domain—a traditionally male domain. Amma's economic independence also sets her apart from many of the female patients she meets.

The fourth woman I will describe is a specialist I met only the night before I left Hyderabad in the summer of 1995 after almost a full year of fieldwork. As often happens in the serendipitous processes of fieldwork, I did not meet the person who took me to this specialist until the last week of my fieldwork. My contact was a highly educated Muslim man (he had a Ph.D. in food sciences) whom I met in the "court" of a famous *pīr* in Hyderabad, whose renown is partially based on the fact that he has met with and given *tāvīz* to numerous politicians. The food scientist had been bringing his mentally ill daughter to this *pīr* for treatment for several months, after allopathic and psychiatric treatments for schizophrenia had failed. She had been amenorrheic for several years but had started her period again after two months of treatments from this *pīr*, drinking from saucers on which he had written Quranic verses and names of God. When I told the scientist of my work and asked if he knew of any women like Amma, he said yes, there was a *pirānimā* who lived near the airport who meets the 'public' every Tuesday and Thursday night and he would be happy to take me to meet her.

This female healer fits the criteria I have outlined as distinguishing a professional from a lay healer: she meets the public, including men and Hindus, and charges money for her services. She differs from Amma in one very significant way, however: she does not write. Her diagnostic process is to "read" lemons. On a first visit, she gives the patient several lemons that the patient should bring back the next week; then, depending on how the lemons have shriveled (or not), the healer makes a diagnosis. She also goes into trance, during which time she prays over and for the patient. The man who took me to this healer had before and after pictures of the lemons the healer had given to his daughter, which showed a significant difference; he thought that the treatment had helped, but it was not as strong as that of the famous *pīr* they were now visiting. He was, of course, very interested in Amma and visited her after my departure, but Amma reported that her prescription had been house exorcism and that the scientist had thought it was too expensive and had not followed through with it.

Amma views herself as distinct from and superior to these female religious specialists, whose domains of practice are more restricted than hers. She expresses disdain for the *pirānimā* associated with the women's *dargāh* as someone whose service was not of the same quality as her own, which is distinguished by its written product. Amma asked me directly, "What does she give? Does she write *tāvīz*? No! Does she write *fālitā*? No! She gives nothing. She's only a 'food-eater' [i.e., she takes money without giving anything in return]."

Amma's Qualifications as a Female Healer

Both Amma and Abba agree that Amma's access to her particular healing profession, particularly meeting the 'public', is first dependent upon Abba's ritual/religious position as a *murśid*. Amma's position as *pirānimā* is a minimal, albeit not sufficient, requirement for her ritual role, and few *pirānimās* become healers. Abba asserted many times that it was only with his permission that Amma could sit in this position; if he took that permission away, she would have to stop. Early in my fieldwork in 1990, I asked Amma if the young man sitting across the table from her was her disciple [*murīd*]. She seemed hesitant to respond but finally said "No, not really." The young man interjected, "I am a disciple of *both* Amma and Abba." During those first days that I sat at her healing table, Amma seemed to have difficulty acknowledging to me (perhaps because I was an outsider) that she had her own disciples, since this is part of the role of a *pīr* but not of the role of a *pirānimā*. However, by the end of the seven weeks I spent with her in 1990–1991 and in the years that followed, she talked of her disciples more easily. Both Amma and her disciples experience her as a guru/teacher; however, this is not a formalized, named role available to her as a woman in these contexts.

While literacy is seldom a requisite in mystical traditions such as the Sufi tradition to which Amma and Abba belong, it *is* a requisite of the particular healing system within which Amma practices, and it is the qualification Amma often emphasizes in differentiating herself from other female healers. It also distinguishes her from Abba, who does not and cannot fill the role of healer because he is not literate in the Arabic script. The requirement of this level of literacy stands in stark contrast to that required of many male and female Hindu healers whose authority (and diagnoses and prescriptions for patient action) is derived from possession by the goddess and has no orientation toward a written text. Abba says he had an opportunity in his youth to learn the Arabi script but at that point in his life he simply had no interest in it; he proudly added, however, that he did learn the 'roman' script when he served in the British army during the 'German war'. Two of his brothers are also *mursids*, but they know Arabi script and use it in healing practices.

Amma's literacy in Arabi script is not unique for Muslim women of her generation; many were given a traditional education at home (a few in secular schools) so that they could read the Quran. Arabi literacy is increasing among younger women in Hyderabad, who acquire it in both formal and informal educational settings. However, even among younger women, Amma's active use and manipulation of the script—the production of writing—is unusual; such manipulation of pen to paper characterizes a male sphere of ritual activity from which women are excluded. In later years Amma taught her youngest daughter, Rehma, how to "read the *tasbi*" [prayer beads; reading implies interpreting how they swing]. But, Rehma told me, she does not know about *abjad*: "I use *tasbi* and diagnose women's problems only." Her husband has made clear his disapproval of women meeting the public and has not given his wife permission to do "this kind of work." But Amma is his elder and his mother-in-law, so he does not criticize her directly.

When I first asked Abba if he also healed or could heal if he wanted to, he did not give his lack of literacy in the Arabic script as the reason he did not do so; rather, he attributed it to his gender. He said that he *could* heal and does heal children, but since most of the patients are women, it is better that Amma, as a woman, touch their heads:

I can do children, but if you're sitting over there saying, "I have trouble here; I have trouble there," I can't put my hands on you, right? More women come here. They can't tell me things about the night; women can't tell me certain things, "It's like this, my husband's done this; he's done that." Mostly it's women's matters that go on here. There's some benefit in that.

Several female patients concurred when I asked them if they came to Amma because she was female. They nodded their heads. "If it's a man, you have to sit far away from him and he doesn't listen to you. Amma listens carefully."

On another occasion, Abba elaborated on the benefits of being a female healer in this context:

Khalid used to do this kind of healing work independently for a while. But look: like he used to work here in front of us, he would do the work quickly, quickly [as opposed to Amma's relaxed style]. But it didn't work to do it independently [without Amma]. It's like when the prime minister was Indira Gandhi. When she was no longer living and someone else wanted to become minister, it didn't work, right? Isn't that right? The thing is this: Amma is Amma; Amma is Amma. Just because you sit there doesn't make you Amma, does it? It's like this. I don't sit there because mostly women come here. Because women come here, I can't sit there. And they say "I have a problem here, a problem there," and you have to put your hand there and you have to pray over them. Then look, people will say, "What is this? He's a *mursid* [a man]; what is this? He puts his hands on women." And they'll give him a bad name. So she sits there [at the healing table] and I sit here [in the store]. That's the way it is.

In actuality, at least one-third of Amma's patients are men; the objection that a woman who "should be observing *parda*" is touching male patients in such a healing context would seem to be potentially more objectionable than the objections to a spiritual male leader touching women. Amma herself said that there is nothing wrong with a man touching women's heads if he's a *murśid*, such as Khalid, who does bless women by putting his hand on their heads. Although Abba is always in the room when female patients are "confiding female problems" to Amma, the perception is that it is a women's space. A female patient confirmed Abba's perceptions of gendered accessibility to Amma: "I come to her because she's a woman. If it's a man, you have to sit far away from him and he doesn't listen to you. Amma listens with her full attention [*dhyān*]."

A Hindu engineer who had brought his wife to Amma answered my query about why he brought her here rather than to a Hindu healer: "I heard about her great *muhabbat* and *śakti* [love and spiritual power]." Other patients agreed, comparing Amma's patience with the impatience of Khalid, who periodically helps her at the healing table:

He's 'express,' and Amma is 'passenger' [making reference to express and passenger trains]. [Amma laughs with the patient speaking and adds] Yes, and there is more 'public' [more people] on the 'passenger' train. He should go into business with me, and then he would become famous.[11]

Abba identified his own style with that of his son:

My rule [*rāj*] is one thing and hers is another. If you come to Hazur [Abba], I get angry, and you say, "Don't go to Hazur." If you go to Amma, she speaks with great love. [She says,] "Today your illness will go away." [The patients who are listening laugh and agree.] What did I tell you earlier? Love. Love is the greatest thing. Her love is greater. What do I have? One, two; I do the work and tell them to go. What does she do? [She says], "No, my son, it's like this; it's not like that." They come crying and go away laughing.

Abba continued by suggesting that Amma's love—a mother's love—is a reflection, a small fraction of, the love of God itself:

Amma has the love of sixty mothers. . . . If a mother is all dressed up for a wedding and her child falls, she'll pick him/her up without worrying about her sari. The work of a mother is the greatest. But still, government officials ask for the name of a child's father, not the mother [for official records]. [It is said] "*Khilāfat* is a man's; *vilāyat* is a woman's." A woman's *bhakti* [lit., devotion; i.e., spiritual power] stops every month [when she menstruates], whereas a man's goes on and on. That's the only difference.

Through the use of the term "*khilāfat*," this commentary identifies the male world as the official, legal one. *Khilāfat* literally refers to the office or title of the leader, the caliph, and implies succession, or the right of succession to that office. In the context of the Sufi traditions in which Amma and Abba participate, it refers both to the authority to become a *murśid* and make disciples and the physical piece of paper that grants this authority (given by the *khilāfa's* own *murśid*). *Khilāfat* implies external institutional authority. This right of succession, hence to become a *murśid*, is denied to women.

What do women have? According to the saying, women have *vilāyat*. The most common meaning of this word in colloquial Hindi/Urdu is literally "foreign land" or "outlying province," and this is the way I first interpreted the saying. Using this definition, I thought *vilāyat* was making reference to the fact that women have no rights in the realm of spiritual succession in the same way that they do not have a right of formal "succession," or patrilineal inheritance in their natal homes; they are given to another home, a "foreign land," upon marriage. The implication in this reading of the saying, taking into account the next phrase regarding women's devotion, is that even though women are "foreigners" in spiritual succession, they still have some spiritual strength that is interrupted by the pollution of menstruation.

However, there is another more specialized meaning for *vilāyat* that is closer to the Sufi context in which Abba is speaking. The term "*vilāyat*" is related to "*walī*," which in Arabic literally means "one who is near, who is protected." The term has come to be applied to Sufi saints and in western scholarship on Sufism is traditionally translated as "friend of God." Using this definition, Abba's saying can be interpreted as being much more supportive of Amma and other women as spiritual practitioners than the first interpretation: "External, institutional religious authority belongs to men, but proximity to God [spiritual authority, wisdom] belongs to women."[12] However, for an Urdu speaker, a shadow of the meaning "foreign land" may linger even if "proximity to God" is the primary meaning, since women's spiritual authority must be negotiated as soon as it enters a public realm such as the one in which Amma practices.

Abba continued:

A woman has a very big heart. It's even bigger than a man's. She's ahead of a man in bravery [*bahāduri*]. There have been some very brave, bold women who lived in earlier times, two to three hundred years ago. There was Chand Bi Sultana [a female ruler of Ahmednagar] and the Rani of Jhansi. . . . They waged big battles. Women, too, are courageous [lit., have big hearts: *dilwāle*]. Allah has sent them into the world, too; He's also given them the law [*qānūn*].[13] It's not that [i.e., that they are discriminated against]. This is how it happened.

Murśids or *pīrs* are often characterized as being either *jamāli* or *jalāli*—cool and passive or heated and active. Abba calls himself *jalāli*, as do some of his disciples. He told me that *jalāli murśids* do not make good healers because people are afraid of them. Recognizing this, he is willing to "sit in the service" of Amma and fold *tāvīz* and *fālitā* for her.

Positions of Authority Negotiated

Abba does not sit in Amma's service passively, however. The healing room is often charged with a low-level, albeit usually good-humored, tension between two religious authorities: Abba the *pīr* teacher and Amma the *pirānimā* healer. Amma's position is directly dependent upon Abba's in the traditional hierarchy of *murśid-pirānimā*. But the fact that he does not have the literacy qualifications to heal in this system puts Amma in a superior position, both within the setting of the healing room and economically. Sharing authority in this way is an unusual situation for which there is no readily available cultural model. It is a story under construction, one bound to create tension. The unique nature of the relationship between Abba and Amma, one of dialogue, argument, and mutual respect, plays an important role in that story.

Abba periodically reminded those of us sitting in the healing room

151

of the interdependence of men and women, as dictated by Allah, and, further, the symbiotic relationship between himself and Amma. First, of the importance of honoring one's mother:

It's like this. I'll explain it to you—why the entire world lays at the feet of the mother. Her blood, her liver, blood—we've drunk her blood [in the womb]. [However] if there's no father, then how would a mother be born? This is also true. Adam. First Adam came into the world. The one we call Adam, then Hava [Eve].

When I asked Abba if he, too, had the knowledge to heal, he responded, "If I didn't learn, how did she learn? After becoming a guru [myself], I gave her my *bhakti* [devotion]." Another time, he explained, "She sits with great devotion [*bhakti*]. But if I get angry, her *bhakti* decreases," implying that her healing power is associated with her devotion to God, which is, in turn, interwoven with her relationship with Abba. He continued,

It's like there's a king [*bādśāh*] and there's his minister [*wazīr*]. I'm the king and she's the minister. The children are the subjects. If the king asks [for taxes, etc.], the subjects will give them to him through the minister. If the subjects do whatever they want [i.e., not follow the appropriate protocol for accessing the king] there will be a fight. What will the king do then? He'll be upset. If the king and minister cooperate, the subjects will stay under control.

In 1994–1995, Amma said her average monthly income from her healing practice was Rs. 7,000–8,000, whereas Abba's monthly retirement benefits were only Rs. 1,500. Amma's economic earning potential and independence sets her apart from most of her female patients and gives her a certain independence from Abba, too, regarding the decision-making in her practice. However, Abba continually verbalizes concern about the financial aspect of Amma's practice. He keeps track of the number of patients who are waiting and reprimands Amma for slowing down her pace (by making *pān*, for example) if the crowd is growing too big. One morning, Amma started healing much later than usual because her married daughter had just arrived for a visit and Amma was chatting and drinking tea with her. Patients were lining up, making Abba nervous. He kept calling to Amma, reprimanding her, "How long are you going to keep talking? Look at everyone waiting." Another day he complained that it was already noon and Amma was only on her fifth patient, "You should work and talk at the same time. That's why Hindustan [India] is behind [because people can't do this]." But Amma is rarely deterred from her own pace and style by criticisms such as these. When Hussein told her to hurry up—because "a lot of 'public' is sitting," her answer was, "Let them sit! The work is big, so how can it be accomplished in a hurry!"

For many years, I remembered with some skepticism Abba's comments about Amma's dependence on him and his permission for her to practice, thinking that surely Amma would be able to practice in the way that she does independently of Abba if only she had the appropriate title. I was sadly proven wrong after Abba died in 1998; only in his physical absence did it become clear to me how unusual Amma and Abba's relationship was and how her ability to practice such healing as a woman *was* dependent, to a great extent, on Abba's openness to new ideas and willingness to "let" Amma meet the public. After Abba's death, his disciples needed another male authority, and many of them whose first loyalties had been with Amma now abandoned her, no longer coming regularly to the healing room. They transferred their loyalties to her son Khalid, who was now the spiritual male authority. Amma felt the loss keenly.

Differentiated Gendered Speech Forms

Amma and Abba's differentiated ritual roles are reflected in their differentiated speech and narrative genres. As a *muršid*, someone who "shows the way—how one should live," Abba takes his role as a teacher seriously. As storekeeper, he has time to give frequent philosophical teachings, which he illustrates with religious and folk tales, to those congregated in the room. Abba often took it upon himself to answer the questions I was asking directly to Amma, a role she seemed content to let him assume. A standard opening for his teachings is: "How should we live? First we should do 'research' on ourselves: what should we do?" or:

If God sent you into the world, then why? If you're born, they why were you born? This is an important question. Why were you born into the world? If we're here, then what should we do? Allah wants us to remember him. He's given us ears to hear and feet to walk. First we should do 'research' on ourselves. Allah has sent us here—why? What should we do? What is the duty of parents? Of a sister? Of a brother? Or of elders and children?

Breath comes and goes. This much you should understand. If breath doesn't come for even two minutes, then it's all over and you die. If you understand this, you understand everything . . . [and he continues with a teaching on *nafs,* the lower nature of humans, and anger].

Other teachings elaborate on the importance of love or honesty or hard work, and these are often supported by Quranic narratives, stories of the saints, or folktales (see chapter 5 for extended examples).

Amma has little time for speech unrelated to the healing situation at hand, although she also gives short teachings periodically and assured me she knew the folktales in Abba's repertoire. She sometimes "co-performs" Abba's narratives, clarifying facts or even taking over dramatic moments of narration. However, Amma's speech genres in the healing room primarily consist of prayers, whispered or silent Quranic recitation, explanations of treatments, and conversational interaction with patients. She performs primarily personal narratives and what I have called "testimonials" to her spiritual authority and healing power rather than stories of saints or folktales. Her frequent use of personal narratives contrasts sharply with Abba's rhetorical and conversational genres, which include very few personal narratives of childhood, becoming a disciple and then a *murśid,* or any miracles he might have effected. His narrative and ritual performances focus on and are drawn from his ritual role, his identity as a *murśid,* rather than on his own individual history or personality. Once he became a *murśid,* his authority and right to be there were not questioned. Amma's authority and right to sit in a public ritual role, on the other hand, is never a given. Amma and Abba's differentiated genres of storytelling reflect their differentiated roles of teacher and healer (*pīr* and *pirānimā*) as well as the traditional constraints and freedoms of their gendered *jātis.*

Amma's Personal Narratives

Amma's personal narratives analyzed here are either answers to questions about her life and experience or are narratives performed as an integral part of her healing rhetoric. The narratives Amma performs begin to build up a shape and quality quite distinct from the life narratives of her female age-mates in the neighborhood. One of these women, Khalid's mother-in-law, with whom I ate many meals and drank many cups of tea, frequently tells unelicited narratives that are filled with personally drawn vignettes of her everyday life: the fear and dread of early marriage she experienced when visitors came to "look at her" as a young girl; the embarrassment of breastfeeding when her breasts were overflowing with milk and drenching her sari, which resulted in her hiding under a mosquito net while feeding her baby; an old deaf grandmother-in-law being teased by her grandchildren; the grief experienced over the death of a teenage son and the subsequent rounds from *dargāh* to *dargāh*, looking for relief from her grief.

Most of the personal narratives Amma told in response to my early direct questioning about her life were, in contrast, carefully chosen and constructed to provide a context for her life as a healer; many highlighted her uniqueness, both as a girl/woman among other women, and her unique spiritual qualities among both men and women. For example, when Amma first met my husband, she introduced herself with a description of her birth: "I was born during a big storm [*tūfān*]; they often told me about the big storm during which I was born. Ever since then, I've continued to be a big *tūfān*, and I deal with the *tūfāns* of others, here in the healing room." Amma takes pride in her high energy and activity level, telling me that she was "born to work. I'm strong because of my habit of working hard. It's not my habit to sit lazily in one place."

On another occasion, Amma fondly reminisced about her love of learning as a child, an inclination that might have contributed to a special relationship with her father, one that her five sisters did not share with him (Amma also had two brothers): "I know how to do everything—climb trees and ride a bicycle. The only thing I don't know how to do is swim. My father taught me everything. My father used to call me son, not daughter [*beṭā, beṭī nahīn*]. He always loved me like a son." This distinction between the terms *beṭā* and *beṭī* is an example of Amma's self-conscious positioning of herself on the male side of the distinction between male and female *jātis*. In colloquial Urdu, "*beṭā*" is a term of endearment, something like "my dear little one," that parents use to address little girls as well as boys. The usage is so common that most people would not give any significance to a girl being called *beṭā*/little boy, but Amma has chosen to make the grammatical gender distinction significant.

When I asked Amma how she got into this work, she told me she had followed "Allah's *bhaktī*" [devotion] from a young age; she would often sit for long periods and "remember Allah." According to her, the first external recognition of her unique qualities came from a Hindu teacher at the government school she attended until sixth grade. He observed her and encouraged her parents to keep her in school: "Watch this girl. She will become famous; she will become a good scholar." But her parents withdrew her from school at the end of sixth grade; most girls did not study beyond that level in those days. She got married at age 13, and the first of her eleven living children was born by the time she was 15. Even while raising a family, she said, "I remembered Allah. I had to take care of the house, the store, the children. I had to run everything. The children grew up. Then I took up this work. After taking this up, one more daughter was born." She caught herself, "No, the youngest was born, and *then* I took up this work." Amma continued her narrative:

My Nizambad guru, Mahmud Alam, gave me instruction, Allah's instruction. Learning from that, I received Allah's love. Receiving that, I began healing people. All kinds of people began to come, with *kartūt*, *bānāmati*, *asrat*, and all kinds of problems. . . . Removing their problems, I continued to receive Allah's love. If you don't love Allah, then can you do this work? Can you? Until you receive His love, then how can you do this work?

When I first met Amma in 1989 and asked her about her early life, she told me that she had had a vision [*nazar*] soon after she was married in which she saw words "like the credits on the screen at the end of a movie" and that this had propelled her to her healing practice. When I asked her about the words of that vision, she said that she had had many visions but could not tell me more about the contents of this particular one. She did, however, describe others:

Do you know what happened once? When I was playing with my breath [meditating], I had a vision of my guru, a vision of light [*rošnī*]. From this, love was born. Love comes from light [*bijlī*; the same word used for electricity]. When I'm talking to you, it's not me talking, but my light. Everything is light [*rošnī*]; without light, I wouldn't exist, you wouldn't exist. Allah is light [*bijlī*]; He is radiance [*nūr*].

Whether or not she reveals their contents, it is clear that visions are an important element of Amma's life story to which she attributes much of her healing authority.

Amma first went to a guru when she was about 30 years old, when she "secretly" visited and obtained teaching from a guru in Nizambad.[14] She had seen the guru in a dream and he had told her various things. When she woke up, the guru was gone, but she remembered what he had said, identified him, and went to visit him.[15] After visiting the guru, she returned to Abba and told him that she had made a great mistake by visiting this guru without telling Abba first. Instead of being angry as she had expected, he said, "Take me to him. I, too, will learn." This guru initiated Abba first as a *murīd* and, at age 40, as a *muršid*. When Amma expressed her interest in learning the specific mantras necessary for healing, the guru referred her to his own guru, and it is through the latter that Amma learned the specifics necessary to become a 'public' healer. Amma laughed when she thought about the implications of her receiving teaching from her guru's guru: "My [first] guru is my *pīr bhaiyā* [*pīr* brother] and Mahmud Alam is my grandfather *pīr*." According to Amma, her initiation from her first guru and then learning the healing techniques from *his* guru fit into a broader interest in learning all kinds of new things:

I'm like you. I love to learn. Sitting here [at the healing table], hear and learn everything going on here. You'll learn and then you'll become like me. One should always keep on learning. Even now, I have a great passion [*šauq*] to go on increasing my knowledge [*ilm*]. One should learn everything that one can. But what to do? I don't know English. Who's going to take the time to teach me English and Hindi? There's no end to learning. I've been interested in learning ever since I was small. But what to do? Now my eyes have become weak. Otherwise, I used to take books and read every night, late into the night.

On another occasion, she attributed her love of learning to God himself and to those spiritual elders around her, "Like you, I have the desire for everything. It's a desire from God. I also got it from humans, from the pious ones [*buzurgān*] around me. I also got it from my husband, didn't I?" But, Amma acknowledged, learning was a process that would never be complete:

Jo-ice, no matter how many books you write, even then, it will be too little, there will still be knowledge that is not included. Leaving my small children, that's all I did: write, write, write. Twenty-five years have passed. But even then, I haven't learned everything. So no matter how much you write, it won't be enough. Even if you used all the trees in the universe as pens, even then. . . .

Amma first practiced her healing among extended family and friends, as many women do (except that other laywomen do not write). It was only after her last child was born, when she was about 35 years old, that she began to meet the 'public' like she does now. Her practice and renown have grown considerably over the years I have worked with her, along with the financial remuneration which accompanies such success. Between 1989 and 1991, success was marked by a shift from sitting on the floor in front of a low wooden table to "moving up" to a folding table and chairs. Amma told me that her success greatly angered her first guru and that he sent the evil eye [*asrat*] toward her. However, she successfully deflected and returned it to him, and Amma has had no further contact with him. She considers her "grandfather guru" to be her real guru. This guru, Mahmud Alam, died around 1984, at the age of 90. When this *pīr*'s very elderly widow (who was said to be 100 years old at the time) visited Amma in her home, several other women who had taken initiation with the *pīr* came to greet her and sit at her feet. The *pīr* sisters began exchanging stories of their experiences with the *pīr*, each story claiming some kind of special relationship with him through physical objects they had received from him, such as pieces of clothing. Amma proclaimed that she had received a *kurtā*, a much larger piece of cloth than the handkerchiefs and scarves the other women had received. She interpreted this as a sign that she had been favored by the *pīr*, and she continued to assert boldly her uniqueness: "While he may be dead to the rest of you, to me he's still living."

Once when I was trying clarify exactly when and at what stage of child-rearing she had begun her public healing, Amma again used her life story to frame her unique position as a healer:

I've followed Allah's *bhakti* ever since I was small. Then I got married. Even after I got married, I kept on praying [lit., reading] continually. When I had children, I sat out for forty days; then I'd start up again. Then I started the store; since I started it, I've never left it. I worked in the house and raised the children—it's a 40-year-old store. Then I met a guru and became a disciple. I became a disciple, then I, too, became a guru. I'm also making disciples. And I'm continuing on.

After I had known Amma for nearly ten years, I heard quite a different account of her life as she and I were sitting together alone in her courtyard on a Friday morning, her day off. She began by reporting the disappointments each of her sons had been to her, but by the end she had "broken into performance" (Hymes 1975),[16] a mode marked by her heightened body language and tone of voice, elaborated imagery and, perhaps most important, her own sense of the narration as a performance, as she concluded: "And so, Jo-ice, this is my big story; it would make a good 'film', wouldn't it?"

I used to be so independent. Now I can't manage to do everything myself. Otherwise, I've been such a hard worker all my life, such a worker. It's no easy thing that I've raised so many children. But, unfortunately, all my sons aren't educated. Even though I tried so hard and it was my wish to educate and make good all my children, only one [Khalid] did it; the rest didn't study. One quit school after seventh class, the other after sixth, and another after ninth. What can I do if my family isn't good, if my offspring aren't good? Who can I ask about this?

When I ran the store, weighing things again and again on the scale, my hands would get sore. This entire neighborhood would take things on credit. They still owe me a lot of money. But I thought, "Okay, I've done it all in the service of Allah." Then I took up this 'line' [her healing practice]. Everything in the house went [by the wayside]. I sat in His service. The children were very small then; that youngest one had been born only forty days before. I even stopped nursing her.[17] I sat in the room for four years [meditating]; only after four years, I came out and started this work. I used to eat just one date early in the morning and one in the evening.[18] All my fat disappeared and just bones remained; only my face stayed the same.

Joyce: Did your *murśid* ask you to do all this?

Amma: My *murśid* asked me to do *zikr*. I got permission to do so from above [from God]. My husband found a piece of bread and tried to force it into my mouth, but it came right out; taking a single swallow, I started throwing up immediately. Since then, he's stopped interfering in my affairs. Since that [youngest] daughter was born, we've stopped being husband and wife [stopped having sex]—nothing. After that, I kept on menstruating for a while. I prayed to Allah and that, too, has stopped. Now it's been fifteen years, and that, too, has stopped. Now I'm just like a man; there's nothing; I'm like a man, without [menstrual] pain [*ab marad kā hai, na dard kā hai*]. Now there's only Allah, only Allah. It's a wonderful life, isn't it? Just do your work, eat a bit, do the *zikr*, wash your face, have a bit of *pān*, remember Allah, then come and sit in my place; then get up in the evening, eat a bite, pray again. This is how time passes.

They say, "If there's no sorrow or worry of the world, it's only due to your kindness, oh Lord." It's only due to the work of the *pīr* that I don't have any desires. The children have grown up; I've gotten them all married, so I don't need to worry about any of them. If I die, they'll all gather, take me [to the graveyard], lay me down, cover me up, and return back [to their families]. They'll look after themselves and their families. If any one of them wasn't married, I would be worried, because no one cares for anyone else. Now that all of them are independent, they'll look after themselves.

But the life of the youngest son is in a terrible state.

Joyce: Someone gave him *davā*, right?

Amma: Let them do it; what ever happens, doesn't Allah know it? He [youngest son] used to run after me calling "Ammi, Ammi"; now he's become an enemy. Yesterday he came after not having come [to the healing room] for five days. He just stood over there; he saw me, but he didn't even bother to speak to me. . . . [Amma continues to complain bitterly about her grown sons who are still financially dependent upon her instead of supporting her.]

And so, Jo-ice, this is my big story; it would make a good 'film', wouldn't it? Still [after all this], I keep laughing.

During this reminiscence, Amma was not constrained by the time and rhetoric of the healing room. The opening frame of her narrative was similar to what any middle-aged woman's might have been, "I used to be such a strong woman, but now I'm unable to do everything myself." But it is not her habit to perform a narrative simply of complaint and/or suffering, even outside the healing context, and quite quickly the story shifts to one of her own virtuosity and spiritual strength, juxtaposed with a family life filled with trouble. While Amma begins with a narrative of suffering that might be shared by what she calls the "*jāti* of women," she quite quickly shifts the persona of the self by again setting herself apart when she frames the difficulties with "I've done it all in the service of Allah." She sustains this unique persona, distinct from that of other women who suffer, when she interjects, "It's a wonderful life, isn't it?" and ends the narration of suffering with "Still, I keep laughing."

In personal narratives, Amma only indirectly refers to difficulties she may have encountered as a female disciple and, later, healer, such as in the following narrative:

Jo-ice, this 'line' of work is not easy. When you take up this work, you have to face a lot of problems—you're tested. If you can bear that, then you'll meet God. You have to have patience. Some people will abuse you, some hit you, some say bad things about you, others say other things. You have to pray to God continually. You have to be patient and pray, "Oh Allah, make him a good person, make him understand. Make him good and let me take this trouble. Oh Allah, put him on the correct path. Accept our praise." Like this. There are enemies, but you have to embrace even them.

Once time when our guru came to our house, we had a hen. I slaughtered it; I cooked it. But we didn't have any flour in the house; we didn't have any money. Even so, I went to the bazaar and brought flour, cooked some breads, and prepared everything. [Living in the house] were my husband's sister, my husband, and two of my two sons. All of them were against my guru, saying, "How can he come just like this [without notice]?" Let them say whatever they want. I wouldn't let him go. When he came, I spread things out for him, fed him. He didn't touch any of the food, though. "Allah!" I said to myself, and kept quiet. The people in my house gave me a lot of trouble. My sisters, brothers, children, everyone gave me a lot of trouble. But I've always prayed, "Allah, look after everything." What do I have? Everything is His. Whoever is patient will never be disappointed. God accepts their prayers [duā]. Why? Because He is tolerant. Like mothers. Don't we tolerate our children? Then think, wouldn't God tolerate the world?

In other conversations in later years, particularly as her health and eyesight began to deteriorate and then after Abba died, Amma began to interject more frequently into both her healing and everyday speech comments such as, "All a woman's troubles have visited me: a son leaving his wife, a son leaving his mother, a child dying, and finally a husband dying." I once asked her whether or not she could treat members of her own family, and she answered, "No. I can give light to other people's houses, but there's no light [rośnī] in my own. I haven't been given permission by my guru to treat my own family. Tāvīz don't work for your own family members. A 'doctor' can't treat his/her own family, right? I'm a learned one [āmil], a 'doctor'. I can treat others, but not myself." Performances of personal narratives are a site for articulating and negotiating this tension between personal and professional roles of mother/wife and healer; depending on the context of performance, the tension may or may not be resolved narratively.

Amma's Testimonial Tales

Amma "breaks through into performance" more naturally when she tells what I have called "testimonials"—stories that recount her "miracles," her success as a healer. I distinguish these stories from life history or personal narratives because they are a more natural and frequent part of Amma's healing narrative. She tells testimonial stories as illustrations of her unique healing power and authority and to establish her credibility among her patients, particularly first-time patients.

One testimonial I heard numerous times recounts Amma's power manifest through her induction of labor in her sister, whose baby had died at term in utero. Through repeated tellings, this testimonial has been standardized and given artistic, dramatic form. I provide one variant below:

My sister's labor wasn't starting. Her child had died in her womb. It died in the womb; the child had died. So what did they say? "The child has died, so you will have to have an operation." My brother-in-law told this to my sister.

So I went [to the hospital]. I went there, and what had happened? My brother-in-law had already signed for the operation. He signed and then I arrived. I took the paper and went to Shankar Amma [the female doctor]. I took it and tore it up. "What are you doing?" she asked. I said, "Give me until three o'clock tomorrow afternoon; do the operation then" [i.e., if labor hasn't started by then]. They took a 'TV X-ray' and the baby was dead.

I quickly went home, bathed, took my Book, and went back and sat there [in the hospital room]. The baby had been dead in the womb for seven days. . . . [indiscernible on tape]. I went in and sat down. I put water in a bucket and sat down.

[Joyce: The Book is the Quran, right? Amma: Yes.]

I took [the Book], read it, and sat down. Then, do you know what kind of vision came to me? [It was] of those who had caused it to happen, who had killed the baby [presumably *jinn*, devils, or humans who had cast the evil eye]. And of Malamat and Amma Jan [names of a devil and a female saint who were vying for the baby]. She was wearing a black blouse and sari. [The vision was of] Malamat-Amma Jan, Malamat-Amma Jan, Malamat-Amma Jan, Malamat-Amma Jan, trees, stones. I saw them as I was reading, and they saw me.

They came and sat down. She sat down like a tiger. "Bring some water," she said. "It's a beautiful child." I saw all this while I was reading. I saw the whole 'scene', like the 'cinema'. So I brought the water and drank it [it is not clear if she drank it or caused her sister to drink it]. She said, "The child's hand was causing it; now it's clean."

The Book was finished, and Malamat went and fell under a tree, and Amma Jan went over here, and the devils who had caused the death went over there, and my reading was finished.

[Her voice is competing with that of the screeching parrot outside, and a sentence is lost here.]

Patient to whom Amma is telling the story: So did she have the operation?

Amma: No. Do you know what happened after that? My brother-in-law came in, bringing the Book. It was two o'clock [in the morning of the day of the scheduled operation]. I told him, "Go to sleep." And I sat there eating *pān* [betel leaf], spitting, eating *pān*, spitting. I just sat there.

Al-lah, Al-lah. The pains started. My sister's pains started. They took her to the 'theatre'. At twelve o'clock she delivered. 'Normal', not in bits and pieces. Like her other two children, not in bits and pieces. The delivery happened. The child was blue, blue, blue. The hand was so white; you've never seen one so white. The face was like this [she puffs out her cheeks]. The smell was terrible.

The doctor called me, "Look," she said. "Yes, I saw it. And you said an operation would be necessary, and now the delivery has happened [naturally]."

There was no fever, nothing, and she was 'discharged' in three days.

When I went back [to the hospital] for my second daughter's delivery, she [the doctor] said, "Amma, you go out and I'll come in [into the room]. If I come in, what will the baby do? I'll stay outside." I said, "No, come in Shankar Amma." She said, "No, Amma, you come out and then I'll come in. If you stay in there, I won't come in."

[Amma laughs heartily.]

Other testimonials are only a few sentences, as when Amma re-counted her power to "close a dog's mouth." She had been walking along when she encountered a barking dog. She said some words to close its mouth and it was silenced. The worried owner of the dog came out of the house to see what had caused the sudden change, but Amma told him not to worry—the dog was not harmed, only silenced. The owner recognized Amma as someone special ("You are full of Allah's *bhakti* [de-votion]"), and Amma continued on her way.

Amma is not alone in her performance of testimonial tales; her pa-tients also recount stories of her healing successes as they sit in the court-yard awaiting their turn to see her or at her healing table as they hear problems of other patients. Amma sometimes elicits these stories by ask-ing patients to come back when their problem is cured so that she and other patients can see and hear about the results of her treatment. Mothers frequently bring in pudgy, healthy babies who have been healed from failure to thrive or who are the results of Amma's intense infertility treat-ments [*nahāvan*]. Or wives return to affirm Amma's treatment of failing marriages. One young Hindu mother whose husband had been drinking too much, had mistreated her, and had quit going to work returned to Amma's healing room with her mother to testify to the success of Amma's treatment. She was dressed in a new brightly colored sari and new glass bangles—signs of an auspicious wife—and her face was beaming as she told patients in the courtyard and at Amma's healing table the story of her husband's mouth being successfully "shut." She and her mother brought sweets to offer as *fātihā* [religious offering] at the flagpole, an offering officiated by Abba. The patient's mother then distributed the sweets to all who were present in the healing room and courtyard.

One of Amma's male disciples is particularly fond of dramatically performing testimonial tales of Amma's power. He is a railway worker between the ages of 35 and 40 who comes to sit across the table from Amma and assist her whenever he is not traveling for his work. One of his tales is an example of what might be called a negative testimonial. A patient had come in to ask Amma to diagnose why her baby had died. Amma used the *abjad* technique of diagnosis and proclaimed that the cause of death had been the evil eye [*asrat*]. The disciple immediately reprimanded the mother for not having come in sooner and then told a testimonial of his brother's child, who had died a similar death. The brother had brought the child to the disciple narrating the story and asked for advice, and the disciple had told him to bring the baby to Amma. But his advice was ignored and the baby died.

Negative testimonials about Amma's own treatment are heard very rarely in her presence. An example of one such case is that of a Hindu man with a trembling hand who came back to Amma after three weeks of treatment that had produced no signs of improvement. On this visit, he came back with his rather skeptical father. When Amma told them that the failure meant that stronger, more expensive treatment would be required, they answered that they would make their decision and return the next day. Another man returned to say that he had been three-quarters healed (literally, "three annas better," an anna being a coin that is no longer in circulation) and was coming back, optimistically, for the last quarter. A young female patient whose husband had run off with another woman complained to Amma that even after burning all the *fālitā* she had been given, he had not come back. Amma defended her treatment by saying that it had failed because the patient had not given her the other woman's name the first time. She wrote out another set of *fālitā* with the name now written on it. The patient complained, "How long am I going to have to keep doing this?" to which Amma replied emphatically, "He *will* return!"

The form and content of these testimonials are similar to tales told at the tombs of Muslim saints. When I visited various *dargāhs* and tried to elicit the "story of the saint" from visitors to or caretakers of the tomb, I was rarely given the story of the saint's life (a hagiography) but rather heard a story of his or her miracles [*karāmat*]—the deeds of the saint.[19] It should be noted that these narratives are told *about* the *pīr*, not *by* the *pīr*, and differ in this important way from Amma's performances. Amma structures her own story, however, on a similar model of *karāmat*; she chooses to tell about her deeds, her "miracles," more often than about the details of her personal life.

While Amma's healing room is a context where many stories of the "*jāti* of woman" are told—generally stories of suffering and trouble—and their telling helps to strengthen the identity of that caste, most of Amma's performances of personal narratives, testimonials, and healing rhetoric articulate quite a different story, even those that begin with suffering. Amma identifies this story—of chosen-ness, uniqueness, and acts of authority in the public sphere—as positioned outside the boundaries of a woman's *jāti*. This disclaimer may help Amma reconcile the contradiction between her own life story and the models for gender laid out before her. It may also help give the appearance of story that does not directly challenge the patriarchal traditions within which Amma lives and practices. I suggest, however, that for the women listening to Amma's story, its telling extends the boundaries of gender and that her very presence in a public ritual role embodies an alternative gender ideology.

RELIGIOUS IDENTITIES AT
THE CROSSROADS

5

All these are the same.

While Amma asserts that gender boundaries are impenetrable and rigid, the second half of her assertion maintains that boundaries of religious identities are permeable—that there are no true differences between followers of different religious traditions: "There are only two castes: men and women. Hindus, Muslims, Christians—they're all the same." I was often asked by patients sitting around Amma's healing room what I was writing in my little notebook. I responded that I wrote down whether a patient is Hindu or Muslim, his/her gender and relative age, the nature of the complaint, and Amma's diagnosis and prescriptions. Hearing my answer, Amma often shook her head and expressed disappointment in how little I seemed to have learned sitting at her side, sighing, "Jo-ice, haven't you learned anything? It's not a question of Hindu or Muslim *here* [i.e., in the healing room]. We all breathe in and out, don't we?"

In some contexts, of course, such as marriage and death, political contexts where religious identities might impact voting blocs in elections to legislative bodies, decisions about admissions into universities, and in relation to inheritance rights as determined by different religious systems of family law, differences between Hindus and Muslims matter very much. In other contexts of self-representation, highly educated members of religious communities might identify textual traditions as the crucial identity markers and identify vernacular practices that are not described or proscribed in the texts as extraneous to the tradition, not "real" Hinduism, Islam, or Christianity. In Amma's healing room, these differences are overridden by what is shared, by the crisis of illness. But more is shared between patients than simply human affliction and attraction to a charismatic healer. Patients and disciples also share features of and actors in a cosmological structure that assumes the possibility of spiritual illness and healing; they share knowledge and acceptance of a minimal ritual grammar whose performance impacts the spiritual/physical world. And Amma helps create the inclusive nature of her healing room, the *caurāstā* where there is no Hindu and Muslim, through ritual and narrative performances that draw on motifs and grammars that cross these boundaries of religious difference.

Terms of Religious Identities

Amma and Abba had one male disciple who, in the early years during which I visited the healing room, was consistently referred to as their "Hindu disciple," even though he had become a disciple through the formal initiation ritual with Abba. I was puzzled by this designation since I knew that part of the initiation ritual included reciting the *kalmā,* "There is no god but God and Muhammad is His prophet," and I had been taught that simply reciting this confession of faith made a person a Muslim. I asked Abba if someone necessarily became a Muslim when s/he became his disciple.

Joyce: . . . and Sati, your disciple, is he a Muslim now, or is he still a Hindu?

Abba: No, it's not like that. He's not a Hindu; he has drunk the cup from me [taken initiation][1] and has read the *kalmā.* He had faith, so that's it; it's not a question of Muslim or Hindu. That's all there is to it. It's a matter of conviction [*yakīn*]. If you have faith or conviction, then that's all there is; it's all Allah.

The appropriate designation for this disciple remained ambiguous. On the one hand, Abba firmly stated that he is *not* a Hindu and continued to declare that any designation of Hindu/Muslim was not relevant, yet in other contexts of everyday conversation and appellation, Abba called him his "Hindu disciple." Several years after I had been introduced to Sati as Abba and Amma's "Hindu disciple," after he had already grown his hair and beard (external identity markers as a Muslim), Sati was ritually circumcised with great celebration and feeding of guests. I was not present, but Sati proudly showed me his photograph book of the occasion, and the photographs of the garlanded guest of honor and banquet resembled photographs of a wedding. I realized then that *this* was what was necessary for him to make a total transition to a Muslim identity for purposes outside the healing *caurāstā*. Circumcision was the end of a long *process* of conversion. Only at this point did the disciple change his Hindu name, Sati, to a Muslim one, Mustang. The most important identification throughout the process, even after circumcision, however, was not "Hindu" or "Muslim" as named and bounded categories, but the *pīr/murīd* [master/disciple] relationship between Abba and Sati and the disciple/healer relationship with Amma.

The question of religious identities in South Asia, both self-identifications and identities imposed from the outside, has been the focus of heightened scholarly and political activity over the last two decades, particularly in light of the events during 1990–1992 surrounding the politicization of the Babri Masjid/Ram Janam Bhoomi site in Ayodhya and the destruction of the mosque.[2] Recent studies of both premodern and contemporary South Asia have shown that in practice and performance, boundaries and categories of identities were and are shifting or more permeable than many colonial and traditional academic categories might suggest. A commonly repeated postcolonial argument has been that the colonial census categories and other forms of categorization made religious identities more rigid than they were on the ground (see, among others, Gilmartin and Lawrence 2000; Hawley 1991; Oberoi 1994). The colonial census imposed the identifying term "Hindu" on a wide range of castes and tribes that were not Muslim or Christian but that had not self-identified as a single religious group before. Historians have also criticized the colonial constructions of periodization of Indian history that foregrounded the religious identity of kings and rulers (the Hindu ancient period, the Muslim period, and the British/colonial period) and have begun to suggest alternative ways in which South Asian individuals, communities, and political bodies have self-identified, including according to ethnic, geographic, economic, and linguistic criteria (see Talbott 1995, 1997).

Peter Gottschalk's work in contemporary rural Bihar (2000) similarly challenges a rigidified dichotomy of Hindus and Muslims by analyzing ways individuals negotiate multiple identities based on performatively contextualized narratives of individual and group memory. Vasudha Narayanan's work documents the participation of Tamil Muslims in Tamil literary traditions, both as scholars and composers; participation of Hindus in *dargāh* rituals; and performances by Muslim musicians at Hindu temples and festivals (2000). She observes, however, that while Muslim saints are frequently incorporated into the Hindu pantheon as consorts or friends and Hindus go on pilgrimage to *dargāhs*, Tamil Muslims do not similarly incorporate/reciprocate Hindu deities or sacred personages, rituals, or sites into their own practice on this level (91).

Several of the studies cited above assume and/or acknowledge religious difference (in belief and cosmology), but their authors are more interested in other axes of identity (such as region, language, family, gender, caste, and class) that, depending on context, supersede these boundaries of difference. I want to make room for the possibility that one basis for shared identity might also be *religious,* at the same time acknowledging the contemporary use and meanings of the terms Hindu and Muslim that mark important distinctions outside the healing room. At the healing table itself, narratives, ritual, and cosmology include what are often identified as Hindu and Muslim traditions and motifs, but Amma emphasizes what is shared across traditions and does not consider particular narratives or rituals that she performs to be either Muslim or Hindu. However, these fluid boundaries of identity are specific to the context of this (and other *caurāstā*) sites; as axes of identity move out from the healing room, identities might solidify.

Many scholars of South Asia have talked about elements of traditions that intersect at what I am calling the *caurāstā* in terms of borrowing, syncretization, or hybridization. Tony Stewart and Carl Ernst have care-

fully analyzed the language that is commonly used to describe the interaction of Hindu and Muslim traditions and found it to be condescending
toward and insufficient to describe what is experienced on the ground.
Ernst and Stewart observe that frequently "syncretism as both process and
description hinges on the assumption that those observed have inappropriately mixed cultural and religious categories that are intrinsically alien
to each other." Ernst and Stewart then proceed to examine metaphors
commonly used to describe syncretism and find that they have "generally
negative valuation": borrowing and influence, cultural veneer, alchemy, and
hybridization (2003, 586–587).[3]

Jackie Assayag introduces a different model in his analyses of village
festivals in rural Karnataka where both Muslims and Hindus participate
in each other's festivals (specifically Ugadi and Muharram). He has also
conducted fieldwork at shared sacred sites (shrines) and documented narratives associated with them. His analyses identify the processes at work
in these contexts as "acculturation" and "counteracculturation," in which
"coexistence may be a matter of competition—'competitive sharing'—and
a model of competitive syncreticism—'antagonistic tolerance'—among
Hindus and Muslims" (Assayag 2004, 19). Narratives and rituals that are
shared at these sites of religious activity often reveal competition and
power struggles between the two groups. We have examples of this kind
of tension in narratives performed outside the healing room, but not at
the *caurāstā* itself.

Our task here is to analyze the religious landscape of the healing room
in which Amma practices in such a way as to maintain its integrity without judging it as derivative or secondary to a "pure" or "real" Islam. While
Amma's particular method of diagnosis and prescriptions may be identified as Muslim, patients are not thinking primarily in terms of Hindu or
Muslim. They come to her primarily because of her reputation for healing
successes and spiritual authority to deal with negative spiritual forces.
Exactly *how* healing is effected is less of a concern to patients than their
perception and experience that it *does* take place—although, as we will
see below, they do not have to focus on the how because it is, in its
broadest parameters, familiar to them. None of the patients, Hindu or
Muslim, actually read or know exactly what is written on the amulets,
nor do they ask Amma the specifics of her healing system. So they would

not necessarily know the Islamic content of what is written on the amulets—the various names of Allah and *maukil* and numbers for particular verses from the Quran. Amma's assertion that "here [at this place] . . . all these are the same" implies that Hindu, Muslim, and Christian physical bodies, and the spiritual forces that affect them, exist within an expansive spiritual plane that crosses boundaries of difference; this common space is reflected and created through elements of shared ritual grammar, narrative motifs, and cosmology.

An Encompassing Cosmology

As one might expect, Amma and Abba emphasize through rhetorical performance primarily what is shared rather than what might create division between their patients and disciples. They often articulate an encompassing flexible cosmology that accommodates elements of both Hindu and Muslim worldviews. Part of this encompassing framework is the acceptance of a continuum of power and permeable boundaries between human and nonhuman worlds, as well as what kinds of beings populate the nonhuman world: deities, ghosts, angels, *jinn*, saints, and "devils." Amma and Abba as Muslim religious specialists in this multi-religious context *are* monotheists, but in a very different way than, for example, my Protestant Christian missionary parents, who worked in India for forty years. In Amma's and Abba's cosmology, Allah stands alone and unique as the creator of all things and beings; in this way "unity of God," *tawhīd*, is affirmed. But after the important affirmation of Allah's distinct quality, Amma and Abba do not deny the existence and power of Hindu deities. They imagine a religious landscape in ways similar to that of other South Asian religious traditions (including Indian Christianity), a landscape populated by a wide variety of spiritual beings who are not necessarily or inherently good or evil but simply powerful, and it is at the level of these classes of beings that healing is often effected. Some of these spiritual beings have distinct identities and personalities and can be said to "belong" to one or another religious tradition, although they themselves cross the boundaries of those traditions; others are identified by terms that are translations of Telugu words into Urdu and vice versa for the same classes of spiritual powers that exist in both traditions.

Because of the fluidity of language usage between Telugu and Urdu and the differences between each language's range of meanings and use of some classificatory words, such as *avatār* and *śakti*, what exactly is meant by their use in a given context can be difficult to discern. For example, when I asked Amma once to tell me about the Hindu goddess festival of Bonalu, which was being celebrated in neighborhoods all over Hyderabad at the time, she immediately responded by acknowledging the power of the goddess and then introduced the expansive category of *avatār* (incarnation, specifically the ten incarnations of the Hindu deity Vishnu).

This [festival] is to remind Hindus in the same way that our *ālam* [flags/ standards paraded at Muharram, which had just been celebrated] remind us of the suffering of Hussein.[4] Of course she has *śakti* [spiritual power]. Theirs are *śaktis* [goddesses, female] and ours are *bābās* [male]. [After a long pause she continued,] You know, we, too, have an *avatār*; ours is the seventh. [I asked who that was.] Muhammad. He's the seventh. You know, there are Ram and Krishna. Who were the others? [I listed a few, but she was less concerned with names and numbers than the quality of God that the *avatār* implied.] Yes. Isn't it sweet [*priya*] that God came down in human form [*insān kā rūp*]?

In this case, Amma is equating first *śaktis* and *bābās* and then prophets and *avatārs* as classes (one could even say *jātis*/species) of beings. *Bābās* are human saints who have accrued spiritual power and who perform miracles, particularly after their deaths. Abba himself became (was called) a *bābā* after his death. They are not deities, and by equating *śaktis* with *bābās*, Amma would seem to be acknowledging their spiritual power without granting them the status of goddess, or deity. Similarly, Muslims do not consider prophets to be deities but see them as sent by God, like the Hindu *avatārs*, to teach God's revelation, to correct incorrect beliefs and practices of humans. A Hindu might hear Amma's equation of *avatār* and prophet as implying that prophets are gods, since Hindus consider Vishnu's *avatārs* to be gods (even if they are not the deity in his fullest manifestation).[5] However, a Muslim might make just the opposite inference about the relationship—equating *avatārs* to prophets rather than the other way around.[6] Amma is amazed at the compassionate nature of God, that he would show his nature to humans through human form. She does not necessarily mean here incarnation in a Christian or Hindu sense— god in human form—but God's love being revealed through humans who are extraordinary, filled with God's love and light: prophets and *avatārs*. Another teaching that Abba gave in the context of the healing room helps explain what Amma might have meant by her statement. He asked, "How is it that we can know God's love? Only through experiencing the love between humans." And for many disciples in the Sufi tradition, their *sheikh/pīr* is, as one of Abba's disciples told me, "like God. For me, he is God." That is, because of the *sheikh*'s close relationship with God (a *walī* of God), to know and obey the *sheikh* is to know and obey God.

Just as Muhammad is placed in the expansive *avatār* system, Amma and Abba also contextualize the *avatārs* in a specifically Muslim but similarly expansive category of prophets. The Quran mentions twenty-five prophets by name, including Adam, Noah, Ibrahim, Isaac, Jacob, Joseph, Moses, David, Jesus, and Muhammad. However, Muhammad is reported to have said that there were 124,000 prophets and 315 messengers, creating the possibility of an expandable system of unnamed prophets (Hughes 1885/1988, 475). In one teaching, Abba described a historical line of prophets that included the Hindu deity and *avatār* of Vishnu, Ram:[7]

Before Muhammad, there were devils and angels and many other bad things. Ram and Sita ruled for some time. Ibrahim [Abraham] was born and ruled for some time; many other prophets came. When Ram came, then *dharma* [religion] changed; they became Hindus; they became Reddys; these became their different *jātis*. Only after Muhammad they became Muslims.

Amma makes similar identification of Jesus (Issa) as a prophet:

Even in our Quran there's mention of Miriam Bibi and everything that Issa told us. . . . We accept him as a prophet, but Christians call him god. We call him a prophet. But they understand him to be god.

During a lunch break from the healing room, Amma, Abba, and Amma's Hindu (and best) friend, Munnapa, engaged in a heated discussion about *avatārs*. Munnapa began by saying that Krishna was the greatest of the *avatārs*, although he too changed forms. Amma equated Krishna's changing forms to those of Allah and Muhammad: "Like Allah and Muhammad; like that, Krishna took different *avatārs*." Abba chimed in, saying that the greatest *avatār* is Shankar [Shiva], "You know, the one who takes the form of the *lingam* [sign/emblem of Shiva]; even Ram bowed down before him." But Munnapa repeated that there was only one *avatār* and it was Krishna; all the other seven were *avatārs* of him. She then related the story of Krishna stealing the clothes of the bathing cowherd girls [*gopīs*]; Abba, reluctant to give up the performance floor, tried to tell a little of the story of the Ramayana, about Ravana. But another disciple was still stuck on the number of *avatārs* and interrupted him: "But there are eleven, not seven, *avatārs*, and the last is Kalki, the *jalāl avatār* [lit., the fierce one; in Hindu mythology the *avatār* who rides a white horse and is yet to come]." What followed was a free-for-all debate about the correct number of incarnations in the Hindu pantheon, seven or eleven of the god, nine or seven of the goddess (using the Telugu word "*amman*"). Soon everyone seated around the tablecloth spread for lunch began to laugh at the confusion.

In this conversation, Amma does not explicate her intention and/or meaning in equating Krishna's various forms [*avatārs*] with Muhammad and Allah. However, what is important here is Amma's assertion of like *categories* in both Hindu and Muslim traditions and the theological implication that God has made himself known to both communities and revealed through *avatārs* the path of correct action. To *equate* Muhammad and Allah would be *shirk* (heresy) according to many Muslims, but as the following *hadith* suggests, to know the Prophet and his teachings and actions (*sunna*) is to know God: "Who has seen me has therefore seen the Truth [that is, God]" (Denny 1995, 169).

In some contexts, especially in the healing room, Amma and Abba emphasize equivalencies between Hindu and Muslim cosmological categories and incorporate Hindu deities into the hierarchy of spiritual powers at Amma's service; however, they never blur the distinction between Allah as creator and other powerful beings as created. Abba, in particular, makes sure that his disciples understand this distinction. Speaking in Telugu, Abba engaged in the following debate with a Hindu disciple about the nature of god, arguing that Ram was not god because he had offspring. For Abba as a Muslim, a distinguishing characteristic of Allah is that he is neither begotten nor does he beget.

Didn't Ram get married? Didn't he have children? We don't call him god. He's called a prophet. We don't call him god [Urdu generic word for god, "*khudā*"]. A prophet means he's a human. Allah sent him to show the right path. Allah sent them [prophets]; He didn't come himself.

Ellamma, Posamma, Gauramma [names of village goddesses], these are all *śaktis* [goddesses; spiritual beings with power]. They are *śaktis*. But they sometimes give you trouble. How can they be gods? They demand [animal] sacrifice. We don't give these to Allah,[8] but we have to give to them [the *śaktis*] or they cause problems. How can they be gods [Telugu, *devalu*]?

On another occasion when we were sitting in the courtyard of a *dargāh*, I asked Abba how he understood Hindu deities, whether or not he thought they had spiritual power [*śakti*]. He answered using the nominal rather than adjectival form of *śakti*:

Surely, they are *śaktis*. But there's a big difference between *śakti* and *bhagvān* [generic term for god]. *Śaktis* give problems to humans; they come on their bodies [i.e., possess them]; they trouble them; they cause them to lose their way. But these saints [such as the one in whose shrine we sat; *buzurgān-e-dīn*] don't mislead humans like that. If you go to them and ask, they give it. They make you wealthy. They only punish a person if s/he does something wrong. The situation at a temple is that it's a matter of belief. It's like this: a person can even go to a tree and, calling it god, believe in it. It's all a matter of faith [*yakīn*]. These are the differences between temples and *dargāhs*.

Like *avatār* [incarnation] and *nābi/pegambar* [prophet], *maukīl* [messenger] is another expansive category that can encompass powerful beings from across traditions, although the term itself is a Muslim category. Most

177

of the amulets upon which Amma writes call upon *maukīl*, including the four archangels and various *jinn*, to carry out her orders—to protect a patient from evil eye, remove fevers, close the mouth of an antagonist, and so forth. The Hindu deity Hanuman, known for his powers to fly through space and cover wide distances, is also considered to be such a messenger. One of Amma's disciples calls upon Hanuman in his ritual practice of *hazrat*, which Amma has given him permission to exercise in her healing room. Hanuman is said to find and call upon the saint Suleman Baba, who is beseeched to reveal the location of lost objects. Amma's disciplined spiritual practice has given her power to order a wide range of *maukīl* to carry out her commands. She told me, "I can make Kali [a Hindu goddess] sit. Kali will come and fold her hands in front of me," at which point one of Amma's Muslim disciples interjected:

Kali, Hanuman, and what's his name—Narsimha Swami [one of Vishnu's *avatārs*].[9] They all come. They say *namaste* and go away. We call them *maukīl* [messengers], but these people call them gods [*bhagvān*]. [Amma adds]: We call them *śakti*. [The disciple continues]: Whoever has *śakti* is called a *maukīl*. They call them gods; we don't call them gods. They come when we call them; we have the power to make them work for us. They come to people who are powerful, like Amma. They ask her, "Why have you called us?" And she asks, "Why are you giving them trouble?" And she begins to pray, and they leave 'automatically'.[10]

Abba describes the process of calling these *maukīl*:

It's like I send a letter in your name. Reading the letter you have to oblige me. You have to come. Depending on what's in the letter, you have to come immediately. In the same way, there's a *mantram* to be read. If I know your mother's name, then there will be some effect on you, too.

Scholars and practitioners of Hinduism are used to hearing a Hindu perspective of an expansive worldview that accommodates the "other"— where boundaries of difference become internal, in which one may find room for religious figures or spiritual agents of "other" traditions in an expanding pantheon of deities, a flexible system of *avatārs*, and the mantra "there is one truth and the paths are many." However, a similar inclusivity or encompassment is not commonly associated with Islam.[11] Yet Amma narrativizes and performs just such an encompassing cosmology of powerful beings, one in which Allah is distinguished as the creator under whom is an expansive hierarchy of differentiated powerful beings. In contrast to Amma and Abba, who articulate an inclusive cosmology, most of the patients who come to Amma's healing table have a much more generalized worldview—they share common problems and illnesses and they acknowledge that these may be caused by a wide range of spiritual forces that impinge on the physical world.

Finally, the *pīr* or *guru* is another category of being who stands at an intersection of the human and spiritual worlds, whose boundaries are so permeable. The *pīr*, in ways similar to the prophet, also teaches the "correct path" and may have particular spiritual powers of healing and performing other miracles. And when he dies, he crosses over into another category of powerful spiritual beings who continue to act in the physical and social world. Hindu patients who come to Amma's healing room know this category as *guru* and easily fit Amma and Abba into it. Amma and Abba use the words "*pīr*" and "*guru*" interchangeably. Little explanation or cross-cultural translation of the significance of the *pīr* and the relationship and obligations between *pīr* and disciple is necessary in the South Asian context. Abba, in particular, frequently performs narratives of the power and miracles of the saints/*pīrs* of the lineage to which he belongs as a way of establishing his own authority and providing a framework for the miracles that may be experienced in the healing room.

The Human World

Under the creative authority of Allah, prophets, *avatārs, jinn, maukīl*, and gurus lie on a continuum of spiritual power in the cosmology performed in the healing room, and ordinary humans (patients) are situated on the far end of that continuum. Here in the human realm, Amma asserts that any difference other than sexual difference is made by people, socially constructed, not created by God, and hence insignificant on the broad scale of what "matters"; that is, faith and devotion to God:

You shouldn't doubt Allah, whether you be Hindu or Muslim, or anyone else. Even if someone's a Hindu, but he has *bhakti* [devotion], you shouldn't dismiss him; a Muslim, too, if he has *bhakti*, you shouldn't dismiss him either. One has it and so, too, does the other. One says "Ram Ram" and the other "Rahim Rahim." There's only that much difference, isn't there? One has the call to prayer [*azān*] and the other the [*pūjā*] bell. There's only that much difference. There's *pūjā* and there's *sajdā* [one of the physical positions of Muslim prayer, *namāz*]. But there's little difference between them. Allah likes all this play [*khel*]. Look, in the end he liked this [Islam]; and having preferred this play, all this happened. Isn't that right?

[Amma describes the numbers of Hindus who go to the shrines of Muslim saints (*dargāhs*) and the faith with which they ask for miracles, in contrast to many Muslims, who often go there for "show only." Then she continues:] It's not a matter of caste [*jāti*]. It's all our doing, this caste business [*jāt-vāt*; she proceeds to name various castes]. No one came made from god as a Komati. The Brahmin didn't come [i.e., wasn't created] separately; the Reddy didn't come separately; the Rajput didn't come separately; the Harijan didn't come separately. They were all one mother's son, one father's son.

In the beginning there was only Adam, peace be upon him. As the number [of people] grew, different trades developed. If you did *dhobī*'s [washerman's] work, you were a *dhobī*; if you did *mocī*'s [leatherworker's] work, you were a *mocī*. If you did *pūjā* [a Hindu ritual offering to a deity], you were a *pūjārī* [a temple priest or officiant of *pūjā*], and if you read *namāz* [an obligatory Muslim prayer], you were a Muslim. This is the way it was. In this way, the children of one father were divided. They became separate. . . .

Now I say that the blood is all the same. What are the [true] castes [*jāti*]? A man and a woman. *We're* the ones who have divided all these *jāt-vāt*—that these are Rajputs, they're Komatis, they're Brahmins, they're this, they're that.

Some observations on this teaching: Amma begins by asserting the encompassing superiority of Allah. First and foremost, *he* should not be doubted. But Amma uses the term "Allah" both to refer to the God of

Islam, Allah, and as the generic word for god, like the Telugu word "*bhagvān*" can be used generically. She once chastised an Urdu-speaking disciple for using the term "*bhagvān*" when she was speaking Urdu, not because the term was Hindu but because she perceived it to be Telugu; she told her that if she was speaking Urdu, she should use the word "Allah." This supreme God, who stands outside/beyond humanly created difference can be known in many ways, including through the name of Ram or Rahim, and can be worshipped through the Hindu ritual of *pūjā* [offering flowers, water, and/or food to the image of a deity] or the Muslim ritual prayer of *namāz*. At this point in the teaching, the ambiguity of Amma's use of the term "Allah" would seem to be a strategic choice in the presence of an audience comprised of both Hindus and Muslims.

On this and other occasions, Amma uses the term "play" [*khel*] for the actions of humans, in particular those directed toward God, implying that the difference in *forms* of worship is insignificant, even amusing, in the view of God. God cares only about the devotion behind this "play." On other occasions, Amma calls the actions of God, particularly his creation, "play." While she does not stop to elaborate what she means by "play," this concept that the actions of a deity can be designed or carried out with no particular purpose except to bring him/her joy and delight simply through their existence, called *lilā* in Hindu mythology, is a concept articulated in several of the religious traditions represented at the healing crossroads.[12]

But the primary purpose of Amma's teaching here is not theological; rather, it is to critique differences humans create between one another—that is, *jāti* or caste—and to assert the unity of humans born from "one father." In another context, this characterization of caste as made by humans, rather than created by God, could be interpreted as claiming the superiority of Islam, which does not recognize these kinds of caste differences in its texts.[13] However, Amma includes "Muslim" as a caste distinction equivalent to *dhobī*, *mocī*, and *pūjārī* [Brahmin], and hence Muslims are equally implicated in her critique. When Amma ends the teaching with the assertion, "What are the true castes? A man and a woman," patients and disciples who are well acquainted with her healing-room rhetoric will fill in the second half of the assertion: "All these are the same: Hindus, Muslims, Christians."

On another occasion, Abba discussed caste very differently, justifying the need for its existence as occupationally distinguished groups in a way similar to that in which *varṇāśrama dharma* [the socioreligious duty of humans according to their stage of life and caste level] is often explained by upper-caste Hindus.

For example [says Abba], take the Brahmins. They're always naked [*nangā*; in this case meaning that they do not wear anything over their torsos]. Even if they're millionaires and live in big buildings, they still only wear a *dhotī* [piece of cloth wrapped around waist and pulled between the legs]; they're naked. So all the Brahmins got together and said, "We remember God [*bhagvān*] so much, but still he keeps us naked. There are all kinds of people who don't remember Him, and they go around in 'coats, pants, ties'. Come, we'll go complain to God." So, all the Brahmins went to God. "Why, [they said] are we in this condition when we do your *pūjā* day and night? The others don't do *pūjā* or anything, and they go around in cars, 'coats and pants'. Bhagvan said, "Oh you foolish ones! If I dress you in 'coat/pants', then who would do my *pūjā*? Isn't that right? Who would do my *pūjā*? That's why I've kept you naked. I've given you wealth you can't measure, that's why I keep you naked. . . ."

You should love everyone, be kind-hearted. What does kind-hearted mean? It's like if I come wearing good clothes and they give me respect and seat me on a chair. If someone comes with dirty clothes, they'd say, "Go on, get out of here!" Why should they do that? He's the same as me, right? If you seat him, seat him a little higher, seat him next to you, right? Why are you throwing him out? Isn't that that right? Allah is with the poor, and Bhagvan is with them, too, isn't he? Do you think that there's a fat god with the rich? Is the poor man's god small? No, he's the same. . . .

If everyone were equal, then who would do the work? If my wall fell down and I asked you to build it, would you? You'd say, "Who do you think you're talking to?" It happens like that, right? That's why there are rich people and poor people. If someone gets Rs. 50–60, then he can feed his children. Only then he'll come to work. If you're rich and he's a millionaire, then who would work? No one would. My house would be falling down and no one would come. [Audience member: Yes, you're right; everyone should do his own work.] I can't fix my house myself, because I'm too weak. That room is falling down and will anyone come to take care of it? What will I do? So that's why Allah made some big men and some little men.

Amma affirmed, "We need these differences of *jāt-vāt* in order to get work done—after all, if we were all rich, who would work?"

Narrative Motifs and Performance

One of the ways the shared cosmological plane is created and articulated at the healing crossroads is through Amma and Abba's narrative performances. While Muslims cannot/do not explicitly participate in worship of the physical images of Hindu deities, they may and do participate in an expansive imaginative narrative world that crosses easily across religious boundaries, one that includes traditionally Hindu narratives. Narrative performances also help to establish Amma and Abba's individual religious authority in terms that both Muslim and Hindu audiences would understand.

For example, one of Abba's favorite narratives is one of Sheikh Abdul Qadir Jilani, the founding *pīr* of the Qadiri lineage, to whom Abba traces his own authority. The story's two main characters are Ghaus-e-Azam Dastagir (Sheikh Abdul Qadir Jilani) and one of his contemporaries, Shams Tabriz,[14] both of whom are known for their particularly *jalālī* [fierce] nature, which this narrative illustrates. Abba characterizes *pīrs* as being either *jalālī* or *jamālī* [cool, easygoing, cheerful]; he characterizes himself as *jalālī*, but usually with a twinkle in his eye. The names of Allah are also characterized as *jalālī* or *jamālī*, and invocation of his *jalālī* names in *zikr* can be dangerous for the novice (Ernst 1997, 97). Similarly, in this story, simply speaking the name of the *jalālī* saint's name, "Ghaus," leads to the speaker's head falling off. The narrative variant below was performed soon after I first met Abba, when he was explaining his spiritual lineage to me (and others at the healing table), tracing it back to the *pīr* Gharib Nawaz, who is buried in Ajmer (India), then back to Ghaus-e-Azam Dastagir, who is buried in Baghdad:

Abba: Gharib Nawaz's hand is only on India, whereas Ghaus-e-Qadr's [Ghaus-e-Azam's] hand is over the whole world. Wherever you go, you'll see the green flag [the latter's symbol]. It's like this. When people used to take Ghaus's name, their heads would fall off.

Male patient: He means that if a person was not pure or took his name without thinking—

Abba: —the head would separate from the body.

Patient: The head separated. But who was he?

Amma: Shamsher Tabriz [Shams-i Tabriz].

Abba: There was an important person called Shams-i Tabriz. He used to play with tigers in the jungle. With tigers—in the same way we might play with ten to twelve dogs—he used to play with tigers in the jungle. Do you understand? One day a king had a baby.

Amma: He couldn't have children; the king's wife couldn't have children. The astrologer had told them that even if they did have children, the children would all die during childbirth itself.

Abba: The king asked, "Then who will inherit my throne? How can my children be kept alive?" The astrologer told the king, "In the jungle, there lives a *faqīr* [Muslim ascetic] who is blind. His name is Shams-i Tabriz. He has the power to bring people back to life."

The queen delivered; she delivered a baby son who died soon after. They hung a curtain and put the child behind it. The king called the army and said, "Go to the jungle and bring back whoever's there [i.e., the *faqīr*]." He was playing in the jungle with nine tigers. They surrounded him and caught him. And what did they say? "Come with us; it's the order of the king that you should come." "Why me? I can't come." "No, no, we've been ordered to catch and bring you!" "Okay, let's go then."

They took him and went back. They pulled the curtain back. "Bring this child to life." What did the king say? "Bring this child to life." He [Shams] responded, "Okay. Get up by the order of Allah." But the child didn't get up. Then he said, "Get up by my order." The child shook himself [as if from sleep] and got up.

The king asked, "What is your secret? Why didn't the child get up by the order of Allah, but got up by your order? What is the secret, tell me." [He answered,] "What can I say?" "No, no, you have to tell me," [the king insisted]. He called for the executioners and said, "Come and pull off his skin."

The fat, fat executioners came to remove his skin, but it didn't come off; they couldn't get a hold of it. So what did he tell them? "Once, when I was sitting to pee, a drop fell here. Grab my skin from here and pull it off." Then they pulled off his skin, all of it. They pulled it off, and the king ordered him to leave the city.

Covered with flies, filth, and stench, he began to beg from people, but no one gave him anything. So he went to a butcher. "I'm hungry; give me something," he said. And he [the butcher] gave him a piece of raw meat and told him to have someone else cook it for him. But no one would cook it; no one let him come close because of his bad smell.

People were afraid of him. After all, he was only raw flesh, right? There were flies buzzing around him.

Amma: He was only raw flesh, right? Wouldn't people be afraid of him?

Abba: The poor soul gave him a chunk of meat and said, "Take this chunk of meat and cook it." But whoever saw him told him to move on [no one agreed to cook it]. So he got very angry; being angry, he didn't say anything.

Male patient: He went to a mountain.

Amma interjects: Then Tabriz said, "I'm going to call *shams*" [Arabic, sun; called down to cook his hunk of meat]. Saying this, he called the sun. He said, "*Shams*, come down." But just before the sun came, Ghaus-e-Pak came and stood before him. "Don't call it down; don't call it down! If the sun comes down, the whole 'public' will be burned into ashes."

How did he [Shams] respond? "Okay, I won't call *shams*. But whenever anyone even says your name, his head separates from his body. You, too, shouldn't use the power of your tongue like that." So he [Ghaus-e-Pak] said "Okay" and went away. Now, raising his [Shams's] hand [toward the sun], the meat was cooked. He ate it and went away, and Ghaus-e-Pak went the other way.

Abba: Earlier it was like that: whenever someone said his name, his head would separate from his body. Shams asked Ghaus-e-Pak to control his *jalālī* [fierce nature]; only then he, too, would stop [asking the sun to come down]. So he agreed. When someone is in pain, he says a lot of things; he may say anything [i.e., he may call out the name of the saint Ghaus-e-Pak]. Earlier, in this situation, if you even said his name, your head separated from the body.

Amma: Now look, even in troubled conditions, we didn't use to say his name, didn't say, "*Ya Ghaus*," ' because as soon as you said it, your head separated from the body.

Why does Abba tell the story? Of course, it is, above all, a dramatic story that makes for good performance. But this particular story is chosen from a wide repertoire of possible options; there is a reason it has become a favorite in the context of the healing room. First, it dramatizes, rather than discursively declares, the spiritual power of saints/*pīrs*. And because the narrator, Abba, is himself a *pīr* in this same lineage, its performance indirectly confers the authority of the lineage upon Abba. This is a very different strategy of establishing authority than the performance of personal narratives upon which Amma relies to create her public authority. Second, this narrative about the miracles of saints helps elicit and solidify (unvoiced) assumptions shared among patients about the intercessory power of the *pīr* (and indirectly the *pirānimā*) by dramatically exteriorizing this power: the *pīr* can cause heads to fall off with the mere mention of his name, play with tigers, raise the dead, and call down the sun. Because Abba is a *pīr* in this lineage, he, too, shares in this nature and has access to similar power, albeit diffused (even diluted) from the intensity of that of the *silsilā*'s founder. And Abba can use this power on behalf of his disciples and Amma's patients.

The narrative also indirectly addresses the controversy in some Muslim circles about this very assumption of the possibility of intercessory power by a saint in front of God on behalf of another human. While this is not theologically problematic for Hindus, for some Muslims it may begin to approach a breach of a central concept in Islam—that of *tawhīd*, the singularity of God. The fear is that when a saint displays such power, his disciples might be tempted not simply to honor him but also to worship him. In the narrative, the *pīr* Shams first orders the dead child to raise up from the dead in Allah's name, but nothing happens. Then he says, "Get up by my order," and "the child shook himself and got up." The king notices this seeming discrepancy—that the saint's name is more powerful than that of God's—and demands that Shams explain why the child did not get up in Allah's name. Shams refuses to reveal the secret—and I was reminded of Amma's recurrent pronouncement about such secret things: "These are heavy matters." The king is presumably not initiated and therefore would have been unable to understand the secret even if he had been told. Shams's refusal leads to the dramatic unfolding of the rest of the story. This indirect reference to potential controversy (one that I never heard directly addressed in the healing room) is an example of how Abba often uses narratives to address only indirectly an issue or question with more multivalence than a direct answer would be able to do or how sometimes the narrative gives an "answer" that Abba would be reluctant to say directly.

While it addresses issues of spiritual authority and powers, the narrative performance also creates and draws from a repertoire of motifs and characters Hindu and Muslim narratives share and thus contributes to a shared imaginative identity between various patients and disciples who are its audience. Stories such as this do not sound foreign or strange to the healing-room audience. Even when they first hear them, both Muslim and Hindu audience members recognize certain features, beginning with the physical powers of spiritually powerful humans discussed above. But specific narrative motifs are also shared, such as that of the danger of pollution—in this case the danger of inadvertently leaving a drop of urine on the skin, which provides an entry into the otherwise protected boundary of the human body.[15] A similar motif is found in the Mahabharata story of Nal and Damayanti. In variants of this epic story, Kali, the personification of the Kali Yuga (the present age of darkness when *dharma* is forgotten), enters the hero Nal's foot through just such a (urine-) polluted spot on his foot, thereby causing the hero and his wife Damayanti great suffering. While in other rituals and narratives, the specifics of purity/pollution rules might vary, the general "grammar" of the significance of ritual purity and pollution is shared in many South Asian religious traditions.

The motif of heads falling off is also familiar to Indian audiences and resonates with Hindu narratives of beheadings and exchanges of heads. One such narrative is the widespread and popular South Indian village myth of Renuka.[16] The power of chastity is so great that she can carry water on her head without a pot. One day the shadow of a *gandhārva* [a flying celestial being] falls on her, and the water spills. Seeing this, her husband Jamadagni suspects that her chastity has been compromised, and he orders his son Parashurama to behead her. The son complies but then begs his father to revive his mother. He is given permission to do so himself, but he mistakenly attaches an untouchable woman's head to the body of his mother rather than her own Brahmin head.[17] The Brahmin-headed, untouchable-bodied woman begins to be worshipped as the village goddess Renuka. Of course, even more widespread is the narrative of the deity Ganesh, beheaded by his father Shiva, whose head was replaced with that of an elephant. In contrast to these two stories, in the narrative about the *jalālī pīr* Ghaus-e-Pak, heads fall off without active agency on the part of the person responsible (the saint). And we are not told what happens to those heads and bodies. But because repertoires of narrative motifs and sequences flow across religious boundaries, the idea of fallen-off heads is accepted; rarely is a story entirely new or experienced as "foreign" at this healing *caurāstā*.

Another way Amma and Abba employ common South Asian narrative motifs is to localize, expand, and make familiar Quranic narratives, such as the story of Miriam, mother of Issa/Jesus. In the course of explaining to a patient that spiritual healing treatments probably do not exist in the United States, where "there are no poor people," Amma nevertheless asserted that such treatments would still be necessary for spiritually caused problems. Her son reminded her that most people in the United States were Christians; still, he continued, "Sometimes, even among Christians there are some important [i.e., spiritually powerful] people who pray with folded hands and there is a cure. But there's a little difference." Amma interrupted him, "No, no, this healing power is available to all humans. If they have devotion, why wouldn't this be the case?" Then she launched into the story of Miriam:

Even in our Quran there's mention of Miriam and everything that Issa told us. . . . He was a prophet. As many prophets have come and gone on earth, they have all died. But he didn't die. He went up; he became a star and disappeared. So they call him god, but we call him a prophet.

Bibi Miriam was young. She had neither mother nor father, so she was living with her brother and sister-in-law after her parents died. So Bibi Miriam was living with her brother. She was taking a bath when above her in the sky, Jibrail passed. Jibrail's shadow struck the water. It also hit her and she became pregnant. And what did her sister-in-law say? "She's done bad things." Then her brother said, "No, my sister's not like that. My sister is honest." [But] the sister-in-law gave her a lot of trouble. She gave a lot of trouble to Bibi Miriam. When I read about this in her book, I read it and cried a lot at her fate.

Then the sister-in-law told her husband to leave her in the jungle. Her brother took her to the jungle and left her there, crying as he left. She [Bibi Miriam] said, "Brother, go now. Why are you taking blame for me? I made no mistake [did no wrong]." Then she stayed in the jungle. Her nine months passed there, living on roots and leaves in the jungle. She made a hut with leaves. Her nine months having passed, she started having pains. She held on to some rock, a rock and then a vine. . . . She was in such pain she passed out. Angels came to help her. They came to help her with the delivery. They cleaned and bathed the baby. They washed his hands, and a stream formed; they washed his legs and another stream formed. This all happened when Issa was born. The stream from his hands is called "*zamzam,*" and the water from his feet is called "*kosar.*" When people drink the water of *zamzam,* they gain good health. The water of *zamzam* is still available, but not the water of *kosar.*

The narrative weaves together several Muslim and Hindu motifs and references. The spring/well of *zamzam* is a contemporary sacred site in Mecca said to be the spring from which Hagar and Ishmael drank when they were banished to the wilderness by Ibrahim (Abraham); the spring appeared to them as a miracle in the desert. Pilgrims to Mecca drink from the well and take bottles of its water home with them, in much the same way that Hindu pilgrims take home water from the Ganga River to use in rituals and to distribute some of the blessings of the pilgrimage to those at home. The water of *kosar* [Arabic, *kawthar*] is a river or pool in Paradise.[18] While Hindu patients or audience members listening to this narrative might not recognize these specific references and names, they are intimately familiar with the idea of sacred waters, including the healing power of such waters. And in fact, waters are sacralized right in

Amma's healing room when she blows over bottles of water brought to her, thus empowering those waters to protect and heal those who drink them.

This narrative draws on still another common motif shared with several Hindu narratives: that of the shadow of a celestial compromising the chastity of a woman (more specifically, in Hindu mythology the motif of a *gandhārva*'s shadow causing pregnancy or threatening the chastity of a woman), such as in the story of Renuka. Even more striking is the similarity between the portion of this narrative of Miriam where she gives birth in the jungle and that of Sita at the end of certain versions of the Ramayana. In some Ramayana narrative variants, the pregnant Sita is abandoned in the jungle by her brother-in-law Lakshman (on order of Ram), where she gives birth to her twin sons with only nature coming to her aid.

Many narratives performed by Amma and Abba share more than motifs across traditions; they frequently tell full narratives that are drawn from traditional Hindu mythological stories. Remember Abba's telling of the Ramayana in earlier discussions of *avatārs* and Amma's recounting of the episode of Hanuman bringing healing herbs to a dying Lakshman from the same epic. When I asked Abba how he understood the deity Ganesh, whose festival was being celebrated at the time with the installation of images at neighborhood crossroads all over the city, including a clearing right behind Amma's healing room, he did not answer with a theological pronouncement about the deity and his existence but simply responded with a story, the story of Ganesh's creation. As in Amma's narrative of Hanuman, he did not preface his telling with an identification of the narrative as Hindu or with the statement that "this is what Hindus say." His telling implied that this is simply the way it is.

Abba: Shankar [Shiva] had gone to meditate in the forest. When he was gone, Parvati took dirty bathwater [*mailā pānī* is emphasized; water with which Parvati had already bathed] and formed Ganesh.
Amma: She made a doll [*putlā*].
Abba: Shankar came back from the forest and asked, "Who is this standing outside of Parvati's bath?"

He was born in water and he's thrown back into water [i.e., at the end of the festival, his clay images are immersed in water]. Parvati wanted to get married, but every man said "But you're my mother." At last Shankar came. He said he would marry her if she became a little girl; so she became a little girl. . . . Then Shankar went back to the forest.

In this short performance, Abba actually conflates two distinct narratives, shifting from that of Ganesh's creation by his mother Parvati to one of Adipara Shakti, the primordial goddess who had herself created the gods and so none of them wanted to have sex with her, since as their creator she was like a mother. Abba identifies Adipara Shakti here as Parvati, whom Shiva (Shankar) agrees to marry if she becomes a girl again.

I found the question "how do you understand" [*kase samajte hain*] a particular Hindu deity or festival to be more open-ended and productive than asking whether or not Amma and Abba "believed in" or worshiped that particular deity. Here, Abba's answer through narrative is as ambiguous as my question; narrative provides him a space within which to acknowledge the existence of the deity in an imaginative world without declaring whether or not he is a god. To share a narrative repertoire is not necessarily to imply a shared interpretation of those narratives in the different contexts in which they are performed. Abba does not worship Ganesh like a Hindu might before undertaking a new venture, but Ganesh is fully present in his imaginative world. This particular performance was a much-abbreviated version of the story as it exists in other contexts, leaving out many details, but it answered my question in a much more imaginative and expansive way than it had been asked.

We have found that healing-room narratives most often emphasize a shared worldview and often employ shared motifs or full narratives. However, outside the healing room, when Abba performs for audiences of his disciples, he frequently distinguishes between Muslim and Hindu worldviews and practices. Abba performed one such narrative (whose translation is given below) during a Friday visitation to the home of one of his disciples, where several Hindu men who wanted to become his disciples had come to meet with him. Note that performatively, a distinction between Hindu and Muslim is dramatized by the code-switching between

Urdu and Telugu (the languages spoken by Hyderabadi Muslims and Hindus, respectively, although many Hyderabadis understand both languages). Abba begins in Urdu:

I want to tell you one more thing; but don't be offended. [He switches to Telugu, speaking to the Hindu audience members.] Don't take it badly just because a *sahib* [i.e., a Muslim] is saying this. [Back to Urdu.] Don't be offended. I thought of it and am now telling you. But don't get angry.

There was a stone in the jungle. A man brought it home and began to hit and hit it. Hitting it a million times, he made a form [*śakal*] out of it. By hitting it, he made a beautiful image [*murti*], with hands and feet. He made it and kept it in this room; he kept it inside. He decorated it. He broke coconuts in front of it; he brought bananas; he lit incense. He did all this. He came every day at four and offered incense, coconuts, milk, worship, and all those kinds of things [*agarbati-wagarbati, pūjā-wūjā, nāriyal-wāriyal, dūdh-wūdh*].[19] He brought them to that place and then went home.

One day, the Brahmin came at four in the afternoon and a noise came from inside. [In Telugu]: "My god [*devaru*] is coming; my god is coming." [In Urdu]: "Who? Who's talking? The stone is talking!" And he was worried, this Brahmin. He was looking here; he was looking there. Where was this noise coming from? He came and put all the *pūjā* things there.

Then Hanuman said, "You made me, gave me a place to stay, gave me bananas, coconuts, incense, and milk. You've given me everything and I haven't given you anything. Now tell me, who is god [*bhagvān*]? It's like this: believe in a god from whom you receive something, do you understand? God is one. Allah, the creator [lit., one who gave birth] is one. Just because you perform this kind of devotion doesn't make him god. Can you call him that? You can't call him that! Why? Because you're born from your mother's womb; god isn't born from any mother's womb.

Notice that while Hanuman and other Hindu deities may inhabit Amma and Abba's imaginative narrative world—both Abba and Amma incorporate Hindu personages and spiritual beings into their narratives with ease—the physical manifestation of these beings in carved images,

14. Abba giving teachings in the home of a disciple, 1995.

which are worshiped by devotees, is anathema to them. In this narrative, a clear line of distinction between Hindu and Muslim is drawn around both the issues of image worship and the unique quality of god as creator. That is, for Muslims, the ultimate distinction between Allah and the Hindu pantheon of deities is that Allah is not created nor does he have offspring, as do many Hindu deities. The narrative follows these two axes away from the shared world of the crossroads to their outer coordinates, where difference is most strongly articulated.[20] Similarly, Amma calls upon the goddess Kali or Hanuman to come to her service; but while she acknowledges their power/*śakti*, she does not worship them.

A Shared Ritual Grammar at the Healing Crossroads

While some narrative motifs might be difficult to identify as specifically Hindu, Christian, or Muslim in South Asia, one might expect that rituals and festivals would be more bounded. However, here too Amma's healing-room discourse creates and reflects a shared ritual grammar and permeable religious boundaries. In the following observation, Amma makes note of the mixed-up times in which we live, when ritual categories and roles have been mismanaged. Hindus make a similar assessment of the current times when they identify our epoch as the Kali Yuga, a time when humans do not and cannot fully follow their *dharma*, or ethical duties, because, in part, they have been born in the Kali Yuga.

Muharram used to be a Hindu festival and Dasshera a Muslim one. Narsimha [one of Vishnu's *avatārs*] used to come on [possess] them in Muharram. But they [Hindus] couldn't do the *fātihā* correctly,[21] so Muslims had to take over. When Dasshera was ours [Muslim], many goats were killed, but not now. Times are mixed up! The line of prophets [*pegambar*] came to an end when Hussein died; if he hadn't died [been martyred], people would have forgotten and there would have been a need for prophets to keep coming. But now we have the lineage of *murśid* [religious guides/teachers] instead.

Amma's observation also reflects the complex relationship between Shii and Sunni traditions at this level of vernacular Islam in Hyderabad.

The festival of Muharram is most closely associated with Shii Muslims, and participation in its processions (as well as the custom of wearing black clothing throughout the month) is a distinguishing practice between Shii and Sunni observance. However, Amma claims it as "ours," as Muslim. Numerous oral and written accounts of Hyderabadi life and culture, which are frequently told with great pride as proof that local Hindus and Muslims have "always gotten along," describe Hindus' participation in Muharram processions in villages in the Hyderabad region. With the contemporary politicization of these processions,[22] however, this participation is no longer as common as it once was; in fact, it is practically nonexistent. The importance given to the Prophet's grandson Hussein (here identified as coming at the end of the line of prophets) would also seem to have resonance with Shii beliefs, although more commonly Shiis identify him as the second *imām*, following Muhammad's son Ali, and not a prophet. The lineage of teachers/guides to which Amma then shifts after referring to Hussein, however, is not that of the Shii *imāms* but that of the Sufi *mursids*; they have taken the role that prophets earlier had—of showing the right path, of teaching.

Just as the grammar of many festival rituals (processing a deity or object of reverence, feeding, and eating) are shared across religious boundaries, so, too the basic grammar of Amma's healing rituals is shared, even if the specifics might not be familiar to her Hindu (or Muslim, for that matter) patients. It is rare that a patient questions Amma's prescriptions as something beyond their understanding or experience. New patients are often confused about what to do, when to do it, and which kind of paper amulet to use; their repeated questions often cause gales of laughter among returning patients and disciples around the healing table. But they *do* understand the power of a particularly powerful healer to call upon spiritual forces to come to her aid through the power of the word. I often heard returning patients explain to new Hindu patients that Amma's *tāvīz* were the same as Hindu *mantram*/oral incantations, only one is written and the other spoken. Another linguistically shared ritual category both Muslims and Hindus use refers to bringing someone out of possession or trance: *thandhā karnā* [lit., to cool down].[23] It is also the term used when a clay image of a Hindu deity is immersed in water at the end of the festival, the act that "deconsecrates" the image/sends the deity away.

The ritual grammar of many of Amma's prescriptions is also shared across religious boundaries. For example, the prescription of *utārā* that Amma orders for forms of what she calls "heavy" evil eye—circling an attractive physical object around the head of a person in order to draw away the evil eye—is one commonly practiced in numerous ritual contexts in South Asia—Hindu, Muslim, Christian. This ritual action is frequently performed at various times during wedding celebrations, when cash is circled three times over the head of the bride and/or of the new couple to detract any evil eye that might be drawn to the beautiful and auspicious couple. This much of the ritual is readily accessible and understandable to anyone who comes to the healing table. However, the specific objects that are prescribed in *utārā* might feel unfamiliar (and in the case of the raw liver, even repugnant to some upper-caste vegetarian Hindus). *Utārā* is the ritual in Amma's healing repertoire that is identified most often by some middle-class educated South Asian Muslims as Hindu—perhaps because it does not involve the written word, specifically that of the Quran.

Amma employs two other nonwritten prescriptions that are shared by healers of other religious traditions. One of these is called *davā* [lit., medicine]. The prescription is given when Amma has diagnosed that someone has put "something" in the patient's food to influence the patient's actions. Both Hindus and Muslims who come to Amma's healing table accept the possibility that social and physical illnesses can be transferred through material substance; in this case it is intentionally transferred through food. The herbal prescription of *jarī-būṭī* (not to be ingested, but to be buried or burned) is another example of a ritual substance and action that is shared across religious boundaries. When I asked Amma about the rationale of using herbs (as opposed to the oral or written word, upon which she had almost exclusively relied, except for *utārā*), she told me, "There's great *śakti* [spiritual power] in *jarī-būṭī*" and proceeded to tell a short version of the story of Hanuman (from the Ramayana), who flew to a specific mountain to find such healing herbs to bring the dying hero Lakshman back to life. Like Abba, who told the story of Ganesh earlier, she did not tell this as a *Hindu* story but as a narrative that is part of her own repertoire—one that contextualizes and makes space for what was for Amma an innovative practice.

While ritual grammar may be shared, interpretation of that ritual may differ, particularly the interpretation of the relative hierarchy of spiritual beings and who/what it is that actually effects healing. But most patients do not consciously interpret the ritual at all—they have put their faith in a charismatic successful healer, and whatever she tells them to do, they do. If patients do not fulfill the ritual prescriptions, it is rarely because they do not believe in the possibility of their efficacy; usually it is because there are too many details in the prescription to remember, the patient improves without the prescription, or the patient and his/her family are simply too busy or overwhelmed to fulfill their part in what can be time-consuming prescriptions.

In the healing room, Amma performs and articulates primarily shared grammars/motifs of ritual and narrative, and the boundaries between religious traditions are permeable in this context. But in contexts outside the healing room (and other crossroads), distinctions between Muslim and Hindu might become more accentuated. In this South Indian context, two primary axes of distinction between Muslims and Hindus run through the healing room and solidify identities at their endpoints: image worship and death rituals, particularly the distinction between cremation and burial.

Death as an Identity Marker of Difference

A lengthy and heated conversation between one of Amma's nieces and Amma's friend Munnapa as they were sitting together in Amma's courtyard awaiting the beginning of the Gyarwin Sharif festival celebrations illustrates the ways death might become an identity marker in everyday interactions that creates boundaries between Hindu and Muslim. The niece was visiting from a distant city and was therefore "new" to the context of the healing room and perhaps not in regular interaction with Hindus. Munnapa, on the other hand, spends her days ironing in a lean-to against the side of Amma's room and is intimately connected to Amma's practice. This conversation illustrates the difference between a specialist's and a layperson's understanding of the practices of religious communities other than their own. Had Amma been present, she might

197

have been able to provide a bridge of understanding, finding equivalence or shared understanding across the boundaries of difference, but the two laywomen involved were seemingly unable to do so.

The subject of death was raised when Amma's niece asked what provides Hindus with any moral compass, since at death their bodies are simply burned up and they are held to no accountability [ḥisāb] on a day of judgment. Munnapa was confused because she knew that that was not the case, but she did not have words to offer an alternative. Initially, she appealed to what she knew to be an Islamic authority—the book—by saying, "We, too, have a book, you know. Ours is the Ramayana. It tells us how to live." And she proceeded to give a short summary of the narrative. But Amma's niece was not convinced and reiterated again that the Hindu corpse is simply burned, so what difference does it make how they live. I listened to the conversation go back and forth between the two women, waiting for Munnapa to articulate concepts of ātmā, karma, and saṃsāra, but she seemed stumped. Finally, I stepped out of my role of observer and into one of participant, bringing into the conversation the idea of the soul [ātma] that reincarnates into a next life in a form that depends on a person's action in the previous life [karma; saṃsāra]. Munnapa leaned over and touched my knee, responding enthusiastically and with some relief, "Yes, yes, 'correct, correct'!" Amma's niece seemed to lose interest and walked away from the scene of the conversation to join others in food preparation. (A complete translation of this conversation, which gives the specific terms of debate and conveys its rhythms, can be found in Appendix A.)

Perhaps more commonly, death determines and solidifies religious boundaries and identity when a decision must be made whether to bury or cremate a corpse of someone who in life crossed these boundaries. The following example is drawn from my fieldwork in the city of Raipur, Chhattisgarh (in the early 1980s), but it is relevant in this Hyderabadi context as well. A jalālī, stone-throwing bābā called The Naked One showed up one day on the steps of a Raipur sari store, speaking no language anyone could understand—people guessed he might be from Afghanistan—and lived there for ten years. He was naked and wrapped in a rough wool blanket, which he periodically threw off in exasperation or anger. His primary miracle [*karāmat*] was that he never urinated or defecated. Gradually other miracles began to be experienced by those who simply stood in his presence or offered him cigarettes: students gained admission to postsecondary educational institutions, infertile women became pregnant, failing businesses thrived. While living, this *bābā* was identified as neither Muslim nor Hindu; members of all religious communities came to offer him food (which he always rejected) and lit cigarettes (which he sometimes did accept). The photograph of this *bābā* could be seen in stores and restaurants all over the city, whether they were run by Muslims or Hindus. But when the *bābā* died, there was a dilemma. Should the corpse be cremated or buried? The case was taken to court and Muslims won; his body was buried and a large *dargāh* was built up around his grave. In death he became a Muslim and as his reputation at the *dargāh* grew, his popularity outside that context diminished (as indicated by the absence of his photograph in non-Muslim restaurants, autorickshaws, etc., where it used to be commonly seen).

Amma tells of a similar situation after the death of one of her high-caste Hindu disciples, who was very influential in his community. When he died, she said, there was a big fight between Muslims and Hindus over how to dispose of the body, whether it should be buried or cremated. In this case, the Hindus won the dispute and cremated the body; however, the man's hand did not burn. So the Muslims buried it in their graveyard and miracles began to be experienced at that place. The fifteenth-century *bhakti* poet Kabir was similarly difficult to categorize in life as Hindu or Muslim; he denounced the dishonesty, hypocrisy, and external rituals of both traditions. However it is said that both communities vied for his body after his death; Muslims wanted to bury it and Hindus wanted to cremate it. As the debate was going on, someone lifted the shroud and discovered the miracle that Kabir's body had turned into a heap of flowers; thus it was able to be divided in two portions, one for cremation and one for burial (Hess and Singh 1983, 4). In both Amma's narrative and the story of Kabir, in death the body became (quite literally) multiple in order to enable its multiple identities to be maintained, but these are unusual and miraculous situations. In many cases when a religious identity is fluid in life, it is fixed in death.[24]

There are other contexts (for the living) in which religious identities are confirmed and become significant, as axes of difference move out from the healing room. One of these in Amma and Abba's community is the *samā*, which creates a particularly Muslim space that is rooted in local contexts.

IMMERSED IN REMEMBRANCE AND SONG: RELIGIOUS IDENTITIES, AUTHORITY, AND GENDER AT THE *SAMĀ*

It is the poetry that pulls at the heart. . . . A happiness is born
from the poetry and we begin to twirl.

On the twenty-sixth of each Muslim lunar month,[1] the courtyard of
Sheikh Hussain Qadiri, Abba, is transformed from the open-air "waiting
room" of Amma's healing room into a magnetic center of spiritual power
drawing together a core group of disciples of the aging *sheikh*. The occasion is the *samā*, a ritual of devotional song [*qavvālī*] and remembrance
[*zikr*] whose purpose is to arouse mystical love among those assembled
and move them closer to the *pīr*, the saints, and God.[2] It is on the occasion
of the *samā* that Abba's spiritual authority as *sheikh/pīr* is most visibly
performed—he sits on a velvet-cushioned seat/throne [*gaddī*], wears a
special green satin turban, is garlanded by his disciples, and "holds court."
Abba's male disciples are seated in a rectangular pattern around the courtyard; Abba is seated at one end (along with his *murśid* son and heir
apparent, Khalid, and Khalid's oldest son), and the musicians [*qavvāls*]
are seated at the far side opposite him. Amma and female disciples sit on
a raised verandah behind Abba with a curtain separating them from the
sheikh, his male disciples, and the musicians.

In contrast to the healing room, the *samā* courtyard is an explicitly

Muslim performance space: it stands farther out on the axes passing through the healing crossroads. It is, nevertheless, still framed by, even dependent upon, Amma's healing practice and its participants. The *samās* performed in the courtyard of Sheikh Hussain stand in a unique inter-performative relationship with both Abba's teachings as *pīr* and the ritual and verbal discourses of Amma's healing practice as *pirānimā*: each informs and sustains the other. As we have mentioned earlier, Amma is dependent upon Abba's ritual role and his explicit permission to practice in the public domain as she does. But Abba is also dependent on her, as most of his disciples come to him through Amma's healing practice; they were her patients before they became his disciples. While Amma's authority is performatively dominant in the healing room, the dominance of ritual role and rhetoric is reversed at the *samā*; here Abba's authority is most prominently created and displayed.

The *samā* as observed from the center of the courtyard, so to speak, from the perspective of the male *sheikh* and the *qavvāls,* has been wonderfully described in Regula Qureshi's ethnomusicological study *Sufi Music of India and Pakistan* (1986). Qureshi conducted fieldwork at several major shrines of Sufi saints, particularly that of Hazrat Nizamuddin Auliya in New Delhi. Based on this fieldwork, she characterizes Sufism (and, more specifically, *samā* and *qavvālī*) as an "all-male" tradition (xv). Most historical and literary scholarship on Sufism in South Asia has similarly been based on male experience: historically important saints, *silsilās* (genealogies of spiritual descent), and established *dargāhs* (Eaton 1978; Ernst 1992; Schimmel 1975; Troll 1989).[3] Song traditions of *qavvālī* are regularly performed at these *dargāhs* on the occasion of the saints' annual *urs* [death anniversary, referred to as the wedding of the saint, his union with God]. Less-elaborate *samās,* with smaller assemblies and crowds, might be held on the monthly anniversary of a saint's death and/or on Thursday nights, auspicious nights at *dargāhs* during which the saints are said to be particularly close (Thursday is also the day for remembrance of the dead). Abba's courtyard provides us with another kind of context for the *samā*—a private (even domestic) rather than formally institutional context—a context not yet described in scholarly literature.[4] In this performance context Amma and female disciples are very much involved, even if they are not in the courtyard center.

While they follow the basic structure of *dargāh*-based *samās*, the religious practices described here represent vernacular Sufi ritual practice that is not institutionally based.[5] Abba's authority and learning are not inherited through a historically identifiable long-standing lineage associated with a particular *dargāh* or Sufi institution (although he asserts that the *silsilā* he follows has continuity back to Gharib Nawaz Sarkar of Ajmer, Ghaus-e-Azam Dastagir of Baghdad, the great Imam Ali, and finally to the Prophet himself). Rather, his authority as *sheikh* is based primarily on inclination and personal charisma recognized by his own *pīr* (and confirmed in being granted his *pīr*'s *khilāfat*) and has not been inherited through an authoritative bloodline.

Mixing of the Colors: Performance and Identity

Perhaps because of their charismatic bases of authority and noninstitutional affiliations, Amma and Abba say that in relationships, practices, and performance, they cross the boundaries of all the Sufi lineages [*silsilās*], "immersing in the colors of all the seven *silsilās*." Just as their immediate guru sat and spoke with all, they affirm, so they, too, may "sit with all." Abba elaborated, "They are just different colors. Water is all the same whether you drink from a cup or hand, right? Like that, they're different *tarīqā*" [lit., paths].

Amma and Abba's patronage of and participation in the *samā* is a performative indication of this "mixing of colors." When I first asked Amma to which lineage she belonged, she took pride in the multiplicity of affiliations she was allowed to make:

God is one. There are those who wear yellow clothing; Qadiris wear green; I'm Qadiri and also Chishti. I'm Sohrawardi and Qalandar. Qalandars wear red; Naqshabandis wear white. And the others wear 'chocolatey'; they are Sohrawardi. There are seven *silsilās*; we are in all of them; we immerse in all of the colors.[6] We can sit in every place.

Joyce: But which one did your guru belong to?

Amma: My guru was like this, too. It's only because he's like this that I received all seven *silsilās*, too. Will we sing the songs of our guru or of someone else? We'll sing the songs of our guru, won't we? Whatever the guru tells us, those are the footsteps we'll follow.

Amma's niece thought I was asking about whether or not her family were Sayyids (descendants from the Prophet's family) and began to clarify. Amma cut her off:

No, we're not talking about Sayyids. Qadiri, Chishti, all these. There's no *qavvālī* among Qadiri. Only Chishtis have *qavvālī*. So we mix with both Qadiris and Chishtis, right? We perform *qavvālī*, right? We wear green scarves [color of Qadiris] and yellow ones [color of Chishtis], too. We also wear black clothes. That's the color of Sophiyanarang. The color of the Sophiyanarang is absolutely black, just like dead people. Even if you're living, you should die. It's like after a person dies, as they lived that's how they will be then, right? So that's how you should take care of your heart. We call them Sophiyanarang; they wear black.

Amma acknowledges that only Chishtis practice *samā*, but she gives no indication that its practice might be controversial or that she is aware of debates over whether or not dancing, singing and listening to music, and the mystical states they might engender are legitimate Muslim practices. One of the controversies over music concerns the danger that its performance will elicit secular emotions that might be dangerous to the believer. (For an overview of some of these debates, see Schimmel 1975, 178–186 and Ernst 1997, 188–189.)

While *samā* is strongly associated with the Chishti *silsilā*, as performed in Abba's courtyard on the twenty-sixth day of the month, it marks the death anniversary of Abdul Qadir Jilani, founding *pīr* of the Qadiris who is loosely associated with other lineages, if not their founder. The timing of the *samā*, then, helps to identify Abba as Qadiri. But most important, the *samā* ritual performatively identifies the core community of Abba's disciples as they gather in his courtyard from dispersed neighborhoods around the city. Disciples come to Amma's healing room throughout the month at different times, some daily and others irregularly, but for the monthly *samā*, the entire inner circle of disciples gathers in one place at one time. Abba says he has between three and four hundred disciples, whom he has initiated over a period of thirty some years, but only thirty or forty regularly attend his *samās*.

Preparing Ritual Space

The *samā* usually begins at around 10 o'clock in the evening and might last until anywhere between 1 and 3 A.M. Before the ritual performance begins, Amma oversees the preparation of the courtyard that transforms it from the waiting room of her practice into the sacred *samā* performance space. The courtyard is swept and straw mats are laid down and overlaid with heavy woven bedspreads; Abba's *gaddī,* or "throne" of authority (a red-and-black velvet cushion), is carefully positioned at one end of the carpeted courtyard, and a curtain is hung behind the *gaddī.* In monsoon rains, the alternative space to the open courtyard is Amma and Abba's crowded living/sleeping room, in which only the men can fit; women crowd into another small sleeping room and tiny kitchen. Once, after the courtyard had been fully prepared and we stood watching the darkening monsoon clouds gather on the horizon, Amma confidently declared that it would not rain—it never rains on *samā* nights, she said, an indication that "Allah is merciful." However, when sheets of rain began to blow across the neighborhood and Amma had moved everyone and everything inside, her confidence and cheerfulness remained unshaken. As if she had not only moments before equated God's mercy with keeping the rain away, she now declared equally confidently that God was merciful in sending rain and taking care of the earth.

The final preparation of the *samā* performance space is the ritual of *dastarkhān lagānā* [lit., spreading the tablecloth]. A narrow green or red cloth is spread down the center of the carpeted space and a pile of dark, smooth, marble-sized seeds poured out on it. *Murīds* who have arrived early, both male and female, sit around the *dastarkhān,* take a handful of seeds at a time, and count them out in individual piles in front of them as they recite the names of God, the *kalmā,* and/or what Amma identified as *āyat-e-karīmā* until all the seeds from the common center mound are counted out. *Āyat-e-karīmā* is a class of Quranic verses, but Amma also called this one the "prayer of Jonah," which would be "There is no God save Thee. Be Thou Glorified! Lo! I have been a wrong-doer" (Sura 21, 87; Pickthall 1994, 334). Amma explained that the ritual protects the *samā* space and its inhabitants against potential malevolent forces [*śaitānī*].

Abba added: "We perform *zikr* [equating *dastarkhān* with *zikr*] in order to purify ourselves. There are filthy [*gandī*] things, and we perform *zikr* to clean those out." This is also an opportunity for the disciples to engage in personal reflection and intercessory prayer [*duā*]. When they arrive, *murīds* often first go up to the flagpole on which the green flag of the *pīr* (Jilani) is hung, clinging to its base, pressing their heads against the platform on which it is anchored.

Abba joins the *dastarkhān* ritual only near its end, having prepared himself by donning a long satin *kurtā*, applying *surmā* around his eyes, and sprinkling himself with perfumed scent. According to Abba, angels do not like bad smells, so he puts on scent to invite their presence. He and his sons and disciples also apply *surmā* and scent before going to the mosque on Fridays. The *surmā*, Abba once explained, reflects away the direct light of God that one potentially could experience in such ritual contexts, which is too strong to sustain directly.[7] Finally, Abba puts on the green turban and a green scarf. Those disciples who have received Abba's *khilāfat* may also wear green *kurtās*, scarves, and crocheted or velvet skull hats; other disciples wear everyday pants and shirts and cover their heads with handkerchiefs. Two elderly men periodically attended Abba's *samās* who wore orange turbans and were given seats of honor next to Abba; they are not Abba's disciples, but age-mates and friends who are *murśids* of other lineages (orange/yellow being indicative of Chishti affiliation).

When the *dastarkhān* is concluded, male and female participants all stand together as Khalid, Abba's *murśid* son, who will inherit Abba's *gaddī*, recites the *fātihā*. The call-and-response recitation of the *salāmat* that follows, a praise recitation of the names of the lineage of saints extending back to Ali and the Prophet himself, establishes and reiterates the spiritual lineage of the present community. Up until this point, Amma and the female disciples participate with the men, out in front of the curtain that has been hung between the courtyard and porch. There might be quite a lapse of time between the end of the *dastarkhān* and *salāmat* and the arrival of the *qavvāls* from the Old City. One night, we waited until 2 A.M. for the musicians to arrive, and they never did, nor did they send word as to what had happened.[8] While this was an anomalous situation, Abba, Amma, and the attending disciples and family members did not seem particularly bothered that the *samā* did not proceed. The evening was spent in easy conversation, drinking tea, and chewing *pān*. Abba engaged in informal teaching, and several disciples took the opportunity to ask specific advice from both Amma and Abba. Their lack of concern over the actualization of the *samā* suggests the possibility that the gathering of the disciples at the ritual, one that embodies the authority of the *pīr* and the hierarchical, but intimate, relationship between *pīr* and disciple might be as important as the *qavvālī* musical ritual itself.

When the musicians arrive, the women move to their position behind the curtain and the men take their places around the edges of the courtyard, with Abba seated on his *gaddī*, his son to his left, and the other *murīds* seated in hierarchical order (based on age and spiritual seniority) on the other two sides. And the *qavvālī* begins. As the musicians warm up and sing an introductory song, one by one the male *murīd* approach Abba to honor him with floral garlands and press their heads against his feet.[9] Significantly, several *murīds* also walk around the curtain to garland Amma. Amma and Abba give back the garlands to chosen disciples, who accept them as signs of approval and love as well as status in the community of disciples. I make note here of the social and ritual status of the musicians, the *qavvāls*. The term "*samā*" literally means "listening," which, as Carl Ernst points out, gives us an indication that the focus of the *samā* experience is with the audience and not with the musicians: "Performance was generally the job of service professionals of relatively low social status, much like actors or dancers in nineteenth-century Europe" (1997, 180). I was often surprised at the way the musicians arrived and set up their instruments, were fed a cup of tea, and began their performance with only minimal social interactions with Amma, Abba, or their disciples. Nevertheless, the musicians are crucial and their performance, in large part, shapes the spiritual experience of *samā* participants (note that taped *qavvālī* does not usually induce trance). According to Sufi tradition, *qavvāls* may even "hold in their hands" the very lives of participants who go into trance.

The *Kalām*: Poetry That Pulls at the Heart

Abba asserts that it is the poetry [*kalām*] of the *qavvālī* that particularly moves the devotee to a particular heightened spiritual state (implying that it is *words* rather than the *music* that induce trance, although the two can hardly be separated, since this poetry does not exist without the music): "It is the poetry that pulls at the heart. . . . A happiness is born from the poetry and we begin to twirl." *Qavvālī* poetry has several identifiable themes: praise to Muhammad, Ali, or the saints (particularly the founding *pīr* of the *silsilā*); descriptions of various states of love and relationship with the *pīr* or God; and physical descriptions of Mecca and particular shrines of famous saints.[10] The *qavvāls* are responsible for choosing appropriate verses and gauging the audience members' reactions and states of mind/heart. The musicians at one *samā* were an elderly grandfather and two teenage grandsons apprenticing with him. On this night, very few disciples went into trance, and the absence of trance was blamed directly on the *qavvāls*. While the audience enjoyed the young boys' performance in a kind of condescending way, they were inexperienced, and Abba's disciples said they did not know how to "arouse emotion." The repetition of phrases over and over with increasing intensity carries audience members beyond the words themselves into the heightened state Abba describes. Because I sat with the women on the opposite end of the courtyard from the musicians, the words of most of the *qavvālī* performances I recorded are not clearly discernable. However, below I provide two typical sequences from a performance; during this part of the performance, I was seated on a small ledge behind a row of male disciples. Every couplet is repeated at least twice (except when someone goes into trance, in which case the lines that have drawn the person into trance are repeated over and over).

1. My heart is full of love [*iśq*] for Muhammad.
   If the heart is at peace, what more do you need?
      My heart is full of love for Muhammad.
      If the heart is at peace, what more do you need?
   I search only in the lanes of Medina;
   I have no care for the rest of the world.
      I search only in the lanes of Medina;
      I have no care for the rest of the world.
   To those who are proud of their beauty,
   Such pride is not a good thing.

To those who are proud of their beauty,
Such pride is not a good thing.
Look, those are the footprints of Muhammad,
Those spots on the face of the moon.
 Look, those are the footprints of Muhammad,
 Those spots on the face of the moon.
My heart is full of love for Muhammad.
If the heart is at peace, what more do you need?
 My heart is full of love for Muhammad.
 If the heart is at peace, what more do you need?
Wait, wait a while, Muhammad.
We haven't taken in our fill.
 Wait, wait a while, Muhammad.
 We haven't taken in our fill.
Our hearts are still thirsty; our sight still thirsty.
Why such a hurry to leave?
 Our hearts are still thirsty; our sight still thirsty.
 Why such a hurry to leave?
My heart is full of love for Muhammad.
If the heart is at peace, what more do you need?
 My heart is full of love for Muhammad.
 If the heart is at peace, what more do you need?

2. Look for God in man; see if His reflection [*jalvā*] is there.
The one you're looking for is there, in your own house.
 Look for God in man; see if His reflection is there.
 The one you're looking for is there, in your own house.
You won't find God through knowledge [*ilm*];
This is a deep, deep secret [*rāz*].
 You won't find God through knowledge;
 This is a deep, deep secret.
Beauty and all that; they're just words, just words.
Look for God in man; see if His reflection is there.
 Beauty and all that; they're just words, just words.
 Look for God in man; see if His reflection is there.

3. Ghaus-e-Azam is the *pīr* of all *pīrs*.
Ghaus-e-Azam is my *pīr*.

Ghaus-e-Azam is the *pīr* of all *pīrs*.
Ghaus-e-Azam is my *pīr*.
The court of the friends of Allah is sparkling.
The court of the friends of Allah is sparkling.
The court of the friends of Allah is sparkling.
The court of the friends of Allah is sparkling.

(The court of the friends of Allah refers to the gathering of the *pīr* and disciples at the *samā*.)

The verses that describe wandering in Medina's lanes and finally finding Muhammad and being filled with love are particularly loved verses in Abba's *samā*; they are performed frequently and often cause disciples to be moved to trance. They also reflect the personal narratives I heard frequently around Amma's table, of patients or disciples wandering from *pīr* to *pīr*, looking for the right relationship, and the joy and contentment disciples experience when they find their *pīr*. And of course, Amma repeated in her teachings (sometimes with words pointedly directed to me) almost verbatim the lines: "You won't find God through knowledge; This is a deep, deep secret." How then are we to know the deep secret of God? The *qavvālī* line gives the answer that is enacted in the *pīr/murīd* relationship so central to both Amma's healing and Abba's teachings: "Look for God in man; see if His reflection is there." As Abba repeatedly teaches, "We know God's love only through observing the love between humans."

Qavvālī is first and foremost associated with the *samā*; however, I periodically heard Amma hum or sing the line that described wandering the lanes of Medina in other contexts. Or she would sometimes sing or make reference to a line or couplet as part of her teachings. For example, she often warned me, singing the verse above, that all the studying I did could not possibly cover God's creation—that it was a deep secret [*rāz*] beyond the reaches of external knowledge. By 1996 Amma had purchased a tape recorder, and her sons often played tapes of *qavvālī* in her healing room. Amma enjoyed the music and often hummed along. (I, on the other hand, was glad she did not have the tape recorder during most of the years I was taping her healing room interactions; the music would have drowned out her words.) *Qavvālī* has also become a popular non-ritual performance genre in South Asia, for which there are formal com-

petitions between singing groups; audiences for these competitions include radio and television audiences, extending beyond traditional Sufi
audiences.

As the *samā* progresses, a *murīd* who is moved by a particular line of
song might express his appreciation by lifting up his hand, palm upward
(the *qavvāls* often gesture in a similar way as they are singing). The
musicians increase their rhythmic pace and intensity when they see an
audience member responding in this way. The *murīd* might indicate a
further intensification of emotion by gifting money to the *qavvāls*; however, he does not present the offering directly. He first approaches another
murīd, draws him to his feet, and the two might then approach other
disciples to come with them. Each *murīd* pulls from his pocket his own
cash contribution (paper notes, not change) and the group, all holding
hands, approaches Abba. He blesses the money with a kiss and sometimes
stands to join the group, which then approaches the *qavvāls* together to
make its presentation, leaving the money on the harmonium lid. The only
indication that the *qavvāls* notice the money is that they often raise the
volume of their singing and gesticulate with their hands a little more
vigorously.[11]

Moved by Poetry into Trance

Finally, the most intense expression of mystical experience is when
disciples enter into a trancelike state called *ramz*. Abba explains the meaning of *samā* and *ramz*:

Sam is the same as *sun*, to listen; *sam* is to remain silent [*khamoś*]. If
someone starts to sway, others will let him do it; they might hold on to
him, but they don't say anything. If anyone calls out, who will that be?
Only the musicians, and they'll keep singing that same line. Even if someone's a Hindu, if he does *zikr* [remembrance of the names of God] and
has faith, then it [*ramz*] can come even to him.

Moved by the repetitive words of the poetry, a male disciple might
enter *ramz* and stand up and begin twirling in the middle of the courtyard.
First Abba and then the other disciples stand up, acknowledging the

15. Abba and disciples giving offerings to *qavvāls* during *samā*, 1995.

presence of the saints [*buzurgān-e-dīn*; their presence is indicated through the *ramz*]. Amma says, "They're present at the gathering; you have to respect them. No one can see them. Only when this state is reached can anyone see them. Then Abba stands up in reverence." Abba and the other disciples form a circle around the disciple, holding hands to keep him from spinning out of the circle. Or the tranced disciple might go over to Abba and pull him up, engaging Abba in the twirling, and other disciples might join them. Abba told me he embraces the disciple in order to cool down the trance [*ṭhaṇḍā karnā*]. Other disciples in "lighter" trance might stay seated (usually in a kneeling position) and simply sway back and forth. In all of these instances, eventually Abba or a senior disciple will hold a small bottle of scent against the nose of the tranced disciple, gently blowing *duā* over him and drawing him out of that state. While someone is in trance, the musicians keep repeating over and over the same line under which the *samā* participant went into trance until he is drawn out of it. Regula Qureshi observes, "For performers this [trance] signals a moment of extreme responsibility, for unless the ecstatic person continues to hear the phrase that so moved him, he may die" (1986, 4). There are numerous oral traditions that tell of saints who died when the line or verse was not appropriately sustained by the musicians.[12]

Not all of the disciples at Abba's *samā* participate in the physical movement of twirling [*wajd*], only those who have achieved a particular level of spiritual development go into trance; it is an external expression of internal spiritual achievement. At one *samā* in which two newly initiated Hindu disciples were participating for the first time, one of the men went into trance quite early on in the evening. The women I was sitting with expressed disapproval, since this new disciple "didn't know anything. This isn't right. He's just become a *murīd*. What does he think? Not *everyone* achieves *wajd*. It's a matter of time." It turns out he was not familiar with the ritual grammar (social conventions) of trance in this context and inappropriately (according to the women with whom I was sitting) continued his trance behavior even after Abba had passed scent under his nose several times. But Abba was patient and finally simply ignored him; the trance eventually died out on its own accord. There were whispers that perhaps it was not a "real" *wajd* at all, but only an act.[13] While an individual *murīd* is ecstatic, he is considered to be under the authority of the *sheikh* and is expected to express himself within the spiritual/cultural framework of the tradition.

Abba himself expresses very little emotion during the *samā*, except to close his eyes as he embraces a disciple and twirls with him. Presumably, he should remain in control, as he is responsible for the decorum and experience of both individual participants and the assembly as a whole (Qureshi 1986, 126). He told me that when someone enters *wajd*, they do not know "right from wrong; they don't where they're falling or what's happening." It is Abba's responsibility to keep order. However, it is also the case, according to Abba, that *jalālī pīrs* (of which he is one) express emotion less openly than *jamālī* ones, and hence it is not as likely that they will go into trance as easily or often as a *jamālī pīr* will. Qureshi reports that among the groups with which she worked, to become ecstatic was not considered to be "proper behavior" for men of high social status (129). This did not appear to be the case among Abba's disciples, perhaps because of their lower- to middle-class socioeconomic levels, or perhaps because of the intimate context of Abba's *samā* (in comparison to *dargāh*-based *samās*).

After a few hours of *qavvālī*, the musicians stop for a rest and all those present go behind the curtain (presumably hung to separate men from women) to be served tea, chat, and stretch their legs before taking their seats again for another hour or two. Some of the women might leave to go home at this point, while others lie down where they are and fall asleep. On a few occasions, even Amma went inside the house to sleep after the tea break, encouraging me to come with her. On one of these nights, Amma justified her leaving by saying that the musicians were "no good," as they only sang a few good verses and then simply sang "Ahhhh . . ." (i.e., nonsense); again, the selection and knowledge of verse, not just music, is crucial to creating the experience of the *samā*. The *samā* ritual ends with recitation of the *fātiḥā* and distribution of sweets, but after the musicians leave, the night often stretches into early morning as a handful of male *murīds* gather around Abba, who advises them and gives conversational teachings. These disciples at some point in the pre-dawn hours simply lie down where they are and sleep for a few hours, and one by one they go home as the sun rises. One early morning, I watched the first male disciple to leave go over to a sleeping Abba and lovingly massage his feet for a few minutes first; stop at the flagpole, bowing his head at its base; and only then depart.

Arousing Love through *Qavvālī: Hāl, Wajd,* and *Ramz*

The highlight of the *samā* is when the mystical experience of love (God's love and that of the *pīr*) manifests itself in the ecstatic trance state of *wajd*. In fact, among the audience members, a primary criterion of whether or not the *qavvāls* are good, whether they successfully choose appropriate poetry and perform it well, is the activation of such a *wajd* state.

When asked how a person goes into the state of *wajd*, Abba explained:

When a person gets something good, some good poetry [*kalām*], then he loses himself [*bekhudī*] and starts going round and round/twirling; thinking only of Him [Allah, Muhammad, and/or the *pīr* Ghaus-e-pak]; he doesn't know what's happening. . . . It is the poetry that pulls at the heart. Then the person goes into *wajd*.

In another context, Abba described specifically the twirling movement of *wajd*, called *ramz*:

Once he [the disciple] loses himself because of the poetry, then he starts to twirl; and they keep singing that same verse and he keeps twirling. We call this a kind of *ramz*, a kind of *jos* [enthusiasm, fervor]. It's like if you get the *jos* of something, won't you be happy? It's the same way, hearing the poetry, joy is born and the twirling starts. . . . It's a kind of *jos*. Isn't it true that happiness is born from this kind of *jos*? It's like that: a happiness is born from the poetry and we begin to twirl. . . . At other times, if you asked someone to do this [twirling], he wouldn't be able to do it. In some [disciples] sadness is born and in others happiness.

Abba elaborated that the repetitious singing of *qavvālī* is like *zikr*, remembering the name of God—the repetition fans the coals, the spark; when the spark flames, the trance state is manifest as *wajd*.[14] According to Abba, when he himself is in such a heated state, disciples embrace him

215

to get some of his *śakti*, or spiritual energy. On the other hand, when he embraces and twirls with a disciple in trance, Abba absorbs the heat of the disciple and the *wajd* gradually dissipates.

Amma also experiences *wajd* behind the curtain, but it is not manifest through twirling. In this state, she says, Allah becomes close [*qurb hāsil hotā*]; her soul [*dil*] leaves her body and she receives visions of the *buzurgān-e-dīn* [i.e., the saints]. But this is an experience she can describe no further because "it is a deep secret." Her daughter once described the vision of the *pīr* that comes to the *samā* participant who experiences *wajd*, "It comes even to Hindus. It comes to those who love Allah. . . . They become senseless; they're not in themselves, these people. If you hit them, if they fall, they break; sometimes their breath also leaves them. This happened once at Afzal Biyabani's *dargāh* and the person died."

Amma and other participants in Abba's *samās* sometimes use the term "*hāl*" [lit., state or condition] interchangeably with *wajd*. Peter van der Veer reports similar usage among Rifai Sufi groups in western India, who distinguish between trance and possession with the terms *hāl* and *hāzirī* [lit., presence]. He describes *hāzirī* as the "struggle between the saint in the tomb and the spirits who 'ride' the afflicted person" (1992, 555); that is, possession by *jinn* or Hindu goddesses that causes illness, requires healing, and is not interpreted to be a state of heightened spiritual awareness. One of Amma and Abba's disciples, Hussein, in anticipation of an upcoming *samā*, volunteered that "when people say the *bābā* comes to them [i.e., the *pīr* Abdul Jilani enters their body through possession] and they start twirling with joy and enthusiasm, this is wrong. They *are* dancing from joy, but no *bābā* comes to them. *Maukīls* may come, but not *bābā*. He is way too *jalālī* to come to a person like that. [If he did so,] they would become ashes." I remind the reader of the narrative in chapter 5 in which people's heads fall off from simply saying the name of the *jalālī* saint. One can imagine, then, that the tradition would not accept that a human body could sustain the saint's physical presence; humans can sustain only a vision of such a saint.

Because I had heard Amma once distinguish between the male ecstatic experience of *ramz* (twirling) and that which women experience, which she identified as *hāl*, I asked her what the difference between *hāl* and *wajd* was and whether it was gender-specific. She seemed surprised that I had ever heard this distinction and in this conversation equated *hāl* and possession/*hāzirī*:

No, no. *Hāl* is the dance of the devil [*śaitān*]. What we are talking about is *wajd, wajd-zikr*. . . . The dancing at the *dargāh*, that's *hāl* [when persons are possessed by devils/satans and come to the shrine for healing]. What happens at the *samā* is *wajd*. There's a distinction between evil things [*śaitānī*] and beneficent things [*rehmānī*]. When you get *śaitānī* you dance and dance. But when you get lost in Allah, that's *wajd*; your heart flutters. Hearing the poetry, the heart flutters. When the line is finished, the person has a vision, and then he cools down. Someone says a prayer [*durūd*; a prayer of benediction, asking for mercy on the Prophet Muhammad and his descendants], someone blows on him, and we give scent. Then he gets back his strength and says, "*Allah ho, Allah ho*."

[One of Amma's disciples warned that if I watched someone in *wajd*, I would "get it, too." Amma countered,] No, no, no. Her heart is clean; she has great faith [*aqīdat*]. But she won't get it because she isn't a *murīd* yet. [The other disciple: She has trust/*itikāl*.] She won't get it because she isn't a *murīd*. If you recite *namāz* and remember Allah, then you'll stay calm. When you bow down in prayer [*sajdā*], then you cool down. That's what happens at the *qavvālī*; *wajd* happens and then they cool down. [I ask what is blown into the person's ear that brings them down from *wajd*.] It's *durūd*. First a person begins *wajd*, and then when he is satisfied, when he has seen it and his heart is satisfied, then what does he say? Ahh. He's received peace [*sukhund*], hasn't he? He's received what he wanted, right? After that, he remains only a little intoxicated [*naśā*].[15]

Whichever term is used, "*wajd*" or "*hāl*" (their usage seems to be inconsistent and context-specific),[16] it is important to keep the distinction, in the Muslim context, between trance and possession, although the physical manifestations of these states on their participants might look similar. Allah and the saints do not possess, though they might be present; only *jinn* and devils possess and take over a person's body. In *wajd* a person is said to become so "heated" by the presence of God or the *pīr* so as to enter into another state. One could say that the human soul ascends rather than the deity descending; the distinction is subtle, but from a Muslim point of view it is very important.[17]

Female Participation in the *Samā*

Although Amma and the other women are seated behind a curtain during the *samā*, they are nevertheless active participants. The negotiation between Amma and Abba of gender roles and authority present in the healing room is also palpable at the *samā*, although the dominant voice shifts from one to the other. As mentioned earlier, Amma oversees the physical preparation of the courtyard for the *samā*, the careful laying out of the *gaddī* and the hanging of the curtain behind which she and the other women will sit. The physical manipulation of the curtain itself is an evocative image for the negotiation of gendered positioning at the *samā*. On several occasions when male disciples were hanging the curtain, Amma manipulated how low it hung to the floor so that when she was seated directly behind it, she would be able to lift it or peek under or around it to be able to see what is happening at the *samā*, rather than just hearing it. Once, as she and the disciples were literally pulling back and forth on the curtain, she exclaimed, "What are you doing? Don't you think we women want to see?" Amma herself often sits at the entrance of the curtained area (the curtain does not extend all the way to the wall, leaving a walkway), where she can both see and be seen.

The women do not sit behind the *pardā* until the *qavvāls* arrive; they sit with the men around the *dastarkhān* and participate in the antiphonal recitation of the *salāmat*. Further, during the tea break in the middle of the *samā*, male disciples come back behind the curtain, serve tea to the women, and often sit to converse with Amma and their female relatives and other female *murīds*. I once asked Amma why they hang the curtain at all when all of the men sitting on the other side (other than the *qavvāls*) are either relatives or disciples, in front of whom neither she nor the other female relatives and/or *murīds* veil. Further, in the healing room she openly sits unveiled to meet both known men and strangers. Amma laughed at my question and rather quizzically affirmed, "Yes, you're right!" But then one of the other women sitting with us explained that it is not right for men to see women in trance/*wajd*, when their saris might be mussed up and fall off their shoulders; this is why the curtain is hung.

The informal atmosphere behind the curtain, where the women are crowded together, is very different than that of the formally laid out male "court" where the men sit very still and quietly unless in trance or making offerings. Women might quietly converse, and several of the younger ones often fall asleep. But they are, nevertheless, also immersed in the song; and it may suddenly move them to trance. Because of the sometimes uncontrolled bodily movements of trance, there often exists certain ambivalence toward *wajd*, particularly on the part of women. Remember the warning of one of Amma's disciple that I, too, might "get it" if I witnessed someone else in *wajd*, as if this was a state into which I would not *want* to enter. Amma first replied that my "clean heart" would protect me, as if *wajd* is something one would want to deflect. Only secondarily did she imply that I would not be affected by *wajd* because I am not a disciple; that is, that only someone who has reached this spiritual state (of commitment) will receive *wajd*. A similar ambivalence is often expressed about possession in Hindu ritual contexts, even in the same words warning me that I might become possessed by the goddess if I attended possession rituals and festivals (this advice is given by both higher-caste Hindu and Christian friends, who themselves are not involved in possession rituals). That is, even if it is the goddess making herself present, and thus presumably possession is an honor and something one would seek, "You never know what you're going to do," as one Chhattisgarhi woman told me.

Both Hindu and Muslim women are concerned that such altered states of consciousness might cause them to move in such a way as to be "immodest"; and usually a possessed or tranced woman will have a female companion with her to keep her sari appropriately wrapped. In Abba's *samā*, I saw only three women enter *wajd*: Amma, her oldest daughter, and an age-mate and good friend of Amma's. The number of men entering *wajd* far outnumbers that of the women, although like the three women, the same men consistently enter trance from *samā* to *samā*. All three of these women already have social and spiritual status in the community of *murīds*, so presumably they have nothing to lose by giving themselves to *wajd*; it also confirms their spiritual status and strength.

The first indication of female *wajd* is a swaying movement from the waist; as soon as there is any hint of *wajd*, the woman's hair is loosened (in the same way that Hindu women's hair is loosened when they are possessed by the goddess). Hair is an entry into the body; when it is bound up, the body is believed to be controlled.[18] In this case, the woman wants to be open to the spiritual experience of *ḥāl*, to the presence of her *pīr* and of God. When women achieve *wajd* or *ḥāl* during the *samā*, they do not twirl (there would not be space for them to do so, as the women are seated very closely together); rather, they stay seated, swaying back and forth. Amma and her daughter often raise a stiff arm to the sky, pointing upward with their index finger, calling out the name of God, "*Hai Allah, hai Allah, hai Allah.*" Or she might call out to her *pīr*, "*Hamāre pīr, hamāre pīr* [Oh, my *pīr*]." Amma's friend and daughter often fling their arms and head around and around and eventually lie down and roll back and forth wildly. Another woman sitting next to her puts her arms around her to try to control the movements, and someone may attempt to keep her sari draped modestly. Finally, Amma moves close to the woman in trance and holds the scent under her nose; if Amma is in trance, her friend does this. Often the women have to call out to the *qavvāls* to keep singing the particular line they were singing when the woman went into trance (the singers would not necessarily know that a woman has gone into trance).[19] When Amma's daughter comes out of trance, Amma lovingly blows on her and pats her chest as she lays exhausted from the trance experience (both physically and presumably emotionally and spiritually).

There is continual communication from one side of the curtain to the other during the course of the *samā*. Abba, seated right in front of the curtain, is aware when a woman on the other side of the curtain enters trance and hands back a small bottle of scent to apply to her nose, to cool down the trance. When she is moved by a particular line or verse, Amma periodically hands forward monetary offerings to one of the disciples on the other side of the curtain, gesturing for him to take it forward to the *qavvāls* on her behalf. Further, Amma herself often goes into trance at the same time as a heightened moment when *ramz* occurs in front of the curtain. Her *wajd*, in particular, impacts the male company seated in front of the curtain; they often shift in their "seats" and attempt to look back to see what is happening. But the *samā* court is, ultimately, not Amma's arena of primary authority. While her presence is marked and her *hāl* punctuates every *samā* performance, she is not at the center of the performance. The *ramz* (twirling) of the courtyard is not available as a performance genre to her. Amma explained, "*Ramz* is joy [*jos̄*]; isn't joy born from that? But women don't do this. [The implication from her other teachings may be that a woman's life is suffering, not joy.] They get *hāl*; that's just the way it is." But it seems apparent through Amma and Abba's commentaries that love/*muhabbat is* available to women in other ways, and the success of Amma's healing practice is testimony to this.

The *Samā* Contextualized in Abba's Teaching

During a two-month interlude in my fieldwork in 1994–1995, I attended a performance (also called *samā*) in Atlanta, Georgia, given by a touring group of the Turkish Mevlevi Sufi order (more commonly known in the United States as the "whirling dervishes") on a secular performance stage. I attended another Mevlevi performance in an Atlanta church in 2003, which was explicitly more "spiritual."[20] I was struck by the contrast in movement of the dance/whirling of the Mevlevis and that of the participants in the *samā* of Sheikh Hussain in his small Hyderabadi courtyard.

The Mevlevi whirling is controlled and singular—that is, the participants whirl independently around the *sheikh*, although all doing the same movement simultaneously. Further, *all* of the participants whirl (except the musicians and the *sheikh*). The performer begins to whirl before achieving a state of trance, and it is not obvious to the observer when or if the performer achieves that state. Presumably, the whirling itself both guides the performer into trance and is an expression of that trance. When the music ends, so does the whirling, and participants seem to come right out of the trance state without a transitional stage. In contrast, in Abba's *samā*, only those few who enter a trance state, individually or in twos or threes, whirl, circle, or "dance," and their movements are significantly different than that of the Mevlevi performers. Here, instead of whirling alone, the male participant in trance is embraced by another disciple or the *sheikh* and both twirl round and round together. Sometimes the rotations are slow, almost at a standstill, and other times the movement is extremely fast, so that the centrifugal force causes the pair to lean backward, holding each others hands' instead of embracing, the weight of each holding the other up. The rest of the disciples stand to form a circle around those twirling in trance, holding hands, to keep the tranced participants from falling over.

If one takes seriously both the creative and reflective capacity of performance, as suggested by scholars of ritual and performance (see Briggs 1988; Flueckiger 1996; Kapchan 1995; Schiefflin 1985), then the difference in the form of movement is significant. It would seem to suggest a different spiritual experience and goal between the two Sufi traditions. The goal of the Mevlevi mystical experience, as expressed in Maulana Jalaladdin Rumi's poetry, is that of *fanā*, variously translated as annihilation, union, immersion, death in ecstasy, and/or nullification of self in God.[21] The earlier mystic Hallaj used the image of the moth being attracted by and flying into the candle flame to express *fanā*.[22] Rumi images *fanā*:

> Like the flame of the candle in the presence of the sun,
> he is (really) non-existent, (though he is) existent in formal calculations.
> (Schimmel 1975, 145)

Abba's teachings articulate quite a different spiritual purpose and goal than those of Rumi and other classical Sufi poets. He consistently teaches that the purpose of human life, particularly that of the Sufi, is love [*muhabbat*]. I never heard Abba or any of his *murīds* speak of *fanā* or use the term Qureshi heard for spiritual union, "*wisāl.*" The love Abba speaks of is articulated not as union but of relationship, both with God and one's fellow human beings. Abba often begins his teachings with a series of questions such as, "Why are we here? What is our purpose?" and his answer is almost always *muhabbat*. He teaches that the only way we can experience the love of God as humans is to experience that love as expressed between humans. A disciple elaborated, "The most important thing is love; it's simply loving your fellow human being as an equal [*barābar*]. When you see someone on the side of the road and stop, *that's* what makes you a human being [*insāniyat*] rather than just a person [*ādmī*]."[23] This love expressed through human relations, made possible only by God and taught by the *sheikh,* is most explicitly visible in the whirling trance state in which Abba and his disciples embrace. We're told that the disciples "lose themselves" when the poetic lines of the *qavvālī* are good; but performatively they are kept, quite literally, grounded in Abba's embrace, which absorbs the potentially dangerous heat [*jalāl*] of *wajd.*

Gyarwin Sharif: The Annual Festival of Abdul Qadir Jilani

Abba's monthly *samā* is a "private" ritual for a close community of disciples who have all taken formal initiation. But once a year, on the annual death anniversary of Ghaus-e-Azam, the twenty-sixth day of the fourth month of the Muslim year, Rabī ath-thānī, Abba and Amma host a community-wide celebration called Gyarwin Sharif (lit., the "auspicious eleventh") to which they say up to 800 to 1,000 people come.[24] This celebration publicly draws Amma back into the center, displaying the authority of both Amma and Abba. It begins in the early evening with the ritual empowerment and reinstatement of the new flags of Ghaus-e-Azam Dastagir, followed by a ritualized feeding of a wide circle of Abba and Amma's disciples and patients, relatives and friends. It ends with a *samā* that lasts into the late night. The meal is called *niyāz,* and lay Muslims, too, might sponsor such a feast (albeit on a much smaller scale than that hosted by Amma and Abba) during the days preceding Gyarwin, in thanksgiving for a particular vow they have taken in the name of the saint that has been fulfilled. If a person cannot afford an entire feast, s/he might cook sweets and distribute them.

As Gyarwin Sharif approached in 1994 (the first time I was to witness it), the great excitement among Amma's family members and neighbors was about the *zarabwālās,* a word I had never heard before. When I tried to figure out who *zarabwālās* were and how the celebrations would involve them, several of the Muslim children in Amma's neighborhood assured me that I should not worry: "Just come and you'll understand everything." (It turned out not to be quite as simple for me to understand as the children suggested.) Amma's friend Munnapa explained that *zarabs* were sharp instruments that the *zarabwālās* put through their cheeks, necks,

223

16. Abba and his disciples in *wajd* embrace at a *samā*, 1995.

and chests; these men, she said, had such spiritual powers that they were able to keep from bleeding when they touched the *zarabs*, unlike "normal" people. Amma interrupted,

They also put it on me last year. [Amma gestured with her finger as if it was something sharp going through her cheek and forehead.] Everyone said, "No, no, don't do it." The *murīds* were saying, "No, Ammi, don't put those [*zarabs*] in." But I said, "No, go ahead." When you're lost in the thought of God, then even if a scorpion stings you, you won't feel the pain; if a snake bites you, the poison won't affect you.

Amma laughed, seemingly taking great pleasure in breaking the "rules" of who did and did not have the power to sustain the *zarabs* or who should submit to them. Both the act of successfully sustaining the *zarabs* with no sign of blood and its performed narrative (which has now entered Amma's repertoire of stories of her *karāmat*) mark Amma as particularly courageous and spiritually powerful. The traditional Gyarwin Sharif *zarabwālās* are from the Rifai (Qalandar) order and are said to be direct descendents of the Prophet—presumably only they should/do have the power to sustain the *zarabs* without any blood dropping from the puncture wounds.[25]

Abba explained that the purpose of calling the *zarabwālās* was to cool the *jalāl* of the *pīr*, much like his embrace of his disciples does during *wajd*. Abba told again, in abbreviated form, the story of people's heads falling off for simply saying the name of Ghaus out loud:

He was powerful like this ever since he was a child—he could raise the dead even when he was a child. Once when his grandfather was chasing him, he called all the bodies in the graveyard to rise up. The corpses got up and ran. It happened that a woman was there crying over her dead child. The angel of death was carrying the bag [with corpses in it] away. The *pīr* snatched the bag from the angel, and it split open and all the corpses came to life. His grandfather said, "You *jalālī* one, you shouldn't do this." But God said, "Don't reprimand him, because he is my friend [*yār*] and I am his friend."[26]

225

So, see. He was important right from his birth. . . . [Abba then tells the story of when the Ghaus-e-Azam was in his mother's womb and tickled her so that she would move and not get bitten by a snake.][27] . . .

His mother died after giving birth to him. Saints' mothers never live after they give birth to them, these *pīrs*. [Joyce: Why?] No, they never live. *Pīrs* do things like play in the forest. Their mothers can't tolerate these kinds of things [i.e., they're afraid for them]. They would want to tell them not to go here or there. Even the Prophet's mother died after giving birth to him. She gave birth and then she died immediately thereafter.[28]

This is the powerful *pīr* who provides reason for the celebration—his heated *jalālī* character is the motivation for the performances of the popular *zarabwālās*. But Gyarwin Sharif does more than honor Ghaus-e-Azam Dastagir; it places Amma and Abba in his spiritual lineage and performatively identifies and recreates that power in their own social and physical bodies. In fact, visually and performatively, particularly for the 'public' that attends the Gyarwin Sharif rituals, Amma and Abba would seem to be at the ritual center of the festival rather than the great saint Jilani.

Early on the morning of Gyarwin, Amma's family members and close disciples begin to prepare food and water for the feast that evening: water is hauled and poured into large barrels (this neighborhood does not have running water in homes, only public water pumps from which they haul water), piles and piles of garlic cloves are peeled, vegetables are cut, and fires are lit outside in the courtyard over which large pots are placed for cooking rice and vegetable and meat curries. (The movement of women peeling individual garlic cloves and stacking them in piles is remarkably reminiscent of the ritual counting and piling of dark seeds during the *dastarkhān* ritual.) Men, women, and older children are all involved in these outdoor food preparations, and there is lots of laughter and good humor as water is sloshed onto someone's clothes or someone loses count of the rice measured into the cooking pot. On such public cooking occasions, women are most involved in cutting up vegetables and garlic while men are the "cooks" who stir over big cauldrons and fires. (This is a common gendered separation of duties at large public functions such as this throughout India, including wedding feasts, school picnics, etc.) Most of the younger women and girls have had henna designs drawn on their hands the night before, as they do for weddings.

One year on Gyarwin Sharif I noticed that one of Amma's daughters was nowhere to be seen, the daughter who usually took me under her wing when Amma was too busy coordinating activities to spend much personal time with me. I asked where Sultana was and was told to go behind the house to the single room where Muhammad now lived. I found her sitting on a cot by herself, delighted to see me and have some company. I thought she was sick, but she quickly told me that the reason for her exclusion from the Gyarwin celebrations was that she was ob-serving menstrual taboos; she could not even help with the cooking, much less, she said, be near the flags when they were reinstalled.

Although Amma's healing room is closed on Gyarwin, in the early part of the morning she sees patients who have come from distant neigh-borhoods, not knowing the significance of this day (as she is also willing to do on Fridays, when the healing room is also closed). One year, after Amma had given instructions for the various food preparations, seen to the measurements of rice, and made sure everyone knew what their tasks were, she donned her *burqā* and told me she would be back shortly—she was going to the bazaar to buy bangles for her daughters and daughters-in-law. She had already put away new saris and sari slips for the women of her family, some that she had purchased and others that had been given to her by disciples.[29] Amma always has a stack of new saris in her steel almira and thus is never caught off guard by an unexpected guest to whom a sari should be gifted on such occasions—a custom kept by many Indian women who can afford to do so. Meanwhile, Abba sits in a folding chair out in the middle of the courtyard, watching preparations and being greeted by disciples and guests as they arrive to help in preparations. He becomes more involved in organizational tasks when the tent [*śāmiyānā*] is set up in the open field adjacent to Amma's courtyard, under which the *samā* will be held. This is, quite literally, *his* court where he takes his seat of honor during the late-night *samā*.

Renewing Ritual Flags and the *Zarabwālās*

The flag rituals begin at sunset when Gyarwin is celebrated in fall, winter, or spring (earlier than sunset when the festival date falls in the summer; the Muslim calendar is strictly lunar, so the celebration cycles through the solar year over a period of years). At this point, participants are limited to family and close disciples. The faded old flags from the previous year are taken down from the courtyard *cillā*; and the flagpoles are repainted a bright green and new flags are attached to them. Amma has made a sandalwood paste mixture that she applies both to the flags themselves and the silver flag standards (which resemble the Shiite *ālams*, whose shapes include the *panjā* and crescent moon). She has also prepared a clay pot of hot coals over which she sprinkles resin, then passes the flags through the billowing smoke. The flags are raised as high as they can be in Amma's small living space. Family members and disciples squeeze into the small space, and Khalid begins the *salāmat*, a praise litany of all the saints of their lineage, beginning with the Prophet Muhammad, his two grandsons Hassan and Hussein, the twelve Shii *imāms*, the saint Qadir Jilani, up to Muinaddin Chishti and Abba's own *pīr* Sayed Shah Mehamud Alam Husseini Sailik.

By this time, a large crowd has begun to gather in the courtyard and the *zarabwālās* have arrived from the Old City. As the flags are carried out to the courtyard by Abba's disciples, the *zarabwālās* begin to beat their drums, play tambourines, sing, and stand in front of the highly held flags. They bring their *zarabs* to be prayed over by Abba, and then, one at a time, each of them takes a *zarab* in hand, twirls it, and squats down to pierce his eyelid, cheek, chest skin, or tongue. He stands up and carefully, slowly turns around for all to see that not a single drop of blood has fallen. The *zarab* is traditionally a metal skewer or spike or a mace with thin chains attached to the circumference of the ball.[30] A single performer might insert ten to twelve *zarabs* in his body at one time, through the skin of his upper arm, his chest, and his cheeks. While such piercings (and their ritual grammar) are familiar in Hindu contexts of possession, in which the ability to sustain piercings is attributable to the presence of the deity in the person, what might be unfamiliar to Hindu audience members is the fact that these Rifai men do not seem to be in any kind of altered state of consciousness or possession. They are aware of those around them, including me with my camera—and several of them posed in front of me, gesturing other audience members to clear the way. The power to sustain the *zarab,* one that prevents blood from dropping, is the Rifai hereditary *barkat;* as descendants of the Prophet, Rifai are said carry his blood, however diluted, in their veins.[31]

While the *zarabwālās* are not in an altered state of consciousness, Amma and a few senior disciples often do go into trance during the performance of the *zarabwālās,* hitting their chests or holding their arms out stiffly, crying out *"lā ilāha illā allah"* and *"hamāre pīr."* Amma told me that she loses consciousness because of the powerful and palpable presence of the *pīr* (Abdur Qadir Jilani); he is called by the performance of the *zarabwālās* and his presence is another reason given for their ability to perform without any blood dripping. At the end of the *zarab* performance, the flags are carried to the *cillā* and reinstalled, *fātihā* is led by Khalid (responsively with the entire audience participating), and then Amma and Abba are prominently seated for all present to greet them,

17. Rifai *zarabwālā* performing at the festival of Gyarwin Sharif, 1996.

one by one, bowing down and holding on to their feet, while Amma and Abba bless them. Some of the audience members are disciples who have taken formal initiation, others are former and current patients and neighbors; there is no distinction between them during this meeting except, perhaps, for how long they bow or the intensity with which they hold on to Amma and Abba's feet. It was during this part of the ritual celebrations, when the *zarabwālās* had come to take leave of Amma the year before, that Amma took a *zarab* and put it through the skin on her forehead. Many disciples bring large garlands to honor Amma and Abba, and the garlands stack up until they almost hide their faces. Periodically, Amma or Abba takes a garland and gives it back to an honored senior disciple or guest.

During this time of meeting-greeting-blessing, Amma engages in longer conversations with those who come to receive her blessing than does Abba—individuals often ask for her advice or tell her stories of their

18. Amma and Abba garlanded by disciples and friends at the annual celebration of Gyarwin Sharif. Son Khalid is standing behind Amma and disciple Mustang (Sati) is to the right of Abba, 1996. Mustang received his *khilāfat* on this occasion.

particular troubles or family transitions and she, too, inquires of their health and families. Abba, on the other hand, is more remote and formal with those who greet him. This "meet-and-bless" lasts for over an hour, and then the ritual feeding of guests begins. While Abba stays seated during the feasting, Amma walks around greeting guests individually and making sure they have enough food. Honored guests and disciples are fed in the courtyard and the more general 'public' is seated under the *sāmi-yānā*, men and women separately. Male disciples run back and forth with plates of food and take back dirty plates to be washed and put out again. Guests are fed in shifts of up to 100.

The Gyarwin *Samā*

Most guests go home after being fed, but a larger-than-normal group of disciples and close friends stay for the *samā*, which on Gyarwin nights often does not begin until 11:30 P.M. or midnight. As one of my Hindu retired professor friends, who had accompanied me to a Gyarwin cele-bration, observed as we waited patiently for the *samā* "scheduled" for 9 P.M. to begin, "It's a gentle movement in readiness, as if they have the whole night," which, of course, they do. The setup for this annual Gyar-win *samā* differs from the much smaller monthly *samā* in that the per-formance space is much bigger and the male space is up on a platform, which means that the women sit much farther away (although they are visible because no curtain is hung). The Gyarwin *samā* is more formal than the monthly rituals, in part because the group of participants is larger (fifty men rather than the fifteen or twenty that is typical at the monthly *samā*) and in part because of the prominent participation of Abba's *āmil* son-in-law. This son-in-law, who does not attend the monthly *samās*, is given a seat of prominence next to Abba and starts out the ritual with a sung recitation of *nāt* poetic verses, which adds to the formality of the occasion. Further, perhaps as a result of this increased formality, fewer disciples go into trance and the entire ritual is more sedate than monthly *samās*.

Initially the women seem to attempt to hear the *qavvālī* and see what is going on up on the male stage; however, with the words of the songs being blared from loudspeakers above their heads, it is not long until they

231

create their own ritual world without trying to synchronize their activities with what is happening in the male space. Even before the tea break at 1:30 or 2 A.M., many women have drifted into conversation and have ceased to pay attention to the *qavvālī* at all. After the tea break, most of the women either go home or simply lie down with their children where they have been seated, sleeping until early morning.

Initiation: Becoming a *Murīd* and *Khalīfā*

When I arrived in Hyderabad in early September 1996 for only a month, Abba greeted me with the exclamation that surely I had been "called," for I had come just in time for Gyarwin, and this year's celebration would be a special Gyarwin because he was going to "give his *daunī*" (green scarf) to five new disciples and his *khilāfat* to four senior disciples. That night of Gyarwin, after the ritual feasting, at about 10 P.M., Abba called into his room the three men and two women who were to become his *murīds* [formal disciples]. One couple was Hindu and the others were Muslim, and Abba treated them all the same. The sequence of the initiation ritual was as follows: 1) the perspective disciples were told first to perform *namāz*; 2) they garlanded Abba and he returned the garlands to them; 3) Abba wrapped a date for each *murīd* in the corner of his own *daunī* and each disciple held his/her date and repeated after Abba the words of the *kalmā*; 4) each *murīd* held a cup of warm milk into which Abba blew recited Quranic verses and then spit some of his own saliva; 5) Abba told the disciples to repeat after him phrases of the *kalmā* and the *fātihā*, take a sip of milk, repeat after him, then take another sip, and finally drink the entire glass. This last ritual act becomes symbolic of the whole initiation, so that to become a disciple of *pīr* is expressed as "to drink from his cup."

Then Abba told them to be seated and said that he had "just a little thing to give them; but it's a very deep thing. It's like an ember that will leap into flame if you blow on it, but will die out if you neglect it." And he gave them a *zikr* to repeat: *Allah-hū*. He instructed them to breathe in and out with each syllable, swinging their heads from side to side on each syllable. Abba then asked the disciples to practice the *zikr* in front of him so he could check their breathing. One male disciple didn't breathe loudly until Abba insisted that he do so. Another breathed too loudly on the "*hū*" and everyone in the room laughed when Abba told him he would extinguish any life he had if he continued breathing that way. After he was certain that each *murīd* knew the correct method of *zikr*, Abba sent them out of the room, saying, "Now you're new people. Go out and meet your *pirānimā* [Amma] and your new *pīr* brothers and sisters [fellow *mur-īds*]." The five were now officially Abba's *murīds*, but the Hindus were not necessarily identified as Muslims.

Later that evening when I saw photographs of Abba's Hindu disciple Sati's ritual circumcision celebration and heard the commentary about it from Amma, I realized that simply becoming a disciple does not immediately change one's religious identity, even though a Hindu man or woman says the *kalmā* when he or she "drinks from Abba's cup." Sati had been called a "Hindu *murīd*" for many years, even though he had started to come to Amma's healing room as a teenage boy and had been closely associated with Amma for close to twenty years. Gradually, he began to grow his hair and beard, wear more Muslim-identified clothing (long *kurtās*, often green, and the Muslim *topī*, an embroidered or white crocheted head covering), and regularly observe Friday prayers in the mosque. The final step in Islamization was his circumcision. Only now he was called a Muslim by Amma, Abba, and their other disciples, and he took the Muslim name Mustang. It is unclear to me what a female equivalent to circumcision would be or is in this context. In the years that I have known Amma and Abba, I have not heard of a Hindu woman "becoming" a Muslim in quite the same way as Sati/Mustang did. The Hindu woman who "drank from Abba's cup" asked him whether or not to wear the red forehead marking associated with Hindu women. He told her to do so in the presence of her in-laws so as not to cause family stress, but not when she came in front of Amma and/or him. (Amma's friend Munnapa said that she had not become a disciple of Amma and Abba's because she did not want to give up wearing the *bottu*.) Hindu men, too, should not enter the healing room or attend the *samā* with vermilion powder on their foreheads (for men the red mark on their forehead is a sign of having performed the Hindu ritual of *pūjā*). Sati tells the story of coming into the presence of Amma having forgotten about the *bottu* on his forehead; it burned into his forehead and left a scar that is still visible. Since then, he has never applied the vermilion on his forehead. While not applying the *bottu* might be part of the process of Islamization, it hardly seems the equivalent to circumcision in changing one's identity.[32]

When the *qavvāls* arrived later in the evening that Gyarwin night, the four male *murīds* who were to be given *khilāfat* were seated with honor next to Abba, two on each side; each was wearing a long green *kurtā*, a white *lungī*, and a maroon vest. After singing a poignant *nat*, Abba's son-in-law announced the name of each *murīd* who was to be given the *khilāfat*. Abba presented each one with a green satin (prewrapped) turban and an orange scarf (green and orange are the colors of Chishti and Qadiri *silsilās*, respectively). The new *khalīfās* garlanded Abba and touched his feet, then walked over to the women's section, where they garlanded Amma. When the men had returned to their seats and the *qavvālī* began, Amma gave green scarves to the wives of the married *khalīfās*, marking her own authority in the process, before the women settled in for the late-night performance, which lasted that night until 3:30 A.M.

Samā space is physically gendered and segregated; here the patriarchal lineage and public authority of the *sheikh* and his *murīds* and *khalīfās* are performed, marked, and created. However, the boundaries of the formal lineage are, in practice, more permeable and flexible than the image of the *samā* as interpreted from the courtyard center (the male perspective) might suggest. Amma's centrality and visibility at Gyarwin celebrations confirm her inheritance in the spiritual lineage that the festival marks. The two sides of the curtain [*pardā*] are performatively interdependent, reflecting the broader interdependence between Amma's healing practice and Abba's teaching and authority in the initiations of the *pīr*.

234

CONCLUSION: VERNACULAR ISLAM EMBEDDED IN RELATIONSHIPS

What is the most important thing? Love. Love is the most
important thing.

The vernacular Islam practiced in Amma's healing room, in which Amma
and Abba, as *pīr* and *pīrānimā,* heal and teach, is shaped and characterized
by a series of relationships. As Abba so often rhetorically asks in his
teachings: "What is the most important thing? Love. Love is the most
important thing." In other teachings, he emphasizes that what most distinguishes human beings from animals is their ability to recognize and
enact kinship relationships. The ability to form relationships is given to
humans by God, and furthermore, according to Abba, the only way humans can truly know and experience the love of God is to witness and
participate in love between human beings. Because relationships as they
are lived are variable, shifting, and creative, they provide the primary basis
for and site of creativity and flexibility in vernacular Islam as practiced in
Amma's healing room.

First and foremost, in Amma's own articulation, is the importance of
her relationship with God. It is a personal relationship through which she
actively communicates with and receives messages from God, a relationship whose possibility and desirability is accepted by the religious com-

munity in which she lives. Thus, when Amma says she is called by God to this work through dreams and visions, unusual as it might be for a woman, it is difficult for those who may not agree that she should sit in this role to argue openly with her, at least theoretically. Her relationship with God and its demands supersede traditional social/religious gender roles.[1] But this relationship with God would not have been enough to propel Amma into a public healing role had she not been living with a husband who himself had creative vision.

Perhaps the most unusual relationship at this particular South Indian *caurāstā* is that between Amma and Abba. Theirs is a respectful relationship that gives Amma the space within which to follow her desires and her "calling" (as she interprets it) to learn a tradition of spiritual healing traditionally only accessible to men, *pīrs*. Abba regularly reminded me that Amma could do this work only because he had given her his permission to do so. Initially I resisted Abba's statement, thinking it to be only a rhetorical strategy necessary for him to maintain his own honor [*izzat*] in a patriarchal cultural context. However, after Abba died in 1998 and I witnessed Amma's struggle to maintain her ritual position as a woman outside the patriarchal spiritual lineage, since only males can receive the *khilāfat* of succession, I realized that her ability to enter a male ritual position, make informal disciples, and meet the 'public' *had been* dependent, even if indirectly, upon Abba's cooperation and the freedoms he gave or allowed her.[2]

The seeming idiosyncrasy of Amma and Abba's relationship has established a new model for female public action at this level of practice. Abba's son Khalid, who inherited the *gaddī* after Abba's death, has also given his permission to his wife to begin to meet the 'public' at Amma's healing table during the day, when he is at his day job at the university post office. For this younger woman to begin to practice, however informally, was not a big breakthrough that she or her husband had to justify. She rather shyly admitted to her practice when I returned to Hyderabad in the summer of 2003, but she did not perform narratives that identified her as "special" and did she not tell of spiritual visions that called her into the practice. Rather, she seems to have *inherited* a gendered ritual space that Amma's presence and practice had already created, and she is entering into it gradually. While Abba and Amma's ritual roles were based on their charisma and uniqueness, Khalid and his wife entered their ritual positions through heredity.

As dependent as Amma might have been upon Abba, at least structurally, for her ritual position as *pirānimā*, his ritual authority and success were equally dependent on her healing practice. While Abba received his *pīr's khilāfat*, permitting him to make his own disciples, most, if not all, of his disciples came to him through Amma's healing practice. This direction of dependence was less verbally articulated than was Amma's dependence upon Abba's ritual status; however, it was performatively visible on a daily basis. Most disciples first came to know of Abba when they came to Amma's healing table as patients. Gradually some of Amma's patients entered into closer relationships with first Amma and then Abba. When it came time to formalize the relationship, however, the tradition demanded that it be with Abba; only the male has the right to "make disciples." When Amma and Abba were both living, few, if any, disciples perceived their discipleship to be exclusively with Abba. Before I learned that only men could make disciples, I asked some of the *murīds* who regularly came to help Amma at her healing table whether they were Amma's or Abba's disciples. Some of them quickly answered "Amma's" before catching themselves and correcting their answer to be something like "Amma's *and* Abba's"; few answered with only "Abba's." They transformed the male role of teacher/healer *pīr* into a shared role of Abba as teacher and Amma as healer—*pīr-pīrānimā*.

At the healing table itself, Amma relies on relationships with God, with his *maukīl*, and with her patients. Amma has learned the specifics of the numerical system of *abjad kā phāl*, but ultimately, she asserts, this is a mechanical system that must be infused with spiritual authority, knowledge, and love. After Amma learned the mechanics of the healing system from her *pīr*, she "sat *cillā*" [a disciplined meditative practice] for forty days in order to garner spiritual strength and authority. God gave her dreams and visions to identify and create her authority. Throughout her life, she says, she has practiced *zikr* and "read" (meditated, prayed, read, and recited the Quran), serving Allah through the night even as she serves the 'public' through the day—the former sustaining her in the latter. Once she developed a certain measure of spiritual strength, she developed the authority to call upon various *maukīl* [angels, saints, *jinn*, and Hindu deities] to carry out her commands in her healing practice: to close a rival's mouth, to find a lost child, to take away one or another kind of evil eye, to lift a fever.

Presumably many male Muslim healers have developed this kind of spiritual authority and relationship with God and have authority over *maukīl*, as evidenced in their own successful practices. However, many patients come to Amma specifically because they have heard of both her healing success and her reputation for patience and love—for her unique relationships with her patients. She takes the time to listen to them and offers comfort at the same time that she diagnoses the reason for and authoritatively declares the successful conclusion to their tales of trouble. Abba, too, recognizes her unusual patience and loving nature; he says patients "come crying and go away laughing." Although many of her patients identify Amma's loving nature as gendered, Abba says that not all women have such a nature, including others who had become disciples of their *pīr*. Amma, too, draws gendered lines of difference when she declares that there are only two castes/*jāti*, men and women. But she places her healing practice and ritual role on the male side of that impermeable line, since she herself has no female models for such practice.

Many illnesses and troubles brought to Amma's healing table are troubles in relationships or the result of inappropriate relationships, both between humans and between humans and spiritual beings (such as *jinn* or *śaitāns*). Amma's most common diagnosis is the evil eye, which is differentiated between the eye cast by humans or nonhumans, knowingly or unknowingly. Amma's prescriptions deflect potential evil eyes or draw the evil eye away from the suffering patient; other prescriptions close the mouths of adversaries or cause unfaithful husbands or meandering or lost children to return to the family. Evil eye cast by both humans and nonhumans is an (over)attachment to the patient that Amma's prescriptions sever or balance. One could say that her prescriptions reorder human and spiritual relationships. Beyond the written prescription, at other levels, too, Amma's practice incorporates and accounts for the family and social network within which a patient lives. A patient only rarely comes to Amma's healing table alone; s/he is almost always accompanied by one or more family members. And after the patient has been diagnosed and given prescriptions, other family members ask to have their *abjad* opened; it is rare that only one family member is experiencing trouble of one kind or another. Amma works within a family systems philosophy of healing.

When patients experience healing, many of them come back to Amma's healing table again and again, simply to be in her presence and absorb her *barkat*, to receive advice, and, eventually, because she begins to expect their visits. Many patients/disciples tell similar narratives of going from healer to healer, *pīr* to *pīr* or *dargāh* to *dargāh*, until they have finally found Amma and experienced healing only here. The other healers are not usually blamed for unsuccessful healing in these narratives; the fault lies in not finding the right *relationship* with the right *pīr*. Some of these disciples choose to formalize a *pīr-murīd* relationship with Abba. The formal ritual is enacted only with Abba, but Amma is never far away, both figuratively and physically.

Sitting in the presence of the *barkat* of Amma and Abba and serving them over time changes a person and what is required of him/her. For a small number of disciples, this change and deepening relationship with Amma and Abba is exteriorized when male *murīds* begin to grow their hair to shoulder length, grow beards, and wear the Muslim-identified skullcap in a process of Islamization. For Hindu disciples, a deepening relationship with Amma and Abba implies that they begin to leave explicitly Hindu rituals, such as worshiping the images of Hindu deities through offering to and receiving food from them [*pūjā*]. After I had been working with her for several years, Amma's request that I not accept the food offered to the deity [*prasād*] at a Hindu ritual was an instructive moment in how religious identities of her disciples begin to shift and solidify in continuing long-term relationships with her and Abba. She did not give me an explicit teaching about what accepting *prasād* might mean theologically, nor did she make any mention of religious identities of Hindu or Muslim. What was most important was my relationship with her, and this connection was what precluded, for her, my taking *prasād*.

Initially, when a Hindu man or woman "drinks from Abba's cup" and becomes a *murīd*, s/he says the *kalmā*; technically, reciting this statement of faith would "make" a person a Muslim. However, in this context, "conversion" is *process*: of entering and sustaining a deeper and deeper relationship with Amma and Abba, and God, gradually showing more signs of Islamization until finally, for a Hindu male *murīd*, he becomes circumcised and takes a Muslim name. Only then he is considered a Muslim. I never heard Amma and Abba talk explicitly about the necessity to "become Muslim." At the healing crossroads and the axes extending from it, what is most important is to be in relationship—with God; with the *pīr-pirānimā* (Amma and Abba), who show and from whom one can learn God's love; and with one's fellow humans (family, disciples, strangers). Relationships can and do cross religious boundaries, and it is these relationships that enable spiritual healing across boundaries of difference at this *caurāstā* in South India.

EPILOGUE

Now I have to light [shine] my own light, now that Abba's
light has gone.
                                        —Amma, January 1999

Abba died in January 1998, on the twenty-seventh day of Ramadan. But
I did not learn of his death for many months. In the summer of 1998 I
had a vivid dream of Abba borrowing the moped I had driven in 1994–
1995. As he took off with a roar, his long beard and hair, light-green
kurtā, and black-and-white cotton scarf around his neck flew behind him.
And I remember saying to myself in the dream, "He's not *borrowing* the
moped; *he's* not coming back." When I awoke, I was surprised at the
visual and emotional impact of the dream but did not make any attempt
to interpret it. A few months later, one of my Indian-American students
at Emory wanted to go to Amma to ask for help for a particularly persistent psychological illness and asked for directions to the healing room.
I was reluctant to send her, but when I spoke with her and her mother
and realized that they accepted and lived within the worldview in which
Amma practiced—that is, a world in which spiritual forces can impede
on the physical world to cause physical and emotional illness—I gave her
directions and a message for Amma. It was through an e-mail from this
student that I learned Abba had died almost ten months earlier. By this

time I had already purchased an airline ticket to return to Hyderabad for the university winter break, purchased unexplainably, really, since there was no "reason" or agenda to go to India then, when I would be going to India for a year beginning that next summer (1999). But the timing of my ticket coincided, it turns out, with Abba's first death anniversary in January 1999. When I saw Amma, I reported my dream to her and she took great joy in it, repeating it to many visitors to her healing room. We laughed together that I had perhaps been spiritually aware enough to *have* the dream but not aware enough to interpret it, and I had dreamed it several months after Abba's death. I recalled the frequency with which Amma greeted my returns to her healing room with the assertion that she had dreamed of me and I had come. Dreams had been powerful modes and idioms of communication that had crossed "the seven seas."

Abba died on the day that marks the first revelation of the Quran to the Prophet Muhammad, the twenty-seventh day of Ramadan. On that auspicious day, just as it was time for dawn prayers, Amma said he "raised his hands, said '*Ya Allah*,' and breathed his last." The reported timing of Abba's death is a crucial framework to the narrative of his death as a portent of the higher spiritual status he would achieve after death. On the occasion of my first visit to Abba's grave a year after he had died, Amma told me the following story of his death, variations of which were repeatedly performed both in and outside the healing room during my three-week stay in Hyderabad—performed for me, visiting relatives, and the radically diminished numbers of patients. Amma's performances were dramatic, punctuated by sighs, often eliciting tears from her and her small audiences. Abba died of heart failure in a hospital room, as Amma was performing *namāz* just outside his door.

Having spread my prayer mat outside, I was performing *namāz*.[1] Then, what did I see, as I was bowing my head? Mecca was in front of me, and an honorable one [*hazrat*] came there. In his hands were thick, thick chains, like this [indicates with her hands the width of the chains]. I thought, "It must be him, the angel of death [*mālak 'l maut*]. He had thick, thick chains like this; on his neck, too, were thick, thick chains; he had a big head, hair to his shoulders. He was dark-complexioned; he had thick, thick eyebrows, a broad face. He wore a green hat covered with gems. He carried a long, thin stick on which were balanced a saucer, then a stick, then a saucer, then a stick. There was an oil lamp on the top in which a flame was burning.[2] There was the Kaba, right? The Prophet's tomb, right? He came and brought the oil lamp in front of the door [and said to me], "Take this; it is your lamp." I saw all this clearly; I saw it while performing *namāz*. He put it down and went away.

At the very time that he took put it down and went away, Abba's soul took flight. Then what happened? They [others around him in the hospital] were making crying sounds, "*Yuṇ, Yuṇ.*" I was still performing *namāz*, the dawn prayer. I saw them [Abba and his *pīr*] reciting the prayer of praise [*salāt-e-tasbī*]. I was reciting the night vigil [*tahajjud*] when what did I see?[3] A magnificent palace; there was 'lighting' all around—red, pink, yellow, green 'lighting'. His hands were folded; he [Abba], too, was wearing 'white' clothes, and my *hazrat* [*pīr*] was in white. The floor inside was like this, marble stone. There was an arch, and the two of them were inside. When I began to step inside, my *hazrat* said to me, "Don't come in; don't come in with us. I haven't called you; I've called Hussain [Abba]. Hussain is with us," he said. And then my eyes opened.

[Amma sighs deeply.]

My prayers have been accepted. I prayed, and Jo-ice has come to me. Stay until the *sandal* [death anniversary ritual, to be held in two weeks]. Don't go back to America until you've seen Baba's *sandal.*[4] Baba loved you a lot; mentioning your name, he would pray to Allah. You know that I recite *namāz* at night; Allah has accepted my prayers. Allah always listens to my prayers. Up until now, they've always been fulfilled.

Those of my house, however, have not been fulfilled;[5] but it's all according to the desire of God. If Allah has put me in this troubled state, let him do so; but I won't become troubled. I remain here, just sitting and smiling. If the heart cries, let it cry; but the face shouldn't cry. We should pass through the world laughing. The heart may cry, but the face shouldn't cry. It shouldn't despair. You shouldn't cause problems to anyone else. Do you understand, Jo-ice?

[Amma lets out another deep sigh, pulls out her assortment of small *pān* boxes, and continues.]

What have we brought with us into the world; what will we take? There's that film song, right?[6] [she sings the lines]:

Oh good folks, don't tell lies; we have to go into God's presence.
There's neither elephant or horse; we can only go there by foot.

It all stays here; we go out of the world alone. What comes with us? Good deeds and bad deeds—only those two come with us. What are our hands for? To give charity, to give charity to others; this is all we take with us when we leave this world. To give to someone who's hungry; this comes with us. To show the path to a blind person; this comes with us. That's it; the rest doesn't come with us. I, too, want only these things: to be friends with everyone, to be a friend of Allah, right?

Now I have nothing. After all this [Abba's illness and death], there are debts. After repaying them, then I'll sit contentedly. I'll sit contentedly. I'll sit with only hot chili pickles, a piece of bread, and a clay pot. If I'm hungry, that's what I'll eat. I'll sit there praying, praying to Allah.

My heart is no longer attached to this world, Jo-ice. My mind isn't in this world. There's only a little; there's just a little [attachment], and for even that much, I have to try to call it here. If Allah desires it, then I, too, will happy. I'll see his [Abba's] life there [in the afterlife]. His house [grave, *mazār*] there, it has 'lighting', a bed for rest, bedding, everything; you have to see the bedding, the 'light' in that house. What did the woman say yesterday [the woman who lives across the road from Abba's grave]? Abba keeps sitting there [in the grave], and the glow of the 'light' keeps coming from that place. Abba eats *pān*. Having made his light [*rośnī*] shine, Abba left. Now I have to light [shine] my own light, now that his light has gone.

After Abba's death, the issue of male spiritual and worldly inheritance became paramount and highly contentious among his immediate family and circle of close disciples. Amma's son Khalid had technically inherited spiritual succession and authority through having received *khilāfat* from Abba many years earlier, and without Abba's physical presence, Amma was sidelined. Her son boldly took over both family, financial, and spiritual authority. Amma and Khalid vigorously disagreed about the amount of financial debt Abba had left and what was the best way to repay it.

19. Abba's gravesite on his second death anniversary, 2000.

Within that first year after death, one of Amma's favorite and closest disciples aligned himself with Khalid rather than her; the disciple needed a living male spiritual lineage as he set up his own healing practice in a neighborhood adjacent to Amma's. Previously, he had practiced as a carpenter and visited Amma daily, massaging her feet, bringing her small gifts of *pān*, bread, or fruit, and on Sunday mornings helping her in her practice. She says now that she taught him everything he knows, and yet he ignores her. There were a handful of disciples, however, whose loyalties stayed with Amma. We visited several of their homes together, and in each there was a small niche or shelf on which sat a framed photograph of Abba with a lit oil lamp and incense holder in front of it. One of the photographs I took at one of these domestic shrines clearly shows a rather amazing reflection of the lit oil lamp visible on Abba's chest, a reminder of the image Amma had reported of being given the lamp to carry on Abba's teachings (see figures 20 and 21).

Given the dynamism of the healing and spiritual contexts of Amma's life and practice, I was not surprised that when I returned to Hyderabad

20. Amma at a disciple's home shrine (*cillā*); Abba's framed
photograph at the center, 1999.

21. Abba's photograph, placed on a disciple's home shrine, with the flame of the oil lamp reflected on his heart, 1999.

for Abba's second death anniversary in January 2000, the rift between Amma and her son and other disciples seemed to be on the mend, although privately she still complained about their desertion after Abba's death. Amma's healing-room clientele had decreased dramatically; it is difficult to say whether this was because of shifting power dynamics, her own aging, her increasingly poor eyesight and arthritic pain, and/or the demoralizing experience for Amma of Abba's death and subsequent shifts in family and disciple relationships.

Amma's and Abba's interdependence had been dramatically disrupted by death. In Amma's attempt to restore some balance and personal and community healing after Abba's death, her narrative performances shifted dramatically. She no longer performed narratives of exceptional childhood or testimonials of unique healing power; death had changed the dynamics of the healing room and these narratives were seemingly no longer enough to ensure her place in a spiritually authoritative role in a patriarchal system

22. Amma and Abba's gravesite in 2002, now a fully developed *dargāh*.
Amma's grave is to the right in the added screened section. As of
summer 2003, a new settlement had grown up on all sides of the
dargāh and a Saudi-style mosque now fills the plot right next to it.

of lineage and inheritance. Amma's narrative performances began to center on stories that uniquely aligned her with Abba and their *pīr*—it was
she who received the lit lamp from the messenger of death. These narratives, in a new genre of cooperative performance, both spoke *of* and *for*
Abba (rather than with him) and gave Amma a new voice as she struggled
for a new basis for authority.

On the occasion of Abba's first death anniversary, a time characterized
by discord with her son, Amma sometimes speculated that he and other
disciples would probably try to bury her down on ground level rather than
up with Abba on the raised platform that was his *mazār*. But when she
died of heart failure in August 2001, she was buried alongside Abba. The
metallic green screening around his grave was extended to encompass her
grave; a chandelier and several velvet fans were hung above her grave, as

they had been above his. Amma's name, Rukhiya Bi, was added to the sign that is hung on the tin roof of the gravesite (which has a cupola above Abba's grave) that is now an established *dargāh*, at the head of which have been installed ritual green and orange flags, similar to the flags that had first called me to Amma's healing room.

Appendix
Death and Difference: A Conversation

A conversation with Amma's niece and Amma's friend Munnapa while waiting for Gyarwin Sharif rituals to begin, October 3, 1994.

Niece: Everything's in the Quran—*everything's* there. The Hindu scriptures ['canon'] are completely different [*alag*]; the Muslim's is different. But the Muslim one is true. The Hindu 'canon' is false; the Angrezi [English] one is false.

Munnapa [quoting what she's heard many times from Amma]: But when a child is born, s/he's neither Muslim nor Hindu. When we come into the world, there are only two differences. After we get here, only then it's a matter of religious distinction [*jāt*] ...

Niece: But you Hindus don't have any accountability [*hisāb*].

Munnapa: No, no, that's not true; we have it!

Niece: No, you don't have it. Nothing happens if you do something wrong. You don't have our book of accountability [*hisāb kitāb*]; you just burn the body!

Munnapa: No, no!! We burn, but we have that, too—what you have in the Quran, we too have in ours. What's it called? The Ramayana. Each and every thing is in there.

Niece: But among you people, when you die, you burn the body. After we die and are buried, breath comes again and we rise again.

Munnapa: Well, that happens to Hindus, too, even if they're burned.

Niece: The bodies may be raised, but they don't know each other. We're asked each and every thing, if we steal anything, it's written down. Everything is kept in account [*hisāb*], from birth to old age.

251

Munnapa: We have that too!! It tells everything, everything's in the Ramayan.

Niece: But Hindus don't observe fasting [Ramadan *rozā*].

Munnapa: But it's like your *rozā*. We too have a *rozā*: when we worship the moon, then we don't eat in the evening and don't drink water or tea until nine at night. This happens once a year.

Another Muslim friend: And in between you eat and drink and eat fruit.

Munnapa: The day we worship the moon, we don't drink water, nothing, not from evening until nine the next night. Then, when the moon comes out, with great difficulty, we look for it, and seeing the sign, we do *pūjā*. We do the *pūjā* once a year. We have this too [a reference to the *vrat/ nommu* ritual during Kartik Purnima].

Niece: There are some good people who don't do any wrong, who tell only the truth.

Munnapa: Well, we have a lot of truthfulness among us, too. In the Dasshera festival that's coming up . . . [she is interrupted]

Muslim friend [going back to subject of death/body disposal, supporting the religiosity of Hindus]: [Hindus meditate with such intensity] they don't even know what day it is, what the world [*duniyā*] is, where they are; they remain totally immersed in Bhagvan [God]. So, like this, their dead get up; they get up from the earth [*zamīn*]. That's how [powerful] their worship [*pūjā*] is.

Niece: How can they get up without being able to see [without physical eyes after cremation]?

Munnapa: No, you can't see them; in my understanding, you can't see them. . . .

Niece: In America, 300 years ago—it's written in our Quran that there used to be many Muslims there; now, there isn't a single one like that. There were Muslims, but they all died. Two hundred, 150 years ago, there were only three left, three men. Then one man said, "We [Muslim dead] are in water; we're raw [*kacce*]; the bodies are spoiled. We should take ourselves out of here and be buried in a different manner. . . . They went to the mosque. . . . [She tells of a miracle of people digging up dead bodies to bury them somewhere else only to find that they were still living. The miracle converted hundreds of people.] It's all in the book, the story of all this. But what do the Hindus do? They burn everybody and that's it.

Munnapa: We don't burn *everyone*! If they haven't been married, we don't burn those people; only if they're married, we burn them. [Those listening to her laugh.]

Joyce: Still, their belief is that just the body burns, but what they call the *ātmā* [soul], that doesn't burn.

Munnapa: Yes, yes, that's right [claps her hands in delight]. It doesn't burn! You've understood it!

Niece: I know that, but [interrupted . . .].

Munnapa: This hardly burns [points to heart, i.e., *ātmā*] . . .

Niece: God walks forty steps behind us. When He comes to the grave, the breath comes back; the breath comes and the angels come. "Who is that?" they ask. They ask this at the grave, having come from forty steps behind, and the accounting begins. That's how it is among us. In America, do you bury?

Joyce: Yes, and some people cremate, too.

[Niece walks away from the conversation, seeming to have lost interest.]

Glossary

abjad kā phāl kholnā   lit., open the mystery of numbers; Amma's primary (mathematically based) diagnostic procedure; *abjad*

ālim   a scholar in religious learning

āmil   a healer; one who writes amulets and incantations

asrat   an evil eye cast by a supernatural being

bābā   a Muslim saint or ascetic and the term of address for the same

barkat [Persian, *barakat*]   spiritual blessing; a saint's spiritual power, accessible at his grave

bhagvān (Telugu)   god

bhakti   devotion

boṭṭu (Telugu)   vermilion-powder forehead mark traditionally applied by Hindu men and women after worship; a vermilion mark or "stick-on dot" ornamenting women's foreheads

burāq   winged mount (horse, mule) upon which Muhammad rode on his night journey from Jerusalem to the gates of heaven

burqā   long black cloak-type veil worn by many Muslim women in South Asia

buzurg   venerable person; saint

cillā   a 40-day meditative retreat; term used for the physical space (room) for that seclusion/meditation; domestic shrine; seclusion practiced by women for forty days after childbirth

dargāh   lit., royal court; tomb of a Sufi saint or *pīr*; a gate or threshold.

dastarkhān   ritual of counting out seeds onto a tablecloth spread on the ground in order to count the number of *zikr* repeated (usually the names of God or *kalmā*)

devaru (Telugu)   god

dharma   religion; ethics; way of life

duā   personal prayer or supplication; performed independently or at the end of *namāz* and at the end of Amma's healing interactions with each patient

durūd   a prayer of benediction asking for mercy on the Prophet Muhammad and his descendants

fālita   amulet soaked in oil and burned, soaked in water and drunk, or smashed

255

with a sandal; distinguished from *tāvīz*, which is worn on the body as protection

fātihā   opening chapter of Quran, recited as part of *namāz*; also recited independently in the name of saints or deceased persons

gaddī   lit., cushion; throne, royal seat; symbolizes the seat of power that the *pīr* holds; his successor "inherits the *gaddī*"

ḥāl   lit., state or condition; an ecstatic mystical state

hazrat   term of respect, generally to identify spiritual authority; excellence, highness

ilm   knowledge

jalālī   fierce, angry (*jalāl* means "grandeur, power, majesty")

jamālī   easygoing, charismatic (*jamāl* means "beauty")

kalmā   Muslim declaration of faith: "There is no god but God, and Muhammad is His prophet"

karāmat   miracle (lit., deed) performed by Sufi saint or healer

karesu   a type of *kartūt*

kartūt   evil eye cast by a human

khalīfā   the person who receives the *khilāfat* from a *pīr*, after which he becomes a *sheikh*/*pīr* and may make his own disciples

khilāfat   succession; the permission given by *pīr* to a disciple to make his own disciples; also the paper certificate given to the disciple at that time

khudā   god

mazār   tomb of a saint

maukīl [Arabic, *mu'akkal*]   messenger or deputy, often a *jinn* or angel

mirāj   the Prophet's ascension to heaven after his night journey from Mecca to Jerusalem

murīd   disciple of a *pīr*

murśid   spiritual guide; *pīr*, *sheikh*

nafs   human will, lower nature

namāz   Muslim ritual prayer performed five times a day

niyam   custom, rule, law

pān   betel leaf filled with spices (and sometimes tobacco) that is folded up and chewed like chewing tobacco

pardā   lit., curtain; veiling, segregation

panjā   hand representing the family of the Prophet; often represented on silver standards atop the flags of the saints that fly above Muslim ritual sites

pegambar   prophet

pīr   teacher of Sufi path; spiritual guide, saint, *sheikh*

pirānimā   wife of a *pīr*

qavvālī   song genre of Sufi devotional music; devotional songs sung at *samās* to arouse the mystical state of those attending

ramz   trance state induced through *qavvālī* performed at *samā*; specifically, the act of twirling/dancing that is the manifestation of such a state of ecstasy

rūh   soul; spirit

256

samā lit., listening, audition; gathering, assembly; musical sessions of *qavvālī* singing

sheikh title of respect, often used to address a *pīr*; the ritual term by which Abba refers to himself

śaitānī evil forces; misbehavior

śakti spiritual power; female spiritual being; goddess

silsilā lit., chain; Sufi order or lineage

surmā powdered antimony applied to eyes as eyeliner; it is a dark silver color rather than the black color of *kājal* [kohl]

tarīqā path, way; particular teachings of Sufi order

tasbī prayer beads

tāvīz [Arabic, *ta'wiz*] written amulet, generally worn on the body

urs festival celebrating death anniversary of a *pīr*

wajd state of ecstasy, trance

zarab sharp iron instrument (in form of a thin skewer or a mace whose handle is sharpened at the end) used by Rifai performers at the celebration of Gyarwin Sharif

zikr [Arabic, *dhikr*] remembrance; ritual recitation of name of God or a short phrase

Notes

Introduction

1. For readers who know Urdu, an explanation is in order regarding the use of the term of address "Amma" rather than "Ammi" for mother. When I first met Amma, we called her Piranima (a term of address for the wife of a Sufi teacher/guru, *pīr*). I do not remember the exact point when we began calling her "Amma," a Telugu term of address for mother. Many of both her Hindu and Muslim patients (Telugu and Urdu speakers) call her Amma rather than Ammi, and her own children use this term, "Amma," when speaking to me about her.

2. Carl Ernst has pointed out the differences in meaning and connotation between the English word "saint" and the Arabic word "*walī*." The latter literally means "friend of God." "This relational or functional meaning contrasts with the term *saint*, which implies intrinsic holiness or sanctity as a personal quality. The Islamic tradition has no formal equivalent of the Catholic process of canonization of saints" (1997, 59).

3. The term "outside" [*bāhar*] refers to persons outside the regular healing community, those who are new to Amma's healing room. Although Amma rarely took regular patients out of queue, I later observed that she routinely called in strangers, as she did us that first day.

4. While Amma does not "know" English, English words pepper her speech and that of others who come to the healing room. This is a common phenomenon among non-English-speakers in urban India, whose speech patterns are heavily influenced by television and movies.

5. That summer of 1994 had brought severe flooding to parts of south Georgia and a record-breaking summer rainfall to Atlanta. I am interested in the fact that Amma dreams in color, as related in her dream narratives. However, I am not certain of the implications of the color black here. Shii Muslims dress in black during the month of Muharram, and black clothing also identifies members of the Sophiyanarang Sufi *silsilā* [lineage]; but Amma made no direct reference to either of these traditions here.

6. I sometimes illustrated how these kinds of stereotypes about other cultures are common on all sides of the oceans by identifying some similarly misconstrued Indian stereotypes about Americans—one of these about which I have been regularly questioned in India is that American mothers cannot possibly love their children as much as Indian mothers do, indicated by the fact that our children (sons) do not stay with us after their marriage nor do they "take care of us in our old age."

7. See Carl Ernst's excellent discussion of the relationship of Sufism and Islam in his book *The Shambhala Guide to Sufism* (1997), particularly the preface and chapter 1.

8. Although I have no ethnographic data to support this, I would imagine that many Hyderabadi Muslims who travel back and forth to the Gulf as workers have become familiar with non–South Asian practices and views of Islam. Many of Amma's disciples have worked in the Gulf and bring narratives of their personal experiences to her table.

9. When she read a manuscript version of this introduction, Laurie Patton referred me to Wendy Doniger's use of a similar image of a railway roundhouse to think about a "roundhouse of myths," the roundhouse as a site of intersecting traditions. Doniger observes that the roundhouse is "the place where all the tracks of a railway meet so that the trains may pass from any one track to any other track." Similarly, "For mythologists the roundhouse of myths is a place that we must reach in order to get off our track and onto someone else's track, but it is not a place to settle down into" (O'Flaherty 1988, 163).

10. I am grateful for the opportunity to think through some of the ideas in this section at a roundtable in which I participated on "The Case for Case Studies" at the American Folklore Society annual meeting in Baltimore, Maryland, in 1995. Other participants were Margaret Mills, Barbara Babcock, and Deborah Kapchan, all of whom have conducted extensive research on single individuals.

11. In *Writing Culture*, James Clifford had already articulated similar constraints of ethnographic research and writing that keep it from being objective (1986), but Abu-Lughod argues that he does not go far enough in the reflexive move in writing that he advocates. She has specifically criticized *Writing Culture* for its exclusion of female scholars, which Clifford says is because "feminism had not contributed much to the theoretical analysis of ethnographies as texts. Where women had made textual innovations . . . they had not done so on feminist grounds. . . . [and where women had made textual innovation] they did not seem conversant with the rhetorical and textual theory we wanted to bring to bear on ethnography" (20). See Abu-Lughod 1990 for her strong disagreement with Clifford's premises. In turn, Abu-Lughod's case for "writing against culture" has been criticized for drawing generalizations about the use of the term "culture" that anthropological literature has never claimed for it; see specifically Christoph Brumann's essay "Writing for Culture" (1999).

12. This lack of privacy is typical of many kinds of medical interactions in India, particularly spiritual healing contexts, but also in biomedical doctors' offices and hospitals.

13. "Beyond the seven seas" is a phrase commonly used in Indian folklore to refer to unknown lands distant from India.

14. The legend tells of the Chishti saints Yusufayn and Sharif who traveled with the Mughal emperor Aurangzeb's army when it laid siege to the kingdom of Golconda. During the siege, a particularly fierce storm whipped the army tents and extinguished all lamps and candles. Only one tent seemed unaffected, from which the glow of a lamp showed. Aurangzeb himself went to see who was there and found the two saints reciting the Quran. He asked for their blessings on his military campaign, and soon the Mughal army found a way into the seemingly impenetrable fort. Bazaar

posters commemorate the miracle of Yusufayn, showing a glowing tent in a monsoon storm.

15. For example, when trying to figure out his age, Abba dated his wedding by the Police Action of 1948; he thought he was about 25 years old at that time.

16. In the fall of 1990, L. K. Advani, president of the Bharatiya Janata Party (BJP), began a pilgrimage, filled with religious symbolism, from the western Indian site of Somnath to Ayodhya, the birthplace of the Hindu deity Ram, with the intention of building a Ram temple at the site of his birth, where the Babri Masjid (mosque) then stood. He was arrested on October 23 in a government effort to forestall predicted violence. However, many of his followers [*kār sevaks*] were already in the city of Ayodhya, and many were killed in altercations with the police. Communal violence erupted in many parts of India, including Hyderabad. The mosque was demolished a year later. See van der Veer 1994 and Kakar 1995 for an examination of the historical, political, and psychological factors that led up to this eruption of violence.

17. See David Pinault's *The Shiites* (1992) and *Horse of Karbala* (2001) for detailed descriptions and analyses of Muharram rituals and processions in Hyderabad.

In 1995 I stood at a major intersection in downtown Hyderabad watching the hours-long procession of huge Ganesh images being carried to Hussein Sagar (a large artificial lake) on the backs of hundreds of trucks. Accompanying the images of Ganesh were groups of young men with bright pink or orange headbands tied around their foreheads throwing pink powders on the crowds below and yelling aggressively "Jai Sri Ram! Jai Sri Ram!" Several Muslim friends warned me about going out in public spaces on this day when Hindu nationalism was on full public display. Storefronts along the procession route were shuttered and very few women were visible.

18. An important marker of Sufi practice that is not articulated in Amma and Abba's teachings is the stages of mystical/spiritual learning. They talk about the path that a disciple follows [*tarīqā*] and a growing awareness/knowledge upon that path but not about specific, named stages.

19. Multiple affiliation is not uncommon among Sufis, although like Amma and Abba, primary affiliation is usually with one *silsilā* (Ernst 1997, 121).

20. The word "*sheikh*" is frequently transliterated as *shaykh*; I have chosen the transliteration *sheikh* since that is how Abba himself transliterates his title on signboards, invitation cards written in English, and so forth.

1. SETTING THE STAGE

1. The wife of the host family with whom I lived in 1990, Revati Thangavelu, whose home remained a central base for me in my subsequent research trips to Hyderabad, had recently retired from the English Department as a professor when I met her in 1989. She had heard me talk of Amma and Abba for many years before she accompanied me to a *samā* in their courtyard. Similarly, Abba knew of the family with whom I often stayed in Tarnaka, the Thangavelus. Both Revati and Abba were surprised and delighted when they finally met each other, as it turns out they had known each other for years in the English Department but had never called each other by the names by which I spoke of them to each other.

2. The images of the goddesses in both of these neighborhood shrines are covered in turmeric and are decorated in ways characteristic of the Seven Sisters village goddesses; their brother Pota Raju stands guard outside in the form of a nonanthropomorphic rock.

3. The Hyderabadi goddess festival of Bonalu is celebrated at each of these shrines, during which crowds of women carry on their heads clay vessels filled with *pongal* [cooked rice and lentils] that is offered to the goddess. I have also witnessed numerous goat sacrifices at the shrine situated at the university crossroads.

4. The Urdu term "*ser*" can be translated "tiger" or "lion," but the visual representation in Hyderabad is always of a tiger, which makes sense, given the paucity of lions in South Asia.

5. One day over a lingering lunch, I asked Amma and Abba to clarify who exactly was represented by the *panjā*. Abba started by including Allah. Amma quickly contradicted him, and they argued back and forth for some time as to who exactly was considered the "family." Abba lost the argument when Amma insisted that Allah could not be part of the family of five since he has neither been born of anyone nor has he begat anyone. In many parts of the Islamic world, the hand is called the Hand of Fatima (the Prophet's daughter) and is worn as an amulet or drawn on a wall in order to avert the evil eye.

6. I have observed a similar phenomenon in rural hospitals in India, where doctors often call other waiting patients into the examination room while they conduct an initial patient history. One doctor told me that he thought this was one of the most effective means of public health teaching, as he would give explanations for prevention and treatment to all present in the room.

7. In many Hindu contexts, the healer becomes possessed by a deity who speaks through him/her, making diagnoses and prescriptions.

8. This motif of calling a living being to life from a curry is shared with the South Indian story of the Saiva devotee Ciruttontar, who—at the demand of the god disguised as an ascetic—kills and cooks his only son in a curry. As he sits down to eat, the god asks where the devotee's son is and says he will begin to eat only if the son is present. In despair, the devotee calls to the son and he appears, beautiful and alive. See David Shulman's *The Hungry God: Hindu Tales of Filicide and Devotion* (1993) for a full discussion of this narrative.

9. One of the images painted on Amma's courtyard *cillā* in later years was a curved sword, associated with Ali, along with the roaring tiger of Ali.

10. "*Cillā*" is also the term used for the 40-day postpartum seclusion of new mothers, when they are considered to be ritually polluted and are excluded from the same ritual spaces they would be excluded from if they were menstruating. The 40-day seclusion and transformative power of that seclusion is shared between the two contexts mentioned here, postpartum seclusion and meditative/ascetic seclusion.

11. Amma never asked about my own menstrual cycle and I never volunteered this information. However, one day it became unavoidable and I told her that I needed to go home since I had started my period. She asked if I had the necessary supplies with me to take care of this "problem"; if I did, she asserted, there was no reason to go home. I could sit in the healing room, at her table, as long as I didn't touch any of the amulets. I saw then the flexibility of her prohibitions according to a range of contingencies and relationships.

12. I have capitalized the word "God" when it refers specifically to Allah. When the term refers to a category of being, I have not capitalized the word.

13. Hussein's father died when he was a young boy, before his illness manifested itself.

2. The Healing System

1. One of Amma's granddaughters contracted polio as a young baby that left her with one leg shortened, and one her daughters died of heart failure at the age of 35. Abba, too, finally died of a heart attack.

2. See Barbara Metcalf's *Making Muslim Space in North America and Europe* (1996) for discussions of the role of the written word in making and/or identifying space as Muslim.

3. Mantra is primarily an oral rather than written incantation in Hindu traditions; however, here Abba is equating the power of the mantra with the written word.

4. An utterance that is recited before the beginning of many ritual and nonritual activities.

5. See Ewing 1997, 132–138 for an extended discussion of *maukīl* and the ambiguous and multiple usages of the word in the discourse of the *pīr* with whom she worked. In one conversation, this Pakistani *pīr* uses the word "*maukīl*" to refer to both angels and *jinn*, who, he says, are agents of luminous and black knowledge, respectively. Ewing transliterates "*maukīl*" as "*mu'kkal.*"

6. See Schimmel 1975, xix for a list of the Arabic letters and their standard numerical values; also see her Appendix I for a discussion of "Letter Symbolism in Sufi Literature" (411–425).

7. The technique employed by Amma is called *abjud* by the author of *Islam in India* (*The Oanum-i-Islam*; Sharif 1921/1972). The author states that the numerical value ascertained by adding the values of the letters in the names is divided by twelve. The resulting number indicates which astrological sign will dominate the life of the patient. Nowhere in his descriptions of those who practice this technique, who he calls "magicians," is mention made of female practitioners.

8. According to the transliteration she gives, Amma heard Ramoth as Rahmat, meaning mercy. I thank Carl Ernst for bringing this to my attention.

9. Note that Amma did not give the final calculation according to my and my mother's names. Amma never completed *abjad* for my name, nor did I ever ask her to diagnose a specific problem. She did, however, give me several *tāvīz* and sets of *dhuān* and *fālitā* for general protection and to find a job.

10. Sudhir Kakar calls this intricate system of naming and differentiating in the practice of the *pīr* with whom he worked in New Delhi "almost obsessive classifications"(Kakar 1982, 35).

11. Ashes here refers to the ashes of a cremated Hindu body; Muslims are traditionally buried. The disciple speaking comes from a Hindu family.

12. Amma never fully explained to me the logic of the number squares on her *tāvīz*, always saying that we would wait until there was an open, private afternoon together. However, Annemarie Schimmel provides some of the bases of logic for number squares as used in Islamic traditions: "Squares could be formed from [numbers

associated with] divine names, or from the mysterious letters at the beginning of Quranic chapters" (1993, 33).

13. Amma never explained the significance of the numbers seven and eleven beyond the fact that different kinds of beings who cast the evil eye would be attracted by these specific numbers of flowers. However, one can speculate about the origins of at least the number seven by its significance elsewhere in the Islamic tradition. For example, Allah created the heaven and earth in seven layers. According to Schimmel (1993, 154), seven is used in many world traditions as an indefinite number that simply connotes "many."

14. Other "legitimate" occasions for loosened hair are possession by a deity, death rituals, and simply drying it. See Hiltebeitel and Miller 1998 for discussions of the cultural meanings of hair across Asian cultures.

15. Were the patients to go to such an inauspicious place, the *tāvīz* they had been given by Amma would become polluted and have to be replaced with new ones, at a cost of Rs. 35 each.

16. Amma might have been worried not only about me using the texts without adequate training but also about potential readers of this book, who might have tried to find and use the named text.

17. In subsequent *bandīs* I observed, the householders had already broken up the floor in each corner, saving Amma considerable physical exertion.

18. The lack of personal detail or narrative is typical of what is known about many saints whose graves have become *dargāhs*—that is, they are known more for the powers they are able to affect than for their personal narratives. There are, of course, important exceptions, particularly for saints associated with large, well-established *dargāhs*.

19. After Abba died, Sati (now called Mustang) set up his own healing room, with Amma's permission, where he writes amulets and other prescriptions that he has learned from Amma.

20. This statement of intention [*niyya*] before performing a particular ritual is central to Islamic practice; ritual without conscious intention is ineffective, and ritual with mistakes can be effective if performed with the correct (and stated) intention.

21. Sudhir Kakar has observed the same to be true among different kinds of healers he worked with for his book *Shamans, Mystics and Doctors*: "The belief that it is the person of the healer and not his conceptual system or his particular technique that are of decisive importance for the healing process is . . . an unquestioned article of faith for most Indian patients" (1982, 39).

3. Patient Narratives in the Healing Room

1. All cases are drawn from my fieldnotes of 1994–1995, unless otherwise indicated. See Werbner 2003, 226–229 for a listing of patient cases in a Pakistani *pīr's* healing session.

2. For a Telugu-speaking person in pain or sorrow to groan or call out "Amma, Amma" is common and is not necessarily directed toward a particular person or the mother.

3. See Kakar 1982 for description and discussion of the practice (and particular case studies) of a *pīr* living at a *dargāh* in Delhi. This *pīr's* practice is specifically

centered on cases of *śaitānī*, which manifests itself as visitation by "devils" in dreams and/or through possession. The first question the *pīr* asks of his patients is "What do you see in your dreams?" (20). Many of his patients are women who have seen the "same thing" "in their dreams—someone who wants to do 'bad acts' with them" (20). Amma's practice is much broader than that of this *pīr*.

4. This follows a typical scenario of many dowry deaths—the body is burned to cover up the murder as a kitchen accident—but no one here made reference to dowry.

5. Psychoanalyst Sudhir Kakar suggests *becainī* may be an indigenous category for desire in a Freudian sense (personal communication, Fall 2002).

4. NEGOTIATING GENDER IN THE HEALING ROOM

1. For example, in the summer of 1992 when I was first actively thinking about why Amma could practice in a male ritual role, the *Atlanta Journal-Constitution* published a twelve-page spread called "Women of the Veil" whose articles headlined many of these stereotypes: "Islamic militants pushing women back to an age of official servitude," "Women: Political Islam brands them as inferior," "Through a woman's eyes: the veil may be small and symbolic, or a barrier to the word," "Male honor costs women's lives," and "It's dangerous to be born female in the Islamic world," among others.

2. When I was hiking in the Himalayas in 1996 with an American female friend who spoke no Hindi, I heard a similar assertion in a very different context. We had stopped at the edge of a village to ask directions and the woman of the house called us into her courtyard and offered us tea. After several minutes of conversation in Hindi between the householder and myself, she asked why my friend was not saying anything. When I explained that she did not know Hindi, the mountain woman replied, "Well, that doesn't matter. She's a woman and I'm a woman—she should be able to understand what I say."

3. This assertion of the equivalence of Rahim and Ram, and thus the common path to God shared by Hindus and Muslims, is frequently heard in Indian contexts, but it seems to be voiced more frequently by Hindus than by Muslims.

4. Literally, "Even if they draw a lot of blood, they're forgiven."

5. The first couple had one daughter together, and when Amma's daughter got remarried, the new couple had two more children together.

6. This gendered difference in response to "why women don't do something" reminds me of the gendered responses to why women do not take on the guise [*veṣam*] of the goddess Gangamma during her annual festival [*jātara*] in the pilgrimage town of Tirupati (Andhra Pradesh). Men of the family that carries out this ritual said that women did not take *veṣam* because women menstruate; however, women of the family said they did not take *veṣam* because they were "too busy cooking" for the goddess.

7. This same daughter-in-law told me in 1996 that she was indeed interested in this kind of healing practice but that she would need to wait until she was older and had more credibility before she would be able to practice in the ways Amma does. Furthermore, her children would need to be older before she would have the time for such practice. She added, "It's rigorous to have to sit for forty days [in meditation, *cillā*] to live a truthful life, to live on the right path." When I returned to Hyderabad in the summer of 2003 after Amma had died, the daughter-in-law told

me that she had begun to sit in the healing room during the day when her husband Khalid was at work. However, she seems to have started this involvement in the practice gradually and without having taken time out to sit for *cillā*.

8. This contradiction in the telling reminds us that all life histories and experiential accounts are constructions whose shapes shift according to the context and the need of the performer.

9. See Gold 1994 for an example of the ways in which a Hindu female religious specialist stretches the bounds of *pardā* in order to participate in religious practices that are traditionally considered to be outside the limits of *pardā*.

10. A particularly poignant case at this *dargāh* was a young woman who had been staying there with her two-year-old daughter for close to two years. She was using the shrine as a literal refuge from her husband, who had poured kerosene over her and tried to light her afire when she refused to bring more dowry. However, she was also taking action: she had taken her husband to court and her case had gone all the way to the Supreme Court of Andhra Pradesh. She was awaiting the ruling when I met her.

11. Amma is making reference to the fact that her son Khalid tried to establish a healing room independent of hers in another neighborhood which was not successful. Khalid attributes the failure to his not being there enough hours in a day, since he "sat" there only after his government work hours; Amma attributes the failure to his gendered healing style.

12. I thank my colleagues Devin Stewart, Waqas A. Khwaja, and Carl Ernst for their discussions with me about the term "*vilāyat*."

13. I assume Abba means Islamic law—Sharia; but I never heard him use that specific term; he always used the term "*qānūn*."

14. Both Amma and Abba specifically used the word "guru" for this teacher. However, they use the term interchangeably with "*mursid*" and "*pīr*."

15. Being called through dreams or communicating through dreams with one's *pīr* is a common mode of communication in Sufi traditions; see Ewing 1990.

16. Hymes (1975) has identified what he calls "breakthroughs into performance" in the course of everyday conversation that are framed to indicate that the performer is submitting the narrative (or joke, etc) for audience evaluation.

17. Notice that here she says that her youngest daughter was born before she began her healing practice, whereas in a shorter segment of her life history provided earlier in the chapter, she says that this daughter was born after she had begun her practice. The "discrepancy" might be accounted for by a shifting criteria for when her "practice" began, when she began healing informally or when she began meeting the 'public'.

18. Dates are traditionally the food with which Muslims in India break their daily fast during Ramadan.

19. Abba described the following as the process by which *dargāh* come into existence: someone dies, people offer *fātiḥā* [offerings to the dead] at the gravesite and experience miracles, more and more people begin to come and experience similar miracles, and finally a *dargāh* is built.

5. Religious Identities at the Crossroads

1. One of the rituals in which the initiate disciple partakes is to drink from a cup of milk into which the *murśid* has spit some of his own saliva.

2. For example, in 1996–1997, there were at least three such forums in the United States: a conference panel at the Association of Asian Studies in Honolulu titled "Shared Metaphoric Worlds: Religion and Literature in Precolonial India"; a double panel at the Annual Conference on South Asia in Madison, Wisconsin, titled "Setting the Margins of Hindu Identity"; and a conference sponsored by the Dharam Hinduja Center at Columbia University, held at the University of Florida, titled "What is Hinduism"? In 2000 two books with very similar titles addressing Muslim/Hindu identities were published: Peter Gottschalk's *Beyond Hindu and Muslim: Multiple Identity in Narratives from Village India* and a volume edited by David Gilmartin and Bruce Lawrence, *Beyond Turk and Hindu: Rethinking Religious Identities in Islamicate South Asia* (based on a 1995 conference).

3. Stewart elaborates the problem of these analytic categories in an article titled "In Search of Equivalence: Conceiving Muslim-Hindu Encounter through Translation Theory" (2001). He analyzes the use of what might be called "Hindu terminology" in premodern Bengali Islamic texts and finds that in the sixteenth to early eighteenth centuries, "no unambiguously Islamic idiom existed in Bengali during the time. . . . Such specific Islamic technical vocabulary would not prevail until sometime later" (268). Therefore, Bengali Muslim authors used existing Bengali terminology as translations for Arabic Muslim terms, "attempt[ing] to imagine an Islamic ideal in a new literary environment…[attempting] to think Islamic thoughts in the local language" (273).

4. Notice here that Amma is identifying with a Shii ritual tradition of Muharram processions although she herself is not Shii nor does she personally participate in these processions. Her usage of "our" is broadly inclusive of all Muslims; internal differences are not explicitly marked in this context when she is speaking about the relationship of Hindu and Muslim categories.

5. For example, when Vishnu comes to earth in the *avatār* of Ram, he divides himself into four parts to be born as the sons of Dasarath's three wives. Ram is born of two parts, Bharata of one part each, and the twins Lakshman and Shatrugna from the last quarter.

6. I thank Carl Ernst for his reference to a description of the Prophet as *avatār* in a Sanskrit formula on a coin minted by Mahmud of Ghazni in 1018 (Ernst 1992, 52).

7. While this correlation between Muhammad and Vishnu's *avatār* is not a common expression, Richard Eaton cites a similar cosmology and specific association between the *nabi*/prophet and *avatār* in the sixteenth-century Bengali text by Saiyid Sultan, the *Nabi-Bamsa,* in which the author classifies "the major deities of the Hindu pantheon, including Brahma, Vishnu, Shiva, Ram, and Krishna, as successive prophets of God, followed in turn by Adam, Noah, Abraham, Moses, Jesus, and Muhammad" (1994, 286).

8. Muslims do, of course, make goat sacrifices on the occasions of the Prophet's birthday (Id al-Mawlid) and the Feast of the Sacrifice (Id al-Adha). However, many Muslims interpret this sacrifice as commemorative rather than something the deity is demanding.

9. Narsimha Swami is the man-lion *avatār* of Vishnu. He is worshipped as an independent deity in South India, whereas in the north he appears primarily in listings or images of the ten *avatār*s and in narrative form but not is not worshipped independently.

10. Desiderio Pinto describes the *pīrs* with whom he conducted fieldwork at Nizamuddin Dargah in Delhi as telling him that they, too, have control over some Hindu deities, meaning that they can call them to their service. One *pīr* tells a Hindu visitor who has come for help about his government job: "I have done the *jap* (recitation) of Shankar, Ganesh and Hanuman. And they have all come before me and become my slaves. I have them in me. No one can fool around with me, and whatever I say happens. See, I still carry something of Ganesh with me" (1995, 57–58). Another *pīr* advised a female patient to recite the name of the Hindu goddess Radha in order to alleviate problems she was having with her husband (58).

11. Richard Eaton has identified these kinds of processes as the accretion aspect of conversion, in which people add "new deities or superhuman agencies to their existing cosmological stock, or . . . [identify] new deities or agencies with existing entities in their cosmology" (1985, 113). However, he is looking at the process from the Hindu perspective that finds room for Muslim powers, rather than from a Muslim perspective. I am suggesting that these processes may take place without conversion.

12. See Sax 1995 for a series of essays on the multiple connotations of the concept of *līlā* in South Asia.

13. There *are* caste-equivalent, often endogamous, groups in Islam in South Asia: the major ones are Sheikh, Mughal, Sayyid, and Pathan. See Ahmed 1978 for discussions of caste and social stratification among Indian Muslims.

14. This Shams is likely the same Shams-i Tabriz who was the mystical teacher and beloved friend of the thirteenth-century poet Jalaladdin Rumi, although this association was never made explicitly by Abba or Amma. Tazim Kassam has identified three historical figures who are called Shams, whose hagiographies have often been conflated in oral narrative traditions, and who share a hagiographic image as "that of an itinerant, antinomian, and wonder-working *qalandar*: Shams-i Tabriz, the Ismaili Imam, Shams al-Din Muhammad, and the Ismaili preacher Pir Shams" (1995, 76, 82). While Amma seems to have little direct contact with the relatively large Ismaili community in Hyderabad, oral traditions would seem to move more fluidly than people. The one that follows here is shared by Amma's Sufi community and the Ismaili tradition of Pir Shams, originating in western India, described by Kassam: the narrative of Shams raising from the dead a royal child by calling the saint's name, rather than Allah's, the saint being punished by being skinned alive, and then his calling down the sun to cook a piece of raw meat that no one would cook for him because they were disgusted by his looks (79, 378–379).

15. This motif is not found in the narrative version reported by Kassam (1995), an omission that draws my attention to the possibility that the motif has been included for a performative purpose.

16. I heard this myth numerous times in oral variants when I was conducting fieldwork around the Gangamma goddess tradition in Tirupati 1999–2000; textual variants are found in the Mahabharata Bhagavatapurana and Kancippuranam (Shulman 1985, 110–129). For oral versions, see Elmore 1915, 95.

17. Another oral variant tells of Renuka's head falling to earth in an untouchable

village, where it was attached to the body of an untouchable woman. In the oral versions I heard, it was never made clear why the untouchable woman had been beheaded.

18. I thank Devin Stewart of Emory University for identifying this reference.

19. Each ingredient here (incense, coconuts, milk, worship) is followed by an echo word that changes only the first consonant of the initial word into a *w* (*wagar-batī, wūjā, wāriyal, wūdh*). The use of these kinds of echo words in South Asian languages reduces the formality of the initial word and extends its range to include other objects that fall in the same category as the initial word.

20. On another occasion when Abba, Amma, and I visited a popular *dargāh* outside of Hyderabad, I asked them if the kinds of miracles [*karāmat*] experienced at *dargāhs* were also experienced at temples. Abba's answer was "No, they don't occur there because they [the gods] are manmade." Here again, he was drawing a distinction between the god who is the creator and those that are created, specifically implying that the *murti*/image of the Hindu deity has no power. Abba immediately followed this declaration with the caveat that Hindu deities *did* have *śakti*/spiritual power; but, he continued, "There's a big difference between *śakti* and *bhagvān*/god. . . . *Śaktis* give problems to humans . . . they trouble them. . . . And these saints [those of the *dargāh*] don't do that."

21. *Fātihā* is the opening chapter of the Quran, which is also recited as an independent prayer.

22. The equivalently politicized Hindu procession is that of Ganesh Caturthi, where Ganesh images are paraded from temporary shrines to a body of water, where it is immersed.

23. See chapter 6 for a description of this ritual act during the *samā*.

24. Hindu ascetics who have achieved a certain spiritual status are also buried. So burial does not *necessarily* mean a Muslim identity (Christians also bury), but cremation in India does imply a Hindu identity.

6. IMMERSED IN REMEMBRANCE AND SONG

1. The exceptions are the twenty-sixth days of Ramadan and Muharram. On the twenty-sixth day of Ramadan other rituals are being performed since it is the "night of calling out to Allah" [*Allah pukārne kī rāt*], and it is inappropriate to have such a celebratory ritual during Muharram, a month of mourning.

2. Qureshi characterizes the *samā*: "an occasion for Sufi devotees to experience mystical arousal within the framework of the Sufi spiritual hierarchy, through the medium of mystical songs performed by professional functionaries" (1986, 108).

3. There have been some significant recent moves to "recover" the female voice in Sufi experience; see Shemeem Burney Abbas's *The Female Voice in Sufi Ritual: Devotional Practices of Pakistan and India* (2002) and Camille Helminski's *Women of Sufism: A Hidden Treasure* (2003). Abbas carried out fieldwork in at several Sufi shrines in Pakistan between 1992 and 1999 to document female voices and participation. She writes about women participating as professional musicians (singing genres other than *qavvālī*, however, which here, too, is considered a male genre), women's voices reflected in Sufi poetry sung by males, and female characters in Sufi narratives. She mentions women who are caretakers and devotees at the shrines of saints, but her

study does not focus on them. Helminski's study is concerned with primarily literary texts *about* women—rather than women's actual participation in Sufi practices—as resources of empowerment for contemporary practicing female Sufis.

4. I have read of no other description of *samā* or ritual *qavvālī* performed outside of the *dargāh*.

5. See the introduction for a further discussion of a variety of contexts of Sufi practice and thought. For scholarship on popular Islam outside the *dargāh* context in South Asia, see, among others, Katherine Ewing (1980, 1984a, 1984b), Sudhir Kakar (1982), and James Wilce (1998a, 1998b, 1995).

6. These colors are also associated with Allah, members of the Prophet's family, and certain saints. Amma told me white was Allah; green, the saint Ghaus-e-Pak; yellow, the Chishti saint of Ajmer Gharib Nawaz Sarkar; red, the Prophet's daughter Fatima; black, the Prophet's son-in-law Ali; 'chocolatey', the Prophet's grandson Hassan; and finally *sālū* color (brown or reddish brown), the other grandson, Hussein.

7. One of Abba's male disciples told me the story of the prophet Mussa (Moses), who wanted to look directly at God. But he swooned when even glancing at the shadow of God, which burned up the mountain on which it was cast. This burned rock is said to be the origin of *surmā*.

8. This occurred in 1995, when Amma had no phone and there was no way to find out what had happened to the *qavvāls*. Since then, a land-line phone has been installed in the healing room, and by 2003, Khalid had gotten a mobile phone; the *qavvāls* probably had mobiles by that time as well. So the probability of this kind of situation repeating itself is unlikely, although any number of other factors could cause a similar cancellation of the *samā*.

9. A *qavvālī* musical group generally consists of between three to five male musicians: a vocalist, a harmonium player, and a *ḍholak* drummer. A unique handclapping is also a form of *qavvālī* percussion.

10. Qureshi identifies similar categories from the verses she recorded (1986, 86).

11. Ernst writes that monetary offerings are traditionally made to the "master of the assembly" (the *sheikh*) and not directly to the musicians (1997, 188). However, this was not the case in Abba's courtyard. Qureshi argues that the money serves first to "articulate a spiritual relationship," the submission of the disciple to the *sheikh* and the reception of the *sheikh's* beneficence. Only after this has been performed through the *sheikh's* acceptance of the money does the money become a material economic transaction when given to the *qavvāls* (1986, 125).

12. Qureshi tells a particularly intriguing oral narrative that describes a situation when a saint died on the first line of the performed *qavvālī* verse, "but on every second line, he rose to life again. This alternation continued for many hours to several days, but the singing could not stop, until finally the Sufis present had the performers end on the first line to allow the saint to rest in final union with his Beloved" (1986, 128).

13. I witnessed a similar situation in a context of Hindu possession during the festival of Gaura in Chhattisgarh, central India. A man became possessed by the goddess but did not "cool down" appropriately when hot coals sprinkled with resin was passed under his face. When he continued to "dance," the villagers participating in the festival with whom I was standing became disdainful and said he was dancing

only for show. These incidents raise the possibility that possession/trance can be faked, which itself has interesting implications for the traditions.

14. "Classical" Sufi poets have often employed similar images of the flame. Schimmel quotes Ibn ʿAtaʾ Allah: "Ecstasy is a flame which springs up in the secret heart, and appears out of longing, and at that visitation (*warīd*) the members are stirred either to joy or grief" (1975, 178). And the poet ʿ Attar: "What is *wajd*? To become happy thanks to the true morning / to become fire without the presence of the sun (179). See also Figure 21, the photograph of Abba with the flame of the oil lamp reflected in his heart.

15. I provide the Urdu for several technical words in this section for those scholars who are specialists in Sufi traditions and might want to make comparisons with other teachings and case studies of Sufi practice.

16. Shemeem Abbas reports the use of a term that I never heard in Hyderabad, "*kifiat*," which she defines as a "state of spiritual inspiration or mystical delight." She says it is "subtle and covert" in comparison to *hāl*, which is a mystical state "outside the control of the self" (2002, 14).

17. Qureshi (1986, 80) quotes Arberry's definition of *hāl*: "The *maqām* is a stage of spiritual attainment which is the result of the mystic's personal effort and endeavor, whereas the *hāl* is a spiritual mood depending not upon the mystic but upon God" (1950, 75).

18. See Hiltebeitel and Miller's *Hair: Its Power and Meaning in Asian Cultures* (1998) for extended discussions of similar phenomenon.

19. Carl Ernst confirms from his experience that "convention requires that when someone enters ecstasy . . . , it is necessary to repeat the same line of verse until the person returns to his senses" (1997, 186).

20. The Mevlevi order was founded by the son of the Sufi poet Jalaladdin Rumi.

21. *Fanā* can also imply annihilation of ego/*nafs,* and in this sense an annihilation of self (Hoffman 1995, 200ff.). However, Rumi seems to imply something beyond this, an annihilation meaning union beyond distinction between the self and God. Earle Waugh writes that among the Munshidin of Egypt with whom he worked, the term "*fanā*" implies "the lack of differentiation between God and human in mystical union without either disappearing" (1989, 7). These differences in the implications of this single term remind us to be mindful of the regional vernacular differences of Sufi practice and thought even as there are many concepts and terms that are shared.

22. In another context, Amma used the image of flame and moth very differently than Hallaj does when she told me that the *kalmā* is the source of all creation. Then she continued, "All these things are profound secrets; we can't explain them. If we try, we will also get burnt, like the moth attracted to a lamp gets burnt. Isn't it, Joice?"

23. The Chishti founding saint Muinuddin Chishti is said to have claimed that "the highest form of devotion is to redress the misery of those in distress, to fulfill the needs of the helpless, and to feed the hungry" (Schimmel 1980, 24).

24. I participated in Gyarwin celebrations in 1994 and 1996. In 1994 Amma ordered one quintel of rice to be cooked; according to popular wisdom, this is enough rice to feed 500 people.

25. Valerie Hoffman reports that in Egypt, too, the Rifai order is known for the

ability of its members to perform "fantastic miracles," such as handling poisonous snakes and scorpions (1995, 99).

26. The Arabic term for this concept is "*walī*," the translation for which Ernst gives as "a friend, a client, or one who is protected by a kin relationship" (1997, 58).

27. This part of the narrative is unclear word by word, so I have not transcribed it, although its gist was clear.

28. Gordon Newby, who is currently working with early biographies of the Prophet, tells me that it is commonly held that Muhammad's mother died soon after giving birth to him but that he has never heard this as a reason for her untimely death (Emory University, personal communication, January 2004).

29. I was included in this gifting of saris on such occasions. My Hindu friends in Hyderabad often commented on the particularly Muslim color or design of these saris: one was a typical Muslim-green sari hand-embroidered with silver thread. The second year I participated in Gyarwin Sharif, the sari I received was bright pink. On both those occasions, I spent the night at Amma's and as I walked back to my guesthouse early the next morning, I found myself wishing for the first time that I was wearing a *burqā* to cover up the brilliance of my saris and to keep from standing out like a jungle parrot among early morning joggers and walkers on the roads crossing the university. On both these occasions, one of Amma's sons insisted I put on some *kājal* [kohl] to deflect any possible envious evil eye.

30. See Jackie Assayag's description of similar Rifai rituals in Karnataka, South India, in *At the Confluence of Two Rivers* (2004, 132–140). Valerie Hoffman (1995, 99) quotes a 1976 report by Frederick de Jong that describes Egyptian Rifai ritual use these same kinds of sharp iron instruments, in Egypt called *dabbūs*. Like in the Hyderabadi context, in Egypt, the fact that the *dabbūs* does not produce blood or leave a mark is a sign of the spiritual power [*baraka*] of the Rifai performer. Hoffman herself never saw such a ritual in her fieldwork, and when she asked about it, she was told that the "head of the Supreme Council of Sufi Orders had disallowed the practice, explaining that it is improper to make a public display of baraka" (1995, 100).

31. The Rifai adolescent performers whom Peter van der Veer observed in Gujarat attribute the miracle of the piercings with no blood to the saliva of the living *pīr*, which is placed in their puncture wounds (1992, 554). I never heard this explanation or observed this act in Hyderabad. Van der Veer goes on to provide the narrative behind why the *pīr*'s saliva would prevent blood from flowing: "The miracle of the saint's day is based on the legend that Ahmad Rifa'i could turn himself into water. His successors have not retained the founder's full power but only one aspect of it. Water can be pierced without leaving a trace. The Rifa'i pir has the power to transmit this quality of water to the bodies of those who are 'playing' " (561).

On the occasion of an *urs* at a *dargāh* behind the Secunderabad railway station, the *zarabwālās* performed over a white sheet spread out in front of the saint's tomb. When one of the men pulled out a *zarab* from his upper arm, a single drop of blood spilled on the sheet for all to see. The breach of conduct did not cause the consternation I was expecting (at least not in public); the other performers continued and there were only a few whispers suggesting that the man had not been in the "right frame of mind."

32. Islamization of Hindu women would also include ceasing to perform house-

hold *pūjās* as part of their responsibilities as wives and daughters-in-law in an extended Hindu household; but again, this is not the equivalent of "marking" a body.

Conclusion

1. See Lawless 1988 for a similar argument about the ways Pentecostal female preachers are able to preach in public but live in a community that believes a woman's place is in the home and that she should not take public leadership roles.

2. The epilogue that follows this conclusion gives a longer description of what this struggle involved.

Epilogue

1. Amma actually performs this narrative in the present tense; however, the form of Dakani Urdu she speaks does not consistently use present and past tenses to distinguish modes of narrative time.

2. This description of the angel of death suggests his identification as a magician.

3. The narrative implies that Amma's night vigil went through the night until dawn, when it was time for the *fajr* [dawn] *namāz*. Amma often told me that she gave her daytime hours to her patients but saved the night hours for Allah.

4. After his death, Amma, other family members, and disciples all referred to Abba as Baba rather than Abba. Abba is a kinship term, "father," whereas Baba is a title of respect used for Muslim ascetics and saints.

5. She is particularly referring here to her disappointments with her children— that most of them have not found stable lives, either in marriage or employment.

6. From the Hindi film *Tīsrī Kasam.* Amma often interjects sung phrases from devotional [*qavvālī*] and film songs into her teachings and conversation.

Select Bibliography

Abbas, Shemeem Burney. 2002. *The Female Voice in Sufi Ritual: Devotional Practices of Pakistan and India.* Austin: University of Texas Press.

Abedi, Janab Syed Dildar Hussain. n.d. *Anti-Bhanamati Guide.* (n.p.)

Abrahams, Roger. 1976. "Complex Relations of Simple Forms." In *Folklore Genres,* ed. Dan Ben-Amos, 193–214. Austin: University of Texas Press.

Abu-Lughod, Lila. 1990. "Can There Be a Feminist Ethnography?" *Women and Performance: A Journal of Feminist Theory* 5 (1): 7–27.

———. 1993. *Writing Women's Worlds: Bedouin Stories.* Berkeley: University of California Press.

Ackroyd, Peter. 1984. *T. S. Eliot.* New York: Simon and Schuster.

Ahmad, Imtiaz, ed. 1978. *Caste and Social Stratification among Muslims in India.* New Delhi: Manohar Book Service.

———. 1981. *Ritual and Religion among Muslims in India.* New Delhi: Manohar.

Alam, Javeed. 1993. "The Changing Grounds of Communal Mobilization: The Majlis-E-Ittehad-Ul-Muslimeen and the Muslims of Hyderabad." In *Hindus and Others,* ed. Gyanendra Pandey, 146–176. New Delhi: Viking.

Alter, Joseph S. 2000. *Knowing Dil Das: Stories of a Himalayan Hunter.* Philadelphia: University of Pennsylvania Press.

Antes, Peter. 1989. "Medicine and the Living Tradition of Islam." In *Healing and Restoring: Health and Medicine in the World's Religious Traditions,* ed. Lawrence Sullivan, 173–202. New York: Macmillan.

Arberry, Arthur J. 1950. *An Account of the Mystics of Islam.* London: George Allen and Unwin.

Asad, Talal. 1986. *The Idea of an Anthropology of Islam.* Occasional Papers Series, Center for Contemporary Arab Studies. Washington, D.C.: Georgetown University.

Assayag, Jackie. 2004. *At the Confluence of Two Rivers: Muslims and Hindus in South India.* New Delhi: Manohar.

Austin, J. L. 1962. *How to Do Things with Words.* Cambridge: Harvard University Press.

Bauman, Richard. 1977. *Verbal Art as Performance.* Rowley, Mass.: Newbury House.

———. 1992. "Performance." In *Folklore, Cultural Performances, and Popular Entertainments,* ed. Richard Bauman, 41–49. New York: Oxford University Press.

Bayley, Susan. 1989. *Saints, Goddesses and Kings: Muslims and Christians in South Indian Society, 1700–1900.* Cambridge: Cambridge University Press.

Behar, Ruth. 1993. *Translated Woman: Crossing the Border with Esperanza's Story*. Boston: Beacon Press.

———. 1996. *The Vulnerable Observer: Anthropology That Breaks Your Heart*. Boston: Beacon Press.

Bell, Catherine. 1998. "Performance." In *Critical Terms for Religious Studies*, ed. Mark Taylor, 205–224. Chicago. University of Chicago Press.

Biegman, Nicolaas H. 1990. *Egypt: Moulids, Saints, Sufis*. London: Kegan Paul International Ltd.

Bilgrami, Akeel. 1993. "What Is a Muslim? Fundamental Commitment and Cultural Identity." In *Hindus and Others*, ed. Gyanendra Pandey, 273–299. New Delhi: Viking.

Bowen, John. 1993. *Muslims through Discourse: Religion and Ritual in Gayo Society*. Princeton: Princeton University Press.

———. 1998. "What Is 'Universal' and 'Local' in Islam?" *Ethos* 26 (2): 258–261.

Briggs, Charles L. 1988. *Competence in Performance: The Creativity of Tradition in Mexicano Verbal Art*. Philadelphia: University of Pennsylvania Press.

Brown, Karen McCarthy. 1991. *Mama Lola: A Vodou Priestess in Brooklyn*. Berkeley: University of California Press.

Brumann, Christoph. 1999. "Writing for Culture: Why a Successful Concept Should Not Be Discarded." *Current Anthropology* 40 (Supplement): S1–S27.

Bruner, Edward M. 1986. "Ethnography as Narrative." In *The Anthropology of Experience*, ed. Edward M. Bruner and Victor Turner, 139–155. Urbana: University of Illinois Press.

Chittick, William, trans. 1983. *The Sufi Path of Love: The Spiritual Teachings of Rumi*. Albany: State University of New York Press.

Clifford, James. 1986. "Introduction: Partial Truths." In *Writing Culture: The Poetics and Politics of Ethnography*, ed. James Clifford and George E. Marcus, 1–26. Berkeley: University of California Press.

Clifford, James, and George E. Marcus, eds. 1986. *Writing Culture: The Poetics and Politics of Ethnography*. Berkeley: University of California Press.

Crapanzano, Vincent. 1973. *The Hamadsha: A Study in Moroccan Ethnopsychiatry*. Berkeley: University of California Press.

Currie, P. M. 1989. *The Shrine and Cult of Mu'in al-din Chishti of Ajmer*. New Delhi: Oxford University Press.

Das, Veena. 1984. "For a Folk Theology and Theological Anthropology of Islam." *Contributions to Indian Sociology* 18 (2): 293–300.

De Munck, Victor C. 1995. "Sufi, Reformist and National Models of Identity: The History of a Muslim Village Festival in Sri Lanka." In *Muslim Communities of South Asia*, ed. T. N. Madan, 493–522. New Delhi: Manohar.

Delaney, Carol. 1991. *The Seed and the Soil: Gender and Cosmology in a Turkish Village Society*. Berkeley: University of California Press.

Denny, Frederick Mathewson. 1995. *An Introduction to Islam*. New York: Macmillan Publishing Company.

Doumato, Eleanor Abdella. 2000. *Getting God's Ear: Women, Islam, and Healing in Saudi Arabia and the Gulf*. New York: Columbia University Press.

D'Souza, Andreas. 1991. "Thursday at the Tomb: Hindu Influence on Muslim Saint Veneration." *The Bulletin of the Henry Martyn Institute of Islamic Studies* 10 (1): 39–46.

Eaton, Richard. 1978. *The Sufis of Bijapur, 1300–1700: Social Roles of Sufis in Medieval India*. Princeton: Princeton University Press.

———. 1984. "The Political and Religious Authority of the Shrine of Baba Farid." In *Moral Conduct and Authority: The Place of Adab in South Asian Islam*, ed. Barbara D. Metcalf, 333–356. Berkeley: University of California Press.

———. 1985. "Approaches to the Study of Conversion to Islam in India." In *Approaches to Islam in Religious Studies*, ed. Richard C. Martin, 106–123. Tucson: University of Arizona Press.

———. 1994. *The Rise of Islam and the Bengal Frontier, 1204–1760*. New Delhi: Oxford University Press.

———. 1997. "Comparative History as World History: Religious Conversion in Modern India." *Journal of World History* 8 (2): 243–271.

Eickelman, Dale F., and James Piscatori, eds. 1990. *Muslim Travellers: Pilgrimage, Migration and the Religious Imagination*. Berkeley: University of California Press.

Elmore, Wilbur Theodore. 1915. *Dravidian Gods in Modern Hinduism*. Hamilton, N.Y.: Published by the author.

Ernst, Carl W. n.d. "Situating Sufism and Yoga." *Journal of the Royal Asiatic Society*. Forthcoming.

———. 1985. *Words of Ecstasy in Sufism*. Albany: State University of New York Press.

———. 1992. *Eternal Garden: Mysticism, History, and Politics at a South Asian Sufi Center*. Albany: State University of New York Press.

———. 1997. *The Shambhala Guide to Sufism*. Boston: Shambhala.

———. 2003. *Following Muhammad: Rethinking Islam in the Contemporary World*. Chapel Hill: University of North Carolina Press.

———, and Bruce B. Lawrence. 2002. *Sufi Martyrs of Love: The Chishti Order in South Asia and Beyond*. New York: Palgrave Macmillan.

Ewing, Katherine Pratt. 1980. "The *Pir* or Sufi Saint in Pakistani Islam." Ph.D. diss., University of Chicago.

———. 1984a. "Malangs of the Punjab: Intoxication or *Adab* as the Path to God." In *Moral Conduct and Authority*, ed. Barbara D. Metcalf, 357–371. Berkeley: University of California Press.

———. 1984b. "The Sufi as Saint, Curer, and Exorcist in Modern Pakistan." *Contributions to Asian Studies* 18:106–113.

———. 1988. *Shari'at and Ambiguity in South Asian Islam*. Berkeley: University of California Press.

———. 1990. "The Dream of Spiritual Initiation and the Organization of Self Representations Among Pakistani Sufis." *American Ethnologist* 17 (1): 56–74.

———. 1997. *Arguing Sainthood: Modernity, Psychoanalysis, and Islam*. Durham: Duke University Press.

———. 1998. "Crossing Borders and Transgressing Boundaries: Metaphors for Negotiating Multiple Identities." *Ethos* 26 (2): 262–267.

Fernea, Robert A., and Elizabeth W. Fernea. 1972. "Variation in Religious Observance among Islamic Women." In *Scholars, Saints, and Sufis: Muslim Religious Institutions in the Middle East since 1500*, ed. Nikki R. Keddie, 385–401. Berkeley: University of California Press.

Flueckiger, Joyce Burkhalter. 1995. " 'The Vision Was of Written Words': Negotiating

Authority as a Female Muslim Healer in South India." In *Syllables of Sky*, ed. David Shulman, 249–282. New Delhi: Oxford University Press.

———. 1996. *Gender and Genre in the Folklore of Middle India*. Ithaca: Cornell University Press.

———. 2003a. "Narrative Voices and Repertoires at a Healing Crossroads in South India." *Journal of American Folklore* 116 (3): 249–272.

———. 2003b. "Vernacular Islam." In *Encyclopedia of Islam and the Muslim World*, vol. 2, ed. Richard C. Martin, 723–725. New York: Macmillan Reference USA.

Fluehr-Lobban, Carolyn. 1994. *Islamic Society in Practice*. Gainesville: University of Florida Press.

Friedlander, Ira. 1975. *The Whirling Dervishes: Being an Account of the Sufi Order Known as the Mevlevis and Its Founder the Poet and Mystic Mevlana Jalalu'ddin Rumi*. New York: Macmillan Publishing Co.

Gal, Susan. 1991. "Between Speech and Silence: The Problematics of Research on Language and Gender." In *Feminist Anthropology: The Postmodern Era*, ed. Micaela di Leonarda, 175–203. Berkeley: University of California Press.

Geertz, Clifford. 1968. *Islam Observed: Religious Development in Morocco and Indonesia*. New Haven: Yale University Press.

Gilsenan, Michael. 1973. *Saint and Sufi in Modern Egypt: An Essay in the Sociology of Religion*. London: Oxford University Press.

Gilmartin, David, and Bruce Lawrence, eds. 2000. *Beyond Turk and Hindu: Rethinking Religious Identities in Islamicate South Asia*. Gainesville: University Press of Florida.

Gilmartin, David, and Tony Stewart. 1995. "Review of *The Rise of Islam and the Bengal Frontier*." *Journal of Asian Studies* 54 (3) 866–868.

Gold, Ann Grodzins. 1994. "Purdah Is as Purdah's Kept: A Storyteller's Story." In Gloria Goodwin Raheja and Ann Grodzins Gold, *Listen to the Heron's Words: Reimagining Gender and Kinship in North India*, 164–181. Berkeley: University of California Press.

———. 2002. "Counterpoint Authority in Women's Ritual Expressions: A View from the Village." In *Jewels of Authority: Women and Textual Tradition in Hindu India*, ed. Laurie L. Patton, 177–201. New York: Oxford University Press.

Gottschalk, Peter. 1996. "Multiple Narratives and Multiple Identities among Hindus and Muslims in Bihar." Paper presented at Annual Conference on South Asia, University of Wisconsin, Madison, Wisconsin.

———. 2000. *Beyond Hindu and Muslim: Multiple Identity in Narratives from Village India*. New York: Oxford University Press.

Gumperz, John J., and Dell Hymes, eds. 1972. *Directions in Sociolinguistics: The Ethnography of Communication*. New York: Holt, Rinehart and Winston.

Hassett, Philip. 1995. "Open Sama: Public and Popular Qawwali at Yusufayn Dargah." *The Bulletin of the Henry Martyn Institute of Islamic Studies, Hyderabad* 14, nos. 3–4: 29–63.

Hawley, John Stratton. 1991. "Naming Hinduism." *The Wilson Quarterly* 15 (3): 20–34.

Heath, Shirley Brice. 1982. "Protean Shapes in Literacy Events: Ever-Shifting Oral and Literate Traditions." In *Spoken and Written Language*, ed. Deborah Tannen, 91–117. Norwood, N.J.: Ablex Publishing Corp.

Heilbrun, Carolyn. 1988. *Writing a Woman's Life.* New York: Ballantine Books.

Helminski, Camille Adams, ed. 2003. *Women of Sufism: A Hidden Treasure.* Boston: Shambhala Publications.

Hess, Linda, and Shukdev Singh, trans. 1983. *The Bījak of Kabir.* San Francisco: North Point Press.

Hiltebeitel, Alf, and Barbara D. Miller. 1998. *Hair: Its Power and Meaning in Asian Cultures.* Albany: State University of New York Press.

Hoffman, Valerie J. 1995. *Sufism, Mystics, and Saints in Modern Egypt.* Columbia: University of South Carolina Press.

Hughes, Thomas Patrick. 1885/1988. *Dictionary of Islam.* Calcutta: Rupa and Co.

Hymes, Dell. 1975. "Breakthrough into Performance." In *Folklore: Performance and Communication,* ed. Dan Ben-Amos and Kenneth S. Goldstein, 11–74. The Hague: Mouton.

Imam, Zafar, ed. 1975. *Muslims in India.* New Delhi: Orient Longman.

Jakobson, Roman. 1960. "Closing Statement: Linguistics and Poetics." In *Style in Language,* ed. T. A. Sebeok, 350–373. Cambridge: MIT Press.

Jeffrey, Patricia. 1979. *Frogs in a Well: Indian Women in Purdah.* London: Zed Press.

Kakar, Sudhir. 1982. *Shamans, Mystics, and Doctors: A Psychological Inquiry into India and Its Healing Traditions.* New York: Alfred A. Knopf.

———. 1995. *The Colours of Violence.* New Delhi: Viking.

Kapchan, Deborah A. 1995. "Performance." *Journal of American Folklore* 108 (430): 479–508.

Kassam, Tazim R. 1995. *Songs of Wisdom and Circles of Dance: Hymns of the Satpanth Ismā'īlī Muslim Saint, Pīr Shams.* Albany: State University of New York Press.

Kendall, Laurel. 1988. *The Life and Hard Times of a Korean Shaman: Of Tales and the Telling of Tales.* Honolulu: University of Hawaii Press.

Kratz, Corinne. 2001. "Conversations and Lives." In *African Words, African Voices: Critical Practices in Oral History,* ed. Luise White, Stephan Miescher, and David Cohen, 127–161. Bloomington: Indiana University Press.

Kumar, Nita. 1988/1995. *The Artisans of Banaras: Popular Culture and Identity, 1880–1986.* New Delhi: Orient Longman Limited.

———. 1989/1992. "Work and Leisure in the Formation of Identity: Muslim Weavers in a Hindu City." In *Culture and Power in Banaras: Community, Performance, and Environment, 1800–1980,* ed. Sandria B. Freitag, 147–170. Berkeley: University of California Press.

Kurin, Richard. 1984. "Morality, Personhood, and the Exemplary Life: Popular Conceptions of Muslims in Paradise." In *Moral Conduct and Authority,* ed. Barbara D. Metcalf, 196–220. Berkeley: University of California Press.

Laderman, Carol, and Marina Roseman, eds. 1996. *The Performance of Healing.* New York: Routledge.

Lateef, Shahida. 1990. *Muslim Women in India: Political and Private Realities: 1890s–1980s.* London: Zed Books, Ltd.

Lawless, Elaine. 1988. *Handmaidens of the Lord: Pentecostal Women Preachers and Traditional Religion.* Philadelphia: University of Pennsylvania Press.

———. 1993. *Holy Women, Wholly Women: Sharing Ministries through Life Stories and Reciprocal Ethnography.* Philadelphia: University of Pennsylvania Press.

Lewis, Franklin. 2000. *Rumi: Past and Present, East and West.* Boston: Oneworld.

Liebeskind, Claudia. 1998. *Piety on Its Knees: Three Sufi Traditions in South Asia in Modern Times.* Delhi: Oxford University Press.

Loeffler, Reinhold. 1988. *Islam in Practice: Religious Beliefs in a Persian Village.* Albany: State University of New York Press.

Madan, T. N., ed. 1995. *Muslim Communities of South Asia: Culture, Society, and Power.* New Delhi: Manohar.

———. 1975/1995. "The Social Construction of Cultural Identities in Rural Kashmir." In *Muslim Communities of South Asia,* ed. T. N. Madan, 241–288. New Delhi: Manohar.

Mahmood, Saba. 2005. *Politics of Piety: The Islamic Revival and the Feminist Subject.* Princeton: Princeton University Press.

McClain, Carol Shepherd. 1989. *Women as Healers: Cross-Cultural Perspectives.* New Brunswick: Rutgers University Press.

Mernissi, Fatima. 1977. "Women, Saints, and Sanctuaries." *Signs: Journal of Women in Culture and Society* 3 (1):101–112.

———. 1993. *The Forgotten Queens of Islam.* Minneapolis: University of Minnesota Press.

Metcalf, Barbara D. 1982. *Islamic Revival in British India: Deoband, 1860–1900.* Princeton: Princeton University Press.

———. 1995. "Too Little and Too Much: Reflections on Muslims in the History of India." *The Journal of Asian Studies* 54 (4): 951–967.

———, ed. 1984. *Moral Conduct and Authority: The Place of Adab in South Asian Islam.* Berkeley: University of California Press.

———, ed. 1996. *Making Muslim Space in North America and Europe.* Berkeley: University of California Press.

Mills, Margaret. 1995. "Oral Respondent Comments." The Case for Case Studies Roundtable at the annual meeting of the American Folklore Society, Baltimore, Maryland.

Minault, Gail. 1984. "Some Reflections on Islamic Revivalism vs. Assimilation among Muslims in India." *Contributions to Indian Sociology* 18 (2): 301–304.

———. 1994. "Other Voices, Other Rooms: The View from the Zenana." In *Women as Subjects: South Asian Histories,* ed. Nita Kumar, 108–124. Charlottesville: University Press of Virginia.

Morsy, Soheir A. 1993. *Gender, Sickness, and Healing in Rural Egypt: Ethnography in Historical Context.* Boulder, Colo.: Westview Press.

Naidu, Ratna. 1990. *Old Cities, New Predicaments: A Study of Hyderabad.* New Delhi: Sage Publications.

Narayan, Kirin. 1989. *Storytellers, Saints, and Scoundrels: Folk Narrative in Hindu Religious Teaching.* Philadelphia: University of Pennsylvania Press.

———. 1991. "According to Their Feelings: Teaching and Healing with Stories." In *Stories Lives Tell: Narrative and Dialogue in Education,* ed. Carol Witherelll and Nel Noddings, 113–135. New York: Teachers College Press.

———. 1997. *Mondays on the Dark Night of the Moon: Himalayan Foothill Folktales.* New York: Oxford University Press.

Narayanan, Vasudha. 2000. "Religious Vocabulary and Regional Identity: A Study of the Tamil *Cirappuranam.*" In *Beyond Turk and Hindu,* ed. David Gilmartin and Bruce Lawrence, 74–97. Gainesville: University Press of Florida.

———. 2001. "The Strains of Hindu-Muslim Relations: Babri Masjid, Music, and Other Areas Where the Traditions Cleave." In *Hinduism and Secularism: After Ayodhya*, ed. Arvind Sharma. New York: Palgrave.

Oberoi, Harjot. 1994. *The Construction of Religious Boundaries: Culture, Identity, and Diversity in the Sikh Tradition*. Chicago: University of Chicago Press.

O'Flaherty, Wendy Doniger. 1988. *Other Peoples' Myths: The Cave of Echoes*. New York: Macmillan Publishing Co.

Okely, Judith. 1991. "Defiant Moments: Gender, Resistance, and Individuals." *Man* 26 (1): 3–22.

Pandey, Gyanendra, ed. 1993. *Hindus and Others: The Question of Identity in India Today*. New Delhi: Viking.

Patton, Laurie L., ed. 2002. *Jewels of Authority: Women and Textual Tradition in Hindu India*. New York: Oxford University Press.

Peacock, James. 1984. "Religion and Life History." In *Text, Play and Story*, ed. Edward Bruner, 94–116. Washington: American Ethnological Society.

Pemberton, Kelly. 2000. "Women's Ritual Life and Sufi Shrines in North India." Ph.D. diss., Columbia University.

———. 2002. "Islamic and Islamicizing Discourses: Ritual Performance, Didactic Texts, and the Reformist Challenge in the South Asian Sufi Milieu." *Annual of Urdu Studies* 17, 55–83.

Peronne, Bobette, H. Henrietta Stockel, and Victoria Krueger. 1989. *Medicine Women, Curanderas, and Women Doctors*. Norman: University of Oklahoma Press.

Personal Narratives Group. 1989. *Interpreting Women's Lives: Feminist Theory and Personal Narratives*. Bloomington: Indiana University Press.

Pfleiderer, Beatrix. 1988. "The Semiotics of Ritual Healing in a North Indian Muslim Shrine." *Social Science Medicine* 27 (5): 417–424.

Pickthall, Mohammed Marmaduke, trans. and ed. 1994. *The Glorious Quran: Arabic Text and English Rendering*. 10th ed. Des Plaines, Ill.: Library of Islam.

Pinault, David. 1992. *The Shiites: Ritual and Popular Piety in a Muslim Community*. New York: St. Martin's Press.

———. 2001. *The Horse of Karbala: Muslim Devotional Life in India*. New York: Palgrave.

Pinto, Desiderio. 1995. Piri-Muridi *Relationship: A Study of the Nizamuddin Dargah*. New Delhi: Manohar.

Pugh, Judy. 1986. "Divination and Ideology in the Banaras Muslim Community." In *Shariat and Ambiguity in South Asian Islam*, ed. Katherine Ewing, 288–306. Berkeley: University of California Press.

Qureshi, Regula Burckhardt. 1986. *Sufi Music of India and Pakistan: Sound, Context and Meaning in Qawwali*. Chicago: University of Chicago Press.

Raheja, Gloria Goodwin, and Ann Grodzins Gold. 1994. *Listen to the Heron's Words: Reimagining Gender and Kinship in North India*. Berkeley: University of California Press.

Rahman, Fazlur. 1987. *Health and Medicine in the Islamic Tradition: Change and Identity*. New York: Crossroad.

———. 1989. "Islam and Health/Medicine: A Historical Perspective." In *Healing and Restoring: Health and Medicine in the World's Religious Traditions*, ed. Lawrence Sullivan, 149–172. New York: Macmillan.

Raudvere, Catharina. 2002. *The Book and the Roses: Sufi Women, Visibility, and Zikir in Contemporary Istanbul.* Sweden: Swedish Research Institute in Istanbul.

Rizvi, Saiyid Athar. 1978. *A History of Sufism in India.* 2 vols. New Delhi: Munshiram Manoharlal Publishers.

Robinson, Francis. 1982. "Islam and Muslim Society in South Asia." *Contributions to Indian Sociology* 17 (2): 185–203.

Robinson, Rowena, and Sathianathan Clarke, eds., 2003. *Religious Conversion in India: Modes, Motivations, and Meanings.* Delhi: Oxford University Press.

Roy, Asim. 1983. *The Islamic Syncretistic Tradition in Bengal.* Princeton: Princeton University Press.

Sax, William S. 1995. *The Gods at Play: Līlā in South Asia.* New York: Oxford University Press.

Schiefflin, Edward L. 1985. "Performance and the Cultural Construction of Reality." *American Ethnologist* 12 (4): 707–724.

Schimmel, Annemarie. 1970. *Islamic Calligraphy.* Leiden: E. J. Brill.

———. 1975. *Mystical Dimensions of Islam.* Chapel Hill: University of North Carolina Press.

———. 1980. *Islam in the Indian Subcontinent.* Leiden: E. J. Brill.

———. 1984. *Calligraphy and Islamic Culture.* New York: New York University Press.

———. 1993. *The Mystery of Numbers.* New York: Oxford University Press.

Sharif, Ja'far. 1921/1972. *Islam in India, or The Qānūn-i-Islām.* Trans. G. A. Herklots. London: Curzon Press.

Shostak, Marjorie. 1981. *Nisa: The Life and Words of a !Kung Woman.* Cambridge, Mass.: Harvard University Press.

Shulman, David. 1985. *The King and the Clown in South Indian Myth and Poetry.* Princeton: Princeton University Press.

———. 1993. *The Hungry God: Hindu Tales of Filicide and Devotion.* Chicago: University of Chicago Press.

Smith, Wilfred Cantwell. 1988. "Hyderabad: Muslim Tragedy." In *Hyderabad: After the Fall,* ed. Omar Khalidi, 1–25. Wichita, Kansas: Hyderabad Historical Society.

Smith-Rosenberg, Carroll. 1986. "Writing History: Language, Class, and Gender." In *Feminist Studies, Critical Studies,* ed. Teresa de Lauretis, 31–54. Bloomington: Indiana University Press.

Stewart, Tony K. 1995. "Satya Pīr: Muslim Holy Man and Hindu God." In *The Religious of South Asia in Practice,* ed. Donald S. Lopez, 578–597. Princeton, N.J.: Princeton University Press.

———. 2000. "Alternative Structures of Authority: Satya Pir on the Frontiers of Bengal." In *Beyond Turk and Muslim,* ed. David Gilmartin and Bruce Lawrence, 21–54. Gainesville: University Press of Florida.

———. 2001. "In Search of Equivalence: Conceiving Muslim-Hindu Encounter through Translation Theory." *History of Religions* 40 (3): 260–287.

———, and Carl W. Ernst. 2003. "Syncretism." In *South Asian Folklore: An Encyclopedia,* ed. Margaret Mills, Peter Claus, and Sarah Diamond, 586–588. New York: Routledge.

Talbott, Cynthia. 1995. "Inscribing the Other, Inscribing the Self: Hindu-Muslim Identities in Pre-Colonial India." *Comparative Studies in Society and History* 37 (4): 692–722.

———. 1997. "The Power of the Past: Historical Memory & Political Identity in South India, 1400–1600." Paper presented at workshop Constructing and Deconstructing the Hindu Traditions, University of Florida, Gainesville.

Toelken, Barre. 1979. *The Dynamics of Folklore.* Boston: Houghton Mifflin.

Troll, Christian W., ed. 1989. *Muslim Shrines in India.* Delhi: Oxford University Press.

Veer, Peter van der. 1992. "Playing or Praying: A Sufi Saint's Day in Surat." *Journal of Asian Studies* 51 (3): 545–565.

———. 1994. *Religious Nationalism: Hindus and Muslims in India.* Berkeley: University of California Press.

Vitray-Meyerovitch, Eva de. 1987. *Rumi and Sufism.* Trans. Simone Fattal. Sausalito, Calif.: The Post-Apollo Press.

Waseem, M., ed. and trans. 2003. *On Becoming an Indian Muslim: French Essays on Aspects of Syncretism.* New Delhi: Oxford University Press.

Waugh, Earle H. 1989. *The Munshidin of Egypt: Their World and Their Song.* Columbia: University of South Carolina Press.

Werbner, Pnina. 2003. *Pilgrims of Love: The Anthropology of a Global Sufi Cult.* Bloomington: Indiana University Press.

Werbner, Pnina, and Helene Basu, eds. 1998. *Embodying Charisma: Saints, Cults and Muslim Shrines in South Asia.* New York: Routledge.

Wilce, James M. 1995. " 'I can't tell you all my troubles': Conflict, Resistance, and Metacommunication in Bangladeshi Illness Interactions." *American Ethnologist* 22 (4): 927–952.

———. 1998a. *Eloquence in Trouble: The Poetics and Politics of Complaint in Rural Bangladesh.* New York: Oxford University Press.

———. 1998b. "The Kalimah in the Kaleidoscope: Ranges of Multivocality in Bangladeshi Muslim's Discourses." *Ethos* 26 (2): 229–257.

Index

Abba (Sheikh Hussain Qadiri): and Amma's *bhakti*, 152; becomes a *bābā* after death, 174; cosmology of, 173, 177–179; death of, 1, 20, 35, 241–249; disciples of, 204, 237, 239 (*see also samā*); discusses Hindu and Muslim cosmology, 169–170, 175, 177, 182; employment of, at Osmania University, 37; healing activities of, 87, 147–149; income of, 48, 152; interdependence with Amma, 35, 151–152, 202, 218, 236–237, 239, 247; *jalālī* nature of, 151, 183, 214; lineages of, 203–204 (*see also* Chishti lineage; Qadiri lineage); literacy of, 66, 147; monotheism of, 173; photographs of, *v, 123, 193, 212, 224, 230, 247*; Quranic narratives of, 154; role of, as *pīr*, 32, 35, 49–50, 56, 151–153, 179, 201–203, 205–207, 211, 213–217, 230–233; role of, at *samā*, 201, 206–207, 211–215, 230–231; roles of, in Amma's healing room, 40, 44–45, 87, 91, 94–96, *123*, 127–128, 151, 153; service of, during World War II, 147; storytelling of, 154, 183–194, 225–226; teachings of, 152–154, 175, 177–178, 207, 210, 214, 191–192, 216–217, 222–223, 235; tells stories of Hindu deities, 176–177, 190–192; training of, 157

Abdul Jinn, 82–83, 85, 107. *See also maukīl*

abjad (name-number diagnostic system): and childhood illnesses, 121–122; described, 65, 69–72, 74–75, 90, 237; and failing businesses, 128, 132; and "family systems" healing, 87–88, 115, 117, 130, 239–240; and loss of semantic value of numbers, 83, 85; for marital problems, 118, 120; and misbehaving children, 124; not used in possession cases, 109–111

abjad kā phāl kholnā (mystery of numbers). *See abjad*

Abu-Lughod, Lila, 24–25

Adipara Shakti, 191

Ali (Prophet Muhammad's son-in-law), 39, 46, 203. *See also* Tiger of God

allopathic doctors: Amma refers patients to, 65, 112, 114–115, 120; disciples visit, during search for Amma, 60; patients visit, before seeing Amma, 121, 127

allopathic medicine, 3–4, 65, 79

āmil (healer who writes amulets and incantations), 133, 138, 162, 231

Amma Jan, 163–164

Amma (Rukhiya Bi): after Abba's death, 242–249; appeal of, as a healer, 8, 69, 136, 148–150, 172, 238; author's relationship with, 7, 16–22, 90, 113; authority of, as a healer, 63, 67–68, 74–75, 105, 136, 236–237; *barkat* of, 16, 51, 60, 88, 103, 239; as a businesswoman, 48–49, 156, 159–160; clientele described, 54; cosmology of, 8, 174–176, 178–179; death of, 1, 35, 248–249; discusses Hindu and Muslim cosmology, 137, 168–169, 173–181, 188–189, 194, 196; explanation of her *abjad* methodology, 70–73; first healing work of, 158; healing methods of, *see abjad; davā; dhuān; jaṛī-būṭī; tāvīz; utārā* (clay pot) ritual; housing of, 37, 39; identifies with women's *jāti*, 162; importance of intention in healing work of, 73, 264n20; income of, 48, 152; interdependence with Abba, 35, 151–152, 202, 218, 236–237, 239, 247; love of learning of, 155–158; lineages of, 203–204; literacy of, 42, 65–68, 141, 147 (*see also fālitā*); menopause of, 51, 160 (*see also* menstrual taboos); monotheism of, 173; performance of male roles by, 66, 109, 140, 156, 160, 236–237; per-

Index

Amma (Rukhiya Bi) (*continued*)
sonal narratives of, 155–156; photographs of, *v, 43, 47, 62, 87, 104, 230,
246;* pierces self with *zarab,* 230;
prayers of, 154 (*see also duā*); Quranic
recitation of, 154; respect of, for other
healing traditions, 102; role of, at
Gyarwin Sharif festival, 225–227, 230–
232; role at *samās,* 201, 205–207,
214, 218, 220–221; storytelling of,
23, 42–43, 96, 121, 133, 155–164,
174–176, 188–189, 196, 242–244;
testimonial tales of, 164–167; theory
of illness of, 104–105; training of,
157, 160, 237; use of herbs by, 82,
86, 196 (*see also jaṛī-būṭī*); view of,
that understanding is important in
healing, 74, 106; views of, about
caste (*jātis*), 8, 34, 156, 161, 181,
238; views of, about gender roles
(women's *jāti*), 137–138, 161–162,
167; visions of, 156–157, 236–237,
242–243
Amma's disciples: abandon Amma after
Abba's death, 153, 244–245, 247;
Amma discusses, 146–147; choose
Wahhabi reform movement, 13; female, 137; Hussein, 60, 98, 102, 144;
need Amma's permission to use healing techniques, 178; role of, at Gyarwin Sharif festival, 226; roles of, in
healing room, 15–16; roles of, at *samās,* 204–207, 211, 213–214; Sati, 99–
103, 134, 169–170, *230,* 233; search
for a healer before meeting Amma,
142, 239; seek Amma's help with
family matters, 124; study with Abba,
146; testimonials of Amma's work as
a healer by, 165–166
amulets, xii–xiii. *See also fālitā; tāvīz*
Andhra Pradesh, 29
angels: Amma's healing practice and, 12, 68–
69, 237; of death, 242–243, 248,
273n2; intercede on behalf of humans
with Allah, 32; Muslim cosmology
and, 173, 175, 189, 225, 263n5. *See
also* archangels; *jinn; maukīl*
anonymity, 27
archangels, 69, 72, 178. *See also* angels; *jinn;
maukīl*
Asaf Jah, 29
asrat (evil eye from a supernatural being):
and business failure, 131–135; and
childhood illness, 122; defined, 76–77;
and infant death, 166; and jealousy,
158; and marriage negotiations, 87–
88; mentioned, 71–72, 93; and possession, 110. *See also balāyat*

Assayag, Jackie, 172
Auliya, Hazrat Nizamuddin, 202
Aurangzeb (emperor), 28, 260n14
avatārs (incarnations), 174–178, 190, 194,
267nn5–7, 268n9
āyat-e-karīmā (prayer of Jonah), 205. *See also*
Quran
Ayodhya riot, 261n16. *See also* communal
tension

bābās (Muslim male saints): Abba becomes
one after his death, 174; Mustang
Baba, 100–101; The Naked One, 198–
199; sell gemstones for healing, 3, 38;
sheltered at Amma and Abba's resi-
dence, 51–52; who do not write, 66;
and women healers, 143
Babri Masjid, 30, 170, 261n16. *See also* communal tension
Badru, 83. *See also maukīl*
bālā girā (diagnosis that indicates a difficult
marriage), 88
balāyat (action by an evil spirit), 76–77, 97
bandiś (house exorcism): and business failure,
131–135; described, 96–97, 264n17;
and *jaṛī-būṭī,* 102
barkat (spiritual blessings): of Amma, 103; of
Arabic words on amulets, 68; of a
household, 132; of Rifai lineage, 229
Bauman, Richard, 25
becainī (restlessness): of Amma, 41; of
Amma's patients, 92; of author, 6; of
a household, 76; psychoanalytic explanation of, 265n5; and search for *pīr,*
126
Bell, Catherine, 25
bhakti (devotion), 150, 152, 156, 159, 165,
180
Bharata Natyam, 15
Bharatiya Janata Party, 261n16
bhilāvan (nuts), 88–89, 111. *See also* healing
materials
black knowledge, 103. *See also kālā ilm*
Bonalu festival, 174, 262n3
"Book of Service," 67
boṭṭu: worn by a Christian woman, 107;
worn by Hindu women, 9, 61; worn
by Sati, 233–234
Bowen, John, 33
Brahmin caste, 180, 182, 188, 192
bread (*capātī*), 42, 65, 85–86, *87,* 116. *See
also capātī*
Briggs, Charles, 25
burāq, 39
burqā: Amma's clients' use of, 5, 93; Amma's
use of, only on street, 53, 227; and
stereotypes of Muslim women, 9, 135,
265n1

Index

dry-goods store: and Abba's social role, 43–44; Abba's granddaughter takes over, after his death, 44, 53; Amma starts, 159–160; and Amma's healing practice, 40

duā (prayer blessings): Amma critiques other healers' use of, 66–67; and Amma's *barkat*, 59, 103, *104*, 107, 114; for cases of infidelity, 86; for possession cases, 109–110; at *samā*, 206

durūd (prayer), 217

Durga, 38

Ellamma, 177

Ernst, Carl, 31, 70, 171–172, 207

evil eye: and babies, 80, 120–121; cast by people, 71–72, 77 (*see also kartūt*); cast by supernatural beings, 71, 238 (*see also asrat; śaitāni*); deflection of, with amulets, 68 (*see also tāvīz*); as a general term, 75; inherent in a person, 77; *utārā* ritual for, 51, 85, 88–90

Ewing, Katherine, 12, 24–26, 33, 69

exorcism: of buildings (*bandiś*), 55, 96–97, 102, 131–135, 146, 264n17; of people, 108–111, 143

failing businesses, 128–135

failure to thrive, 64, 70, 86–87, 121–122, 165. *See also* children

faith healers, 107–108. *See also* Christianity in Hyderabad

fālitā (amulets to be burned): Amma's use of photocopies for, 73, 103–104; for childhood illnesses, 121; for failing businesses, 130, 134; for family conflict, 115; instructions for use, 79, 82–83, 94, 105; for long-term illnesses, 107; with magic number squares, 65, 83; for marital problems, 117–120; for mental illness with a spiritual cause, 114; for misbehaving children, 124; for missing animals, 126; patients do not read, 7; for possession cases, 111; preparation of, 21, 42; raw materials for, 42

fanā (annihilation of self), 222, 271n21

fate (*kismat*), 76, 90, 113, 118

fātihā (liturgical prayer): Abba offers, on behalf of patients, 49, 122, *123*, 165; and establishment of *dargāhs*, 266n19; recited at rituals, 206, 214, 229, 232

Fatima (Prophet Muhammad's daughter), 39, 262n5, 270n6

finding missing items, 98–101, 126, 178. *See also hazrat; hāzirī; missing children*

Five Pillars, 2

flagpoles, 49. *See also cillā* (ritual flagpole)

flags, 1, 50, 223, 228

flowers: attract evil eye, 264n13; at ceremonial rituals, 207, 230, 232; in healing rituals, 88–89, 111. *See also* healing materials

gaddī (throne), 201, 205–208, 218, 236

Gandhi, Indira, 139, 148

Gandhi, Rajiv, 139

Ganesh, 190–191, 196, 268n10

Ganesh Caturthi festival: and communal tension, 30, 261n17; religious significance of, 269n22; and sacralization of Amma's neighborhood, 38. *See also* communal tension

Gangamma, 265n6, 268n16

Gauramma, 177

gematriya, 70

gemstones, healing and, 3, 38

German evangelists, 107–108. *See also* Christianity in Hyderabad

Ghaus-e-Pak (Ghaus-e-Azam Dastagir; Sheikh Abdul Qadir Jilani), 183–186, 188, 215, 270n6. *See also* Dastagir, Ghaus-e-Azam; Jilani, Sheikh Abdul Qadir

Gottschalk, Peter, 171

gourd (*khādū*), Amma's use of, for healing, 65; and babies who fail to thrive, 86–87, 121–123

Gulf War (1991), 8, 56, 137

Gyarwin Sharif celebration: author's participation in, 20, 272n29; described, 223, 225–234; initiation of *murīds* at, 232–234; and menstrual and postpartum taboos, 138; Munnapa's attendance of, 61, 197; replacement of ritual flags during, 50, 228; *samā* at, 223, 227, 231–232. *See also* death anniversary; *urs*

Hagar, 189

hakīm (practitioner of Unani medicine), 99, 102

hāl, 216–217. *See also wajd*

Hand of Fatima. *See panjā*

Hanuman, 98, 101, 178, 190, 192, 194, 196, 268n10

Hassan (Prophet Muhammad's grandson), 39, 228

Hava: Amma's use of name in *abjad*, 71–72, 74, 103; mother of the world, 152

hāzirī: for business failure, 134; described, 99–101; Hussein practices, 125–126; mentioned, 98

Hazrat Ali. *See* Ali (Prophet Muhammad's son-in-law); Tiger of God

Index

Kali, 107, 178, 187, 194

Kali Yuga, 187, 194

Kalki, 176

kalmā (Muslim confession of faith): Amma's healing practice and, 68, 80, 95, 97; conversion to Islam and, 169; recitation for protection, 205; recited at initiation ceremonies, 232–233; women healers and, 144

karāmat (miracle), 45, 97, 166, 199, 225, 269n20

Karbala, 45, 50

karesu, 88. *See also kartūt*

kartūt (evil eye from a person): Amma describes, 76–77; Amma uses *abjad* to diagnose, 71–72; incorrectly diagnosed, 133; and marital problems, 117–118; and mental illness, 114–115; and misbehaving children, 124; and possession, 111. *See also karesu*

khādū (green gourd), 42, 65, 86–87, 121–122. *See also* healing materials; failure to thrive

Khahar, 83. *See also maukīl*

Khalid (Amma's son): assists Amma in the healing room, 56, 58; assumes authority over Abba's disciples after Abba's death, 153; education of, 57, 159; employment of, at University of Hyderabad, 57; explanation of Amma's *abjad* methodology, 70–71; healing work of, critiqued, 149; healing work of, with women, 148–149; housing of, 39, 57; initial attempt by, to establish himself as healer, 266n11; receives *khilāfat*, 57; role of, as *murśid*, 201; role of, at *samā*, 206; takes over Abba's practice after his death, 244–245

Khamar (Amma's daughter), 56

khilāfat (certificate a *murīd* receives from a *pīr*), 45–46, 50, 232, 244

khilāfat (office of the caliph), 150

khudā (god), 39, 134, 177

kismat (fate), 76, 90, 113, 118

kohl, 98, 125, 272n29. *See also* healing materials

Komati caste, 180

Krishna, 174, 176

Lakshman, 101, 190

Lateef, Shahida, 140

lemons: "reading," 145–146; used for exorcism, 96–97, 109; used for *nahāvan* ritual, 94; used with nails, 88–89; used for *utārā* (clay pot) ritual, 111. *See also* healing materials

Liebeskind, Claudia, 12

lineages (*silsilā*), 31, 203–204

literacy, 147

liver, 88–91, 111, 152, 196. *See also* chickens; healing materials

love: Abba's teachings about, 154, 175, 182, 211, 222, 240; Amma's love of author, 17–18, 113; and Amma's appeal as a healer, 63, 149, 237–238, 240; of God/Allah, 17–18, 32, 156–157; and mystical love at *samā*, 201, 207–210, 215–218. *See also muhabbat*

Mahabharata, 187

Malamat, 163–164

malāmat (evil spirit), 76. *See also śaitāni*

mangalsūtra, as source of a woman's power, 80

marriage difficulties, 64, 86, 88, 115–119, 129, 142, 165

maukīl: as source of power, 69, 72, 80, 82–83, 99, 104, 177–178, 237; and trance at *samā*, 216. *See also* Abdul Jinn; angels; archangels; Badru; Dafe Balad; Israfil; Izrail; Jabbar; Jibrail; *jinn*; Khahar; Mikail; Shafil; Suleman Baba

mazār (tomb of a saint), 248. *See also dargāhs*

menopause, 51, 140–141, 160

menstrual taboos: Amma observes, 138, 262n11; and Amma's healing room, 50–51; and Gyarwin Sharif festival, 227; and Muslim rituals, 138, 262n10; women's explanations of, 265n6

mental illness (*pāgalpan*): and physical causes, 112–113; and spiritual causes, 2, 114–115, 133, 145

Mevlevis, 221–222, 271n20. *See also ramz; wajd*

Mikail, 69. *See also maukīl*

Mills, Margaret, 4, 24

Mir Qamaruddin, 29

Miriam (mother of Issa/Jesus), 175, 188–190

misbehaving children, 124–126, 142

missing children, 69, 101, 105, 125–126, 238

monotheism, 173

muhabbat (love): Amma's, 149, 221; Sufi practice and, 222; women's access to, 221. *See also* love

Muhammad (Amma's son): assists Amma in healing room, 56, 122–123; explains Amma's *abjad* methodology, 70–72; explains *śaitāni kartūt*, 83; practices *jarī-būṭī*, 102; relationship with Amma, 59

Muhammad. *See* Prophet Muhammad

Muharram: communal tension and, 30; described, 174, 194–195; Hindu participation in, 172; mentioned, 128–130, 259n5, 267n4

Index

pūjā, 61, 181–182, 233, 239, 272n32
putlā (effigy), 83, *84*

Qadiri lineage, 31–32, 39, 49, 204. *See also* Jilani, Sheikh Abdul Qadir; Sufi lineages
Qadiri, Sheikh Hussain. *See* Abba
Qalandar lineage, 203, 225. *See also* Sufi lineages
qavvālī (devotional song), 15, 38, 41, 201, 207–211, 231–232, 234
qavvāls (musicians), 206–207, 211, 214, 220; offerings to, *212*
Quran: Amma and Abba expand upon stories from, 188; and Chishti legends, 260n14; and initiation of disciples, 232; prophets mentioned in, 175; and Muslim women's literacy, 147; and *pardā*, 138; power of words of, 67–69, 80, 83, 85, 144, 269n21 (*see also gematriya*); recited to gather healing power, 154, 163, 237; recited for protection, 205; and universal Islam, 2; used in *bandiś*, 97; used on *fālitā*, 6–7, 67–70, 83, 85, 95, 173, 263n12; used in *hazrat*, 144; used with saucers, 145
Qureshi, Regula, 202
Qutub Shahi dynasty, 28

Rahim, 137, 265n3
Rajput caste, 180
Ram, 101, 174–175, 177, 190, 261n16, 265n3, 267n5
Ram Janam Bhoomi, 30, 170. *See also* communal tension
Ramadan, 54, 138
Ramayana, 99, 101, 176, 190, 196, 198
ramz (twirling in trance), 211, 215–217, 221–222. *See also* Mevlevis; *wajd*
Ravana, 176
Reddy caste, 175, 180
Rehma (Amma's daughter), 56, 138, 147
Renuka, 187, 190, 268n17
rice, 89, 111, 226–227, 271n24. *See also* healing materials; *pongal*
Rifai (Qalandar) order, 225, 228–229. *See also zarabwālās*
ritual offerings, 49. *See also fātīhā; pūjā*
rūh (soul), 76–77, 109
Rumi, Jalaladdin, 222, 268n14

Sailik, Sayed Shah Mehamud (Mahmud) Alam Husseini (Amma and Abba's *pīr*), 32, 45, 52, 156–159, 228, 243, 248
śaitāni (devils): as a cause of illness, 2, 17–18, 76–77, 238; and dream interpretation, 265n3; and *jinn*, 69, 97; and possession, 108–111; rituals to protect against, 205
śaitānī kartūt (evil eye caused by evil forces), 83, 86, 105
śakti (spiritual power): of Abba, 216; of Amma, 149; of *bhilāvan*, 89; of Hindu deities, 194, 269n20; of *jarībūṭī*, 196
śaktis (female goddesses), 174, 177–178
salāmat (praise recitation of lineage of saints), 206, 228
samā (devotional musical gatherings): Abba's role at, 201, 206–207, 211–215, *224*, 230–231; Amma's role at, 201, 205–207, 214, 218, 220–221; described, 205–207; defined, 202, 269n2; at Gyarwin Sharif, 231–232; and menstruating and postpartum women, 138; mentioned, 31, 34–35, 56, 61; role of disciples at, 205–207, 211, 214; role of musicians at, 207–208, 214–215, 220
sandalwood oil, 98. *See also* healing materials
sapnā paṛhnā (interpretation of dreams), 67, 76. *See also* dreams
Sarkar, Gharib Nawaz (Muinaddin Chishti): Abba's narrative of, 183–186; color associated with, 270n6; definition of devotion of, 271n23; as founder of Abba's lineage, 39, 203; intercedes for Muslims, 32; praised in *salāmat*, 228; tomb of, 20. *See also* Chishti, Muinaddin
Sati (Amma's disciple): changes name to Mustang, 170, 233; conversion of, 169; mentioned, 134; performs *hāzirī*, 99–103, 134; ritual circumcision of, 170, 233
saucers, 42, 65, 85, 95, 107, 145. *See also* healing materials
Sayyids, 204
Schimmel, Annemarie, 69
semi-precious stones. *See* gemstones
Seventh-day Adventists, 18
Shafil, 83. *See also maukīl*
Shankar (Shiva), 176, 190–191, 268n10
Sharif, 260n14
Shii tradition: *ālams* (flag standards) of, 49–50; shared symbols with Sunni tradition, 45, 50, 194–195, 228; symbols of, 49 (*see also panjā*). *See also* Muharram
shirk (associating anyone/another deity with God), 33, 176
Shostak, Marjorie, 23
silsilā (lineages). *See* Sufi lineages
Sita, 175, 190

JOYCE BURKHALTER FLUECKIGER

is Associate Professor in the Department of Religion at
Emory University. She grew up in India as the child of
Mennonite missionaries and later received her Ph.D. in
South Asian Language and Literature from the University
of Wisconsin–Madison. She is author of *Gender and
Genre in the Folklore of Middle India* and co-editor of *Oral
Epics in India* and *Boundaries of the Text: Epic
Performances in South and Southeast Asia*.